Walk-ins

The
Cosmology of the Soul

by

Sheila Seppi

About the Artists

Audrey and Fernando Ascencio designed and produced the internal artwork in this book. They share their passion for sacred geometry through art and healing.

The flower of life symbol, seen throughout this book, is the symbol for the cycles of creation. Fernando states, "It is the symbol for awakening. It is the pattern of nature, from the smallest particle to the biggest galaxy you will find it. It is the wisdom and knowledge of creation encoded into the symbol itself."

Their website is sacredgeometryhealing.com.

First published 2020 by Sheila Seppi

Copyright © 2020 Sheila Seppi

Flower of life and cosmology of the soul images by
Audrey and Fernando Ascencio

Cover design by Miguel Mendonça

ISBN 13: 979-8656162913
ISBN 10: 8656162913

www.walk-ins.org

To my first spiritual teacher, Jeremie.
May the light of the one infinite spirit be with you
each and every day.

Blessing Prayer

May the stars carry your sadness away,
May the flowers fill your heart with beauty,
May hope forever wipe away your tears,
And, above all, may silence make you strong.

- Chief Dan George, Tsleil-Waututh Nation

Acknowledgements

To my husband Don, for his love and understanding. Thank you for walking the path alongside me. Thank you for taking on a new wife with children and raising them as you own. You are an amazing man, and I am eternally thankful for you.

My wonderful children for hanging in there with me. I am sure it must have been difficult accepting this new person that is your mother. You didn't always understand what I was talking about or sharing with you, but you listened and have always supported me. You have been my cheerleaders and source of encouragement. What a lucky mother I am to have such wonderful children.

Thanks to Barbara Nelson, fondly known to all as Mum. You are one of the greatest joys in my life. You are a blessing to be around and I thank you for your friendship, love, companionship and your support. "Thank you darling."

Miguel Mendonça is one of the most amazing men I have ever met. He is brilliant, kind and generous. I am so grateful for all his guidance and support on this project. He challenged me more than I ever thought possible and made me a much better writer. Thank you, Miguel.

Barbara Lamb and Andrea Perron. Thank you ladies for your encouragement and support in writing this book. You are wonderful, strong women and role models for our up and coming star seed generation. Both of you are very dear to my heart.

Audrey and Fernando Ascencio, thank you for your amazing digital artwork. During the revisions and requests for images, you always smiled. Thank you for your patience and friendship.

Mary Rodwell, what a delight it was to work with you. Thank you for your guidance in discovering and connecting me with other walk-ins. You are a true gift to humanity.

Rebecca Hardcastle-Wright and Gary Gilman, thank you for introducing me to some of the most wonderful people, whom I am now honored to call friends.

To all those that assisted in the transcription process, reading and rereading, I am eternally grateful. These people include Caitlin Kuczko, Jared Dingmann, Nancy Montag, Jenelle Stefanic, Carla Ferrand, Dayna Hurtt, Kara Robertson and Barbara Nelson.

To everyone that participated in any way and endorsed the book, I thank you.

Contents

Foreword by Barbara Lamb

As the Earth and humanity faces growing political, social, environmental, technological and economic threats, humanity needs major help in order to continue and to flourish. In her new book on walk-ins, Sheila Seppi informs us about one particular source of assistance: the phenomenon of walk-ins.

Walk-ins, extraterrestrial-human hybrids, star seeds, star children, etcetera are known to be living with us, and to be helping to raise the consciousness of humanity and shed light amongst the darkness. Many people feel a significant process called Ascension is occurring, in which humanity is advancing into a higher dimension and a finer way of being. As we move through Ascension the truth about our worldly dysfunctions is slowly being revealed. All of this gives us some much-needed hope. Sheila's revelations show us that we are multidimensional beings, and that consciousness from higher dimensions can find ways to dwell here with us and in some instances within us, as in the case of walk-ins.

Through my 45 years as a licensed psychotherapist and regression therapist, and through my own personally transformative experiences, I have gained an expanded picture of reality, exploring other dimensions and the life of the soul. I have conducted several thousand hypnotic regressions to peoples' past life experiences and to encounters with beings from other planets and dimensions. In the course of this journey I have met and worked with a number of walk-ins.

In 1990, through my past life therapy work and my involvement with the International Association of Regression Research and Therapies, I first learned of a colleague's therapeutic work with a walk-in woman. The woman became aware of her walk-in nature by being regressed to the source of her many environmental and food allergies, and her disorientation, which had suddenly begun in her adult life. She discovered that she had come from another dimension and made a 'soul exchange' with a woman already living here (the 'natal' soul in Sheila Seppi's terms), in order to raise the consciousness of human beings. With the help of the therapist she was able to adjust to being in that body, and to adjust to the Earth environment and carry out her mission. At that time this was an entirely new concept for me.

The next walk-in I knew was a woman in her 30s in Colorado. I had met her parents, who asked me why their daughter had suddenly changed from leading a low-consciousness, materialistic life to wanting to establish a metaphysical bookshop and center, and to teach spiritual classes. In subsequently working with the daughter, we realized she was a walk-in from an extraterrestrial (ET) life on a large spaceship. In one regression she connected with her extraterrestrial father and learned details of her former life and her mission of enhancing spirituality on Earth.

Subsequently I met a woman in her 40s who had 'walked into' her human body from a higher spiritual plane to increase peoples' spirituality. She was so different in style, interests, food preferences and ways of being than she ended up getting divorced so that she would be free to carry out her mission.

Next I worked with a woman who had 'walked in' from being a

male extraterrestrial commander/pilot of a space craft. Her mission was to work with people through the hypnosis process in order to clear up past problems and expand their consciousness and awareness of reality. We discovered that at times she returned to her spaceship and temporarily resumed her role as the ET commander/pilot, and then returned into the new body to continue her mission. Her romantic partner had witnessed the 'soul exchange' when it had taken place. Through my continuing regression work I have come to know other walk-ins as well.

I see many aspects of the walk-in phenomenon that are very similar to those of the ET-human hybrids phenomenon. I have worked with a number and co-wrote (with Miguel Mendonça) the book *Meet the Hybrids: The Lives and Missions of ET Ambassadors On Earth*. As with the walk-ins, these hybrids are here in human form to raise the consciousness of humanity, to give helpful service to humans, and to aid in the process of Ascension. These characteristics and intentions are true of star seeds and star kids as well.

I also appreciate Sheila's effort to show us about the life and evolution of the human soul, in and out of numerous incarnations, dimensions and types of beings. Her non-judgemental emphasis on the value of 'experience' is significant in the immensely long journeys of our souls and our relation to the Source. The knowledge she shares with us truly expands our understanding of reality.

My own understanding of the walk-in phenomenon has been greatly expanded and deepened by Sheila's work in this book, and by knowing Sheila herself. I especially appreciate her sharing her own walk-in journey and challenges, as well as the stories of the other walk-ins she has introduced to us. She is a clear example of a soul who has chosen to be here to give service, to inspire, and to uplift people, and she does so in many ways through her multifaceted work.

She is making a valuable contribution to the enlightenment which our world so desperately needs.

Barbara Lamb, MFT.
Co-author of *Meet the Hybrids*, *Alien Experiences* and *Crop Circles Revealed*.

Foreword by Andrea Perron

The most important thing we can do is learn from one another. Not all of us will share like experiences in life, but we are more than capable of absorbing and assimilating the experiences of others and internalizing the conclusions we draw. In this respect, when we engage and interact, we become a part of the other entity we encounter as they simultaneously merge with us, even through the written word. Therefore, each one of us has the opportunity to grow from the union (or reunion) according to our capacity to process information. Any empirical study of humanity yields similar results. We are complicated beings, riddled with emotions. Most people are intellectually adept, predisposed to learning by observation. We look around at the world to determine how we fit in and where we belong.

Though this is true of most, it does not apply to all who walk the Earth. There are those among us who are the misfits, prime examples of beings who have come here specifically with purpose and reason, deliberately so, to gently guide lost and longing souls to a deeper comprehension of self. As a source of pure enlightenment, they are in tune with Source Energy, and are generally known to be healers. Though there are different paths to this level of spiritual cognition, some are graced with it at birth, evolving into a 'Self' awareness of who they are and why they're here. Others struggle with intrinsic knowledge, certain they will never fit in, frequently withdrawing from society for self-protection, all the while questioning their own origin and sanity. It is difficult enough to face the reality of our existence, let alone the feeling of being so alone in the midst of it. However, those who can accept and embrace the transformation as it occurs are most well-equipped to help those who can't cope with the high strangeness of it all. Sheila spent years coming to terms with her power and prowess as a healer. She questioned every element of her existence, explored every emotional reaction to it, and familiarized herself with her new, unusual self well before embarking on this extensive project.

It requires uncommon courage to take such a leap of faith, to declare oneself a walk-in, to be open to the possibilities it provides to share with those unfamiliar with the concept. In so doing, she has enhanced our understanding of what it means to be 'human' in context with our essentially spiritual nature, thus challenging our former notion of reality. Witnessing her old reality through new eyes, she fearlessly details the process and personal progress inherent to her Ascension. A brave soul among a world full of cowards afraid of their own shadow, even the most fear-based individuals find themselves gravitating to her energy because they are disarmed by her presence. Without even knowing what is wrong, what needs to be healed within them, they sense impending peace and the promise of salvation in her arms. She is a conduit, able to absorb and release the pain of others without causing any harm to herself. It is a gift. Observing her doing so with humility, grace and incredible ease is, indeed, a wonder to behold.

Make no mistake about it, we are now in the midst of The Paradigm Shift, currently entering a new Age of Enlightenment unlike anything else humanity has experienced heretofore. There is nothing comfortable about this inevitable transition, a tidal wave of consciousness-raising sweeping the planet. We can either ride the wave into the Fifth Dimension or we will surely perish from the oppressive weight of our 3D world. It is a conscious (and subconscious) choice each and every one of us make during the course of our existence in this incarnation. I consider Earth as Soul School, and no matter how we got here, or why, the curriculum is a tough one. The test always precedes the lesson. Our archaic belief systems will be challenged, perhaps even fractured as we absorb new information and ancient truth imbued by our teachers and healers, the seekers and seers among us who have already traveled an arduous path on a journey none of us can avoid. If you are drawn to this master work of disclosure, then rest assured, there is a reason. Take it in. Rest easy in the knowledge that you are not alone and are actually on your way home in heart, finding your way in the dark, not because it is the Light guiding the way, but because you are becoming the Light you seek, illuminating your own path as you recognize your purpose and brilliance.

Soul is our essence. Love is the answer. Let your conscience be your guide. Allow your moral compass to point you in the right direction, and when the wave is too tumultuous, flip over and float, as the universe knows the destination. Be not afraid to clasp the hand of those who have already experienced transcendental spiritual metamorphosis, those with the courage to share their information and transformation with the world. Sheila Seppi is one such individual. As she healed me with her eyes, she will touch you with her words. Magic being science we do not yet understand, it manifests in many forms. She is my mystical, magical friend, my Soul sister, and my touchstone. It's a privilege and pleasure to contribute my personal thoughts to this remarkable volume, the contribution it will ultimately make to the field of metaphysics will prove incalculable, as immeasurable as Soul itself. I eternally celebrate the day she walked into my Netherworld.

Andrea Perron
Author of *House of Darkness House of Light*

Introduction

Throughout the ages, across the world, innumerable spiritual explorers have stated that our souls are eternal and grow through the experiences they accrue in an ongoing sequence of incarnations. The soul, a persistent, conscious essence, will take one form after another, to fulfil a given purpose each time, and thus contribute to a collective evolution of the conscious, spiritual essence of existence itself.

We will look more deeply into cosmological questions later, but at the outset it is important to acquaint ourselves with the concept of 'consciousness, form and purpose', which will underpin this study. It reminds us of our nature, and our mission here, at this time. It should free up our thinking concerning the relationship between body and soul, and its occasional temporary nature.

This book is focused on the varieties of transient, transacted exchanges between bodies and souls. The original 'natal' soul becomes anchored into the body at birth, and typically experiences a wide range of emotions and life stages until death. But for various reasons, one soul may make an agreement with another to trade forms. When we think of this in the human context, we call these people 'walk-ins', as a new soul has 'walked into' an existing body. It may be that a soul doesn't need a lifetime of experiences, and that it has a more focused mission. Short lives still have major impacts.

How do I know walk-ins exist? Because I am one. I woke up in the body of a 38-year-old woman who was married and had three children. My soul did not need to go through the traditional birth, childhood, adolescence, or young adult phase. I needed an adult form to carry out my mission.

Often when a walk-in arrives, the person is initially unaware of what has happened. They only know that things have changed. Their world may have turned upside down and they are left with more questions than answers. I was blessed to discover who I am in less than six months of arriving. I am now fully integrated into this physical form. The gift of knowing who I am is very profound and powerful. Even as I write, memories and truths reveal themselves to me.

It is my greatest hope that this book will assist those who may be struggling with a lack of understanding as to what is happening to them, and to serve as a beacon of hope and guidance once they discover their truth. For non-walk-ins, I trust this book will expand your understanding and knowledge of walk-ins and the cosmological nature of souls.

This book is an unfolding of spiritual truths that I, and the others written about in this book, remember and share. This is our truth, the universe as we know and remember it. It is written from our perspectives. As you will see, our views and terminology vary. These are our truths, and they may or may not resonate with your truth.

On December 21, 2012, our planet ended a 26,000-year galactic cycle. This cycle was recognized and highly discussed across the world as the completion of the great Mayan cosmological cycle known as the Pleiadian Cycle. We have now moved into the Golden Age, the next 26,000 year cycle, and into an unprecedented time in the history of this planet. Gaia is on the cusp of a major evolution and humanity is about to experience a leap in consciousness. More and more souls - angelics, multidimensional light beings, and galactic star family members - are flooding to Earth through the walk-in process to assist with this transition by helping to raise the frequency and consciousness of both the planet and humanity. It is a very exciting time to observe humanity waking up, evolving and stepping into a new paradigm of understanding. This global event is going to be the greatest show in our galaxy, and I for one, wanted a front-row seat.

The catalyst that led to my writing this book began in April of 2019 when I suddenly experienced liver failure. I am only alive today due to Dr. Randall Frank's Evolutionary Quantum Healing Technique. In less than one hour, from Germany, Dr. Frank, along with a colleague in Hawaii, rebuilt my liver. They also cleared the poison from my kidneys, spleen and pancreas. My recuperation time was only a fraction of what it would have taken anyone else to recover, if they were lucky enough to survive at all.

During my recuperation period I was corresponding with Barbara Lamb, MFT, and she said to me, "You know, this might just be the perfect opportunity to begin writing your book." I took her words to heart and started thinking about how I might approach such a project.

In June, Andrea Perron read the first draft of my story and encouraged me to keep going and offered her support. Then in September, on the Fall Equinox and my 20th-year celebration of being on Earth, I was told by my guides that it was indeed time to bring this information forward and they would be with me every step of the way. So, my writing moved into a more serious stage.

I would be remiss if I did not state that this book is being written during one of the most tumultuous times our planet has ever seen. There is government corruption, COVID-19, major health crises, the biosphere of the planet is diminishing, and the economy is in serious trouble. Despite these events, I view them as one of the first steps of moving into the new Earth. I believe that all the events that have surfaced are coming up for healing. They are growing pains. Because of these events, more and more walk-ins are coming to help show the way, a different way. To offer solutions, love and support.

Initially, I was planning to write only about walk-in souls and to use this book as a platform for sharing my story. However, as I began to write, it became clear to me that I also needed to include stories of other walk-ins. Conducting the interviews for this project was more eye-opening and rewarding than I could ever have imagined.

I found that I was constantly awestruck by the different perspectives each person held, and the individuality of their stories. Yes, there are similarities to my experience, but there are also differences. These differences in remembrances caused me to be more expansive in my writing, which then led to my touching upon the cosmological nature of souls.

As with any book, it has taken many forms over the course of its birthing process. It wasn't until I began to write it all down that I realized that I had finally found a mechanism to bring forward the many thoughts, concepts and knowings that had been swirling around in my mind for the past 20 years. Once I began to write, the words flowed effortlessly. There was no writer's block, no agonizing over how to express myself. Only a sweet flow of expression that came through almost as if the words were unveiling themselves to me.

The writing process allowed me to be totally focused, reducing my thoughts to a single flow of expression. It is in this flow that I was visited and influenced many times by aspects from my higher self and spirit guides. As you read my words, you may notice a hint of their presence as the writing style changes slightly. They helped to guide and mold my thoughts, bringing forth memories long obscured by the veil of forgetfulness that is placed upon us when we incarnate. Their strong presence confirmed to me that the timing for writing this book is now. My collective spirit group helped me to express my thoughts in a way that brought forward a deep sense of remembrance and comfort.

You will read about the trials and tribulations that I experienced after stepping into this body and what it took just to maintain my sanity. And if you, the reader, find that you are experiencing the feeling of going crazy, just know that you are not alone and that you most certainly are not crazy. Take heart, for you may find the reassurance that you seek in these pages.

To expand my perspective on the nature of souls, I began conducting interviews with non-walk-in individuals and people with significant experience in the fields of science and consciousness, hypnotherapy, the paranormal, channeling, extraterrestrial encounters and spirituality. Their stories have added a richness to this book that in the beginning I could not have conceived of and they sent me on yet another journey of self-discovery.

I did not begin reading books about walk-ins until I had completed my basic first draft and submitted it to my editor, Miguel Mendonça. I wanted to keep my knowledge purely my own. When I did start reading them, I felt waves of verification and kinship wash over me as I read the words of each book. It was good to know that I am not alone.

Walk-ins: Cosmology of the Soul may challenge your belief systems, expand your mind or cause you to scoff. The aim, however, is to lead you through an adventure of learning about the different types of souls that are currently on this planet, with a major focus on walk-in souls. I also want to open minds to the broader truth that we are not alone - that we have a galactic star family. In accepting this broader truth about ourselves hopefully we can open our hearts more to accept each other through a non-judgmental, loving perspective. For you see, we are all connected. We are one. We are all members of the galactic family.

This book is presented in two parts. They may prove to be a life raft for newly arrived walk-ins or serve to expand your perspective. Some of the concepts written about are very deep and thought-provoking. Each part is written in short sections to allow you to read a section, put the book down and digest the information.

Part one of this book is designed to acquaint the reader with the concept of walk-ins, the types of walk-ins, the anatomy of the soul and discusses consciousness, form, and purpose as being the foundation for our existence. Here, I share my personal story.

Part two focuses on the stories of other walk-ins. Their interviews describe the walk-in event, their integration process and the mission they brought with them.

To add further perspective on the subject, I also interviewed people in the metaphysical field. We discussed their viewpoints about walk-ins and the nature of the soul, which I summarize in the chapter Additional Perspectives.

In the Conclusions chapter I attempt to bring together all that we have learned in this exploration. It is structured according to the layout of the book, and builds up a picture of the phenomenon as experienced from within, and viewed from without.

In the Appendix I offer the reader a questionnaire, which may help them to answer the question as to whether or not they may be a walk-in themselves.

There are also some recommended readings provided for your

continued education in this subject.

I am grateful for the opportunity to write this book, for in doing so it has expanded my own mind, my own perspectives, my own spiritual growth, and has helped me to remember the universal truths that I hold dearest in my heart.

My Journey

The Walk-in Event

A life-changing event occurred to me during the fall of 1999. During that time I was a very ill person. I had a dysfunctional marriage, three children and worked in a high-profile job. I began reading a book entitled *Ask Your Angels* and learned of spirit guides, helpers and how your angels are always there to assist you. I was born in Virginia and grew up with fundamentalist Christian beliefs, so learning to communicate with angels felt natural and safe. I had never thought of an angel as a guide, helper or teacher before. Even though I did not finish the book, I read enough that the words began to open my mind, provide hope and allow healing to occur. This was the first book I had attempted to read in nearly ten years, so it was a big deal for me.

During the previous two decades, I had been diagnosed with and suspected of having brain tumors, bone cancer, fibromyalgia, chronic fatigue, migraines, multiple sclerosis, sarcoidosis, erythema nodosum and I walked with a cane periodically. I did everything western medicine told me to do and received minimal relief, while the symptoms continued to compound. My work suffered due to an increasing difficulty in holding focus.

One night, in mid-to-late September of 1999, I went to bed a very sick person. Around 7:00 am the next morning, it felt as if someone reached down, grabbed me by the hair and pulled me bolt upright in bed. I felt lightning run through my body and I was in a space of blinding white light. Despite its suddenness, I liked it. It felt comfortable, familiar and safe. I was totally at peace and in no pain. I don't know how long I was in this space, but slowly my vision began to return, first at the periphery, then moving towards the center. I looked around the room in a daze. What just happened? Was I dreaming? Why was I sitting up in bed? Why had the room been filled with white light? Everything looked the same, but everything was different. There was a peaceful eeriness about the room and as I looked around, it was almost as if the objects in the room began to share information about themselves: where they were from, how they got there, who had touched them, who gave them to me. Articles of clothing began to tell me where they were worn last. It was all too much for me.

Settling In

The night before, I had gone to bed with a very firm religious belief system. But now, I knew things that I didn't even believe in! I knew what it was like for the soul to slip effortlessly from the body, and to return. I knew what it was like to be in spirit form. I somehow remembered past lives and spiritual truths that the previous night I did not believe in. I remembered ceremonies and indigenous healing methods that I had never read about, believed or expressed an interest in. My belief system was shaken to its core. I did not understand what was happening to me and I feared I might be having a psychotic break.

I sprang out of bed, expecting to see the kids eating cereal at the kitchen table or watching television but no one was around. It was Saturday, or so I thought. There shouldn't be any school today. Where was everyone? I was dazed and confused.

I then caught my reflection in the mirror. I looked deep into my eyes, half expecting them to shed some light on the strangeness that had become my reality. I marveled at my image. I was fascinated with my hair, my facial features, my skin, my eyes and even my teeth. I felt like I was looking at a stranger, but the stranger was me. I moved about the house aimlessly as if I had never been there before. I looked at the contents of each room with a childlike sense of wonder. I picked up objects and turned them over, feeling their solidity in my hand. Some items were smooth, others rough. Some were hard, some soft. The textures of each item brought an unfamiliar joy. Everything looked so different! So old, so new.

I walked, amazed at the feel of the carpet under my bare feet. I stuck my head in the refrigerator and was greeted with wonderful aromas. I opened the side door to the house and felt the sun hitting my skin. As its rays engulfed me, I felt the warmth of the sun move throughout my body. Again I remembered what it was like for the soul to slip out of the body and return to it. I remembered what it was like to be in a non-physical form. I remembered my sparkling, mist-like essence, and the sensation of peace. I recalled hearing tinkling sounds as I moved; feeling, tasting and being the sound.

And then I started to freak out at these memories.

What is wrong with me?! Am I dying? Am I dead? How can these thoughts be? Where are they coming from? My ears began to ring and I felt dizzy. I felt a tightness in my chest, my breath quickened and I thought I was going to have a panic attack. Though I had never had one before I imagined that this is what it must feel like.

I was jolted from my thoughts by a car pulling up outside. It was my family. And I realized it was actually a weekday and Dylan, my youngest, had been at the babysitter as he was only three and the girls had been at school all day. Where had the time gone today? Why didn't I go to work? Why didn't anyone wake me? What was happening to me? Suddenly nothing felt right. My thoughts were scrambled and my brain felt like it was about to explode.

I tried to describe what I was feeling and what I had experienced to my husband. He just looked at me wide-eyed as if I were indeed crazy. It was obvious that I could not talk to him about this experience, so I decided it was best that I keep everything to myself.

Over the next few months I lived in a state of disbelief. I did not know or understand what was happening to me as the wisdom and power of my new soul began to heal my body and mind. It took only a few weeks for the majority of the symptoms from the various illnesses to leave my body. Although my symptoms were going away, my body was depleted from stress, lack of proper nutrition and poor hydration. Despite these factors, my energy began to return. I discovered a new willpower and a passion for life that had dwindled many years before. I no longer required the periodic cane to walk and could actually play with the kids pain-free. Even though my body and mind were healing, it took well over a year before the newfound clarity became normal and the 'rewiring' of my brain completed.

My behavior patterns, thought processes and personality began to change rapidly. No longer was I gripped in fear. I felt confident and alive. Certain behaviors became unacceptable to me. My eating habits changed. I spoke differently and with more articulation. Things that used to bother me or that I hung onto melted away. My taste in music changed. I walked around with a feeling of love and compassion in my heart. I found it easy to forgive everyone and everything although

I had not yet grasped the skill of letting it go and forgetting. I felt a newfound connection to everything. When surges of anger bubbled up, they were met with empathy and an understanding of the other person's actions. It was impossible to stay angry or to hold a grudge. I found that it took too much effort. I felt empathy so strongly that I knew what the other person was experiencing, thinking and feeling. I was in a state of bliss, and everyone around me noticed.

More often than not, I began to hear voices providing instruction to me. Sometimes the voices were audible, just as if they were in the same room with me. At other times I would feel the message deep inside of me and I just knew what I needed to do or where I needed to go. I was too dismayed to allow the messages to truly sink in but on some level, they anchored themselves and served as a beacon, leading me down an unknown path. People began to just show up in my life just when I needed them. I began to remember snippets of past lives with clarity.

Shirley MacLaine had written a book in the late 1980s describing her spiritual awakening, involving metaphysics. Today, I see it as a very inspiring book. But 20 years ago I thought it was a joke. I did not believe in spiritual awakenings, I believed in salvation. I did not believe in metaphysics. That was the work of the devil. And for sure I did not believe in reincarnation. I saw it as a cop out, for people who did not want to take personal responsibility for their actions. They believe that karma is the true balancing act and that we receive endless chances in endless lifetimes to reconcile the bad karma. Karma can be understood as a person's actions, in this and all other existences, determine one's fate in this or future lifetimes. It is also viewed as patterns of thought and behavior which affect us and those around us. Our actions create energy, and habitual actions reinforce that energy, be it positive or negative. Healing negative patterns through mindfulness, non-judgmental awareness, moves us to create positive energy for ourselves and the world around us. I wanted nothing to do with it. How naive I was. Yet I could not deny the memories that were flooding my mind. The more past-life memories surfaced, the more desperately I would try to submerge them.

I was learning that I had extremely strong intuition. I knew things, felt things, heard things, saw things and I could tell when someone was lying to me. I was right almost every time, even if the person denied the lies or what I shared with them. This was beyond strange to me. I had no means to understand what was happening or why. I had all these thoughts, memories and sudden knowledge of topics that I had never studied. Following my intuition served me well and I was amazed at how, if I followed my gut, everything fell into place for me.

I began to know more things about the marriage, things that I had never considered. It took me less than one month to decide that I was leaving. I focused all my energy and thoughts on an exit strategy and one-by-one eliminated all the 'what ifs'. I researched a new place to live with all the necessary resources for the kids. All the planning was very calming and served as a diversion from the unfamiliar life that I had stepped into.

The Great Escape

The months leading up to my moving out were filled with worry, a sense of being lost and a great deal of planning. I felt like a giant light bulb had gone off in my head and for the first time in many years I was thinking clearly.

I was beyond perplexed by the feelings I was experiencing. Everything felt wrong. I felt like I was living someone else's life, like

I didn't fit in my body. Even my skin felt strangely stretched on my frame. I couldn't sleep. I couldn't eat. I felt like I couldn't breathe. I had zero feelings for the man I was married to and in all honesty, had no idea as to why I was married to him or what had even brought us together. We were so incompatible. These were horrible feelings.

As bad as these feelings were, the worst feeling of all was the sadness, pain and fear that I felt because I could not remember most of my own children's childhoods! I was internally freaking out and convinced myself that this lack of memory was evidence of some suppressed trauma brought on by a psychotic break, among other things. Try as I might, I simply could remember very few details of their lives, only the large overviews. What I did remember was beautiful and heartwarming.

Anna was 12 years old when I walked into this body. One glance at her big chocolate-brown eyes, brown hair and milky white complexion and I was in love. I remembered little details like reading her bedtime stories, her love of bath time, the smell of her hair as she snuggled with me and her fearless, independent personality. She loved to sing, dance and write plays. She was a great artist for her age. I remembered her first day of school, one birthday party, one Christmas and playing Barbies with her. I remembered that she loved to help in the kitchen and how she would pull her little stool over to the sink to help wash dishes. I remember how excited she was when she found out that she was going to be a big sister and how she loved to dance and dress up in my clothes, shoes and jewelry. One of my favorite memories is how she would sneak into my jewelry, take a piece, wrap it in a napkin and present it to me, eyes twinkling and in a sweet little coy voice say, "I have something for you." These memories still bring joy to my heart.

Caitlin was six years old. She was thin, had curly, light brown hair, hazel eyes and loved every four-legged creature on the planet. If she could have had her way, we would have been overrun with animals. Her passion and love for animals continues to this day and I have come to understand that part of her life's mission is to be a caretaker for the animal kingdom. A lot of memories surfaced about her. Her birth was difficult and I had sporadic memories of it, but I think that was because of the pain. She used to fall a lot because her little feet would move too fast for her body to keep up and that I would run her to the doctor constantly - only to be sent home having been told that she was fine. She would climb like a mountain goat onto everything. One time she was climbing and turned a bookcase over on top of herself. She emerged unhurt and mad that she didn't reach the top. She loved to play house and to mimic cleaning with her toy vacuum. She used to type with her toes. I loved to play 'dress up' with her. I would dress her in a matching hat, outfit, shoes and purse. At the age of four she announced that she was going to school. She was so emphatic about it, that I asked the local kindergarten if she could attend one or two days a week for just half a day. Finally they agreed and she was in heaven! What a bundle of joy she was to me.

Dylan was only three when I arrived. He still had whitish blond hair and bluish green eyes that changed when the light hit them just right. He was full of life and I could hardly keep up with him. He was a cute little man. I remembered how his birth was planned and a bit about it. I remembered that just like Caitlin, he scooted before walking and that he mumbled words, then stopped talking and when he resumed, he made full sentences. I remembered how he liked to hide my keys so I couldn't go to work. I remember the joy he brought and his cute little smile. I remember that he was a very ill little boy.

I immediately loved these beautiful children, unquestionably, undeniably and more than I ever thought capable, but I couldn't remember the fine details of their childhoods and that bothered me. A lot! I was filled with fear and convinced that the memory loss was a result of the illnesses coupled with the stress of the dysfunctional lifestyle and marriage which I couldn't remember much about either. I even thought that maybe the suspected brain tumor was the cause.

I also came into this body knowing my parents and had an immediate love for them. But again, I couldn't remember much about them or my growing up years. I knew I had one sister and I knew that my mother had 18 brothers and sisters that had lived to maturity. Between the uncles, aunts and first cousins, we were a clan of 64. I also knew that my dad had one sister with three children. I knew that we were a close family, yet in knowing all these things, I had no emotion towards any of my uncles, aunts or cousins. The only emotions and connection that I felt were for my children, parents and sister.

The only time I could kind-of remember any event prior to my walking in was when I was shown a photograph and then described what was happening at the time. When the memories did emerge, they were like re-watching a movie that had been long forgotten. The more I understood the severity of the memory loss, the more I was convinced that I had had a psychotic break. With practice however, I became proficient at 'faking' memories. When someone would bring up a memory I would laugh and say something like, "That sounds like we had a blast," or, "Tell me about another time when you had that much fun." I became a master of deflecting conservation and have now had many years of practice.

One thing I couldn't fake, however, was being satisfied with the life or marriage I found myself in. Having resolved to leave, I found the perfect house for me and the kids to move into. It was only a few minutes away from work and the new school that the children would be attending. It was very affordable and close to a park. The schools had a good rating and I felt confident that they would make new friends easily. I paid the damage deposit on a house and the monthly rent. The house sat empty, waiting to become our new home when the time was right.

During the fall of 1999 there was a great deal of fearful speculation about the Y2K bug, the potential for computer systems to fail en masse when the date changed from 1999 to 2000. Taking this into consideration, I decided that I would wait to leave until I saw what happened. After all, we lived on a farm and there was a fresh water supply. The mothering instinct kicked in and I stocked up on extra water and easily accessible food for the kids, just in case. If nothing happened, I planned to move out as soon as possible and decided that I would have extra groceries.

On New Year's Eve 1999, I was home with no idea where the husband was or when he was coming home. Finally, he called and said he was at a party. When the kids asked me where he was and why he wasn't home with them for New Year's I told them he was at a party and would be home soon. They were not happy but decided to make confetti and have a New Year's Eve party of their own. This didn't last long and they were in bed asleep by 10:00 pm. That is when the overwhelming urge to begin packing overtook me. I called my parents at midnight to wish them a happy new year and told them what I was planning. My dad said if I still felt the same in the morning that he would be there to help me move. I called him at 7:00 am and told him that my car was already fully loaded and that I would be ready to load his truck as soon as he arrived. The next thing I knew, he was there. We were ready to begin the move by 9:00am. I was completely moved out within the day and ready to begin my new life.

January 2000 was a busy month. The kids chose rooms and we had all the boxes unpacked, each room filled and decorated by the end of the first week in the house. It was a lot of work, but I wanted them to feel comfortable in their new home, so I worked all day and came home and worked many hours on decorating their rooms and the house … just as I had planned before the move. The new school took some adjusting but the kids were settling in nicely. Everything seemed so much easier than I had imagined even with all the work to be done. Things were so much more peaceful and serene.

I thought that once I was settled into the new house that my life would get back to normal and that all the unfamiliar thoughts and knowledge would go away. I was mistaken. More strange things began to happen to me. I began to sense 'others' in the new house and could smell their presence. My psychic abilities began to manifest and I knew when things were going to happen to me before they occurred. I began to hear voices and have strange prophetic dreams.

I even began to experience missing time. At first, it was only a few minutes here and there, but then it escalated to 30 minutes at a time and then as much as an hour. I attributed it to stress, although I felt more relaxed and slept better than I had in months.

One Saturday morning, the three children and I were cleaning their toy room when the brightest, whitest flash of light occurred directly behind my daughter Anna's head. It was so bright that it was like looking directly into a camera flash. All three of us looked around the room trying to figure out what had caused it. It was not raining and there was no storm outside. All the lights in the room were functioning. Eventually, we gave up trying to explain the flash and went back to putting clothes on the Barbie dolls and the toy trucks on the shelves. After about thirty minutes Dylan said he was hungry, so we went downstairs to fix lunch. Much to our dismay it was almost dinner time! We couldn't have been in the room more than two hours yet more than six hours had passed. Where did the time go? What had happened? At the time, we thought we were just seriously into the cleaning mode. It wasn't until years later that I learned we had experienced missing time as a family.

Everything Happens for a Reason

When I moved out, I was working in the field of tourism. Part of my job consisted of some travel and quite a few afternoon and evening meetings. One evening, I had to work and decided to take the kids with me. This meeting led to my meeting a man that eventually offered me a job in an adjoining state. After a few months of being in this body, my marital status changed, I accepted a new job and moved to a different state.

I was super excited. This job would afford me the finances to take care of my three children. I was already finding out that child support would be slow in coming, if at all and being so close to the soon to be ex-husband was proving to be disastrous in so many ways. Looking back, as trying as those times were, they provided so many gifts and I have learned to be grateful for all the lessons that I learned.

Even though I had just settled in the new house, the thought of moving to a different state was exciting. I decided that this job and the move would be the best thing for everyone. I was concerned that the kids would have to go through another move, but I decided to make it an adventure.

My late aunt Mary Lee - or 'Floss' as we liked to call her - agreed to stay with the kids so I could visit the new office and tour the area. During the initial visit, I stayed overnight. Trying to research the new living location, I picked up the local telephone directory. In the back was an ad for a variety of services including one for spiritual counseling, provided by Rev. Jeremie Leckron, PhD. I was compelled to pick up the phone and call the number. It was after hours so I left a message requesting an appointment and a return call as soon as possible. It was my greatest hope that I would now be able to receive the answers as to what was happening with me and put all this strangeness to rest. Jeremie called the next day and an appointment was scheduled.

When the day of my appointment arrived, I was filled with hope and trepidation. I believed in my heart that I had had and was still experiencing a psychotic break and memory loss due to trauma. In actuality, I was hoping she would write me a prescription so my life could get back to normal. But more than anything, I wanted answers. And answers I received. Not the ones I wanted, but the answers I needed.

First, I learned that Jeremie holds a PhD in Psychology, is a Unity Minister and Spiritual Teacher. My education was also in psychology and I was still entrenched in fundamental religious beliefs, so it felt very comfortable working with her. After all, she is a minister. I also learned that she is of Hopi lineage and the first daughter of the first daughter seven generations back of the Bear Clan. Within the Hopi culture, that is a big deal.

As we began our session, I told Jeremie what I had been experiencing and explained my suspected psychosis. Instead of giving me the response I expected to hear, I was assured that I was not having a psychotic break but that I had experienced an instantaneous spiritual awakening. She told me that I needed to reconcile the fact that I was now clairvoyant, clairaudience, clairsentient and claircognizant, was extremely empathic and was a walk-in.

What?! I felt sick, and felt my reality begin to fall away. I had never heard of the 'clairs', or walk-ins. Because I was clearly shaken, Jeremie told me that everything would be all right, to "just breathe," and scheduled the next appointment.

I left the first session mumbling to myself and shaking my head. I could not believe what I had just heard. Not only did I not get any answers that fitted into my belief system, but I was told things that verified that the experiences I was having were real. If I was not experiencing a breakdown and what was happening to me was real, then everything I had previously believed in was an illusion! My paradigm was shattered.

I had been asleep, and was now awake. I was a soul with a body, not a body with a soul. The voices I had been hearing were coming from the world of spirit, not from paranoia, delusions or psychosis. The things I was seeing, like circles of light in my house or people walking down the hall, were actually real. The dreams that I had which came true were actually premonitions. My entire world was rocked. It shifted and was breaking apart. Not in a negative way, but in a way that was bringing enlightenment.

Regardless of the intensity of the experience, I was hooked on this newfound truth. Something inside was screaming, "YES!" And I knew that the words I had heard were true. My soul began crying out for more. Once I moved, I began seeing Jeremie on a weekly basis. I also began to take spiritual classes with her called 'circles' and studied with women from every walk of life. I absorbed the flow of knowledge joyfully. If it had not been for Jeremie and the teachings she provided to me, I would have checked myself into a mental institution during my initial integration.

A few days after my first visit with Jeremie, I was working at the computer when suddenly I became very tired. My mind began to wander then went blank. It was like I was asleep, sitting up in my chair, with my eyes open, only semi-aware of my surroundings. Yet all the while, my fingers were typing. I was stunned when I snapped out of it and realized that I had written several pages. I made a copy of the writings and took them to Jeremie, who explained that I had channeled them. I had never heard of channeling. She explained that I had received and reproduced information from my spiritual guide, teacher or an otherworldly being. That freaked me out too! I was becoming afraid that my life would never be normal again. I channeled many writings over the next few months but lost them when my computer crashed.

I quickly began to understand that everything happens for a reason. Being offered the job and moving to a different state was more about being taken care of by the universe than my qualifications for the job. Yes, I was qualified, but those qualifications only allowed me to walk through a door that had been opened for me by the universe. This move also made it more difficult for the ex-husband to just drop by. Additionally, it placed me closer to Jeremie where I received the emotional and mental support needed to adjust to being a walk-in and it provided me with a spiritual community of women that would support me through the rough times ahead.

Being a part of a spiritual sisterhood made a lasting impression on me. I was blown away by the authenticity and depth of these women. Our clan had women representing every walk of life, including attorneys, teachers and political consultants, and all of them were working to discover their authentic selves. It was amazing. This group of women provided the support I needed and the spiritual family that I craved. All of a sudden, my children had more aunties than they could count. These women helped to nurture and shape their lives. They were babysitters, shoulders to cry on, and they served to verify the fact that I was not crazy. They held my hand during the insane divorce and called me out when I needed it. We became true sisters and there is not one of these ladies that I wouldn't be there for if needed. Time and space cannot break the bonds we forged.

In the circle, I learned about shamanic journeying and meditation, about walking the good walk, about standing in your truth and integrity. I learned how to use and not use my gifts. I became a ceremonialist and developed a deep relationship with my guides and teachers. I learned the magic of letting go and the art of stepping into non-linear time. I had so many unusual experiences during this time. On one occasion, I was showering and a three-foot wide silver eye appeared in the shower with me and I heard that I had been given the gift of discernment. Another time I was visiting a friend and I heard an audible warning: "Get out. You must leave now." Later I learned that this helped me avoid an accident on the road. And one day the Lords of Karma came to visit me in my home. I could write an entire book about my mystical experiences, but the most important thing I wish to share is the fact that throughout these huge shifts, the circle and my sisterhood were always there, supporting me.

The path of shamanism became my anchor and it was the only thing in my life that made sense. My daily prayers served to ground me. The shamanic journeys became my comfort zone and a place to escape to when I became overwhelmed with being in human form and living on Earth. My guides and teachers took me on many adventures and shared multiple truths with me about who I am and my place in the universe. The East taught me all about the new beginnings in my life. The South took me on a path of healing. The West became my release zone and the North gave me the wisdom teachings and knowledge that I needed. Father Sky protected me and Mother Earth nurtured me. All these things were taught under the watchful eye of Jeremie, both in waking and in dream time.

Jeremie helped to interpret my visions. She held me to high

standards and helped shape my gifts. She became my confidante and spiritual advisor. Jeremie had the single biggest influence on my life since coming into this body. I am so blessed to have her in my life.

She always told me the Hopi were a dying people. It is sad, but she has only one living relative left on the reservation and all her Hopi teachers have passed away. The oral tradition that she passed to me is valued more than ever now and I hold its wisdom deep in my heart.

Now that I have moved away, we still keep in touch. I have tried to Skype into circle meetings or to be on a call, but it is just not the same as being there. Jeremie now has a website, which is hopiwisdomteachings.com. I encourage you to check it out. If possible, make your way to one of her gatherings and experience the magic for yourself.

Serendipity

Within a few months of working with Jeremie, she announced to me during a session that she had had a vision that I would remarry. She described the man I would meet as somewhat political, with square hands, and said he would be tall with slightly greying dark hair. Our meeting would involve a vehicle.

Remarry? Was she crazy? I was just getting out of a marriage and I was definitely not looking for another husband. The thought made me almost sick to my stomach, so I decided to not think about it.

My work with Jeremie led me to an in-depth shamanic journey practice. This type of work came easily, and traveling to the upper and lower world became my sanctuary. There, I would work with my guides, teachers, angels or just take a break from the life I now found myself living. I just enjoyed being there and had been instructed not to ask any questions, just to see where the adventure took me.

One of the exercises that Jeremie assigned was to journey or vision for a fellow circle sister. By journeying for each other and not ourselves, we were taught about integrity in the other worlds. We drew names and I pulled my friend Linda's name. I was excited to see what I could ascertain for her.

I started the journey like any other journey when I suddenly found myself in white space. A 20-foot tall red capital letter D appeared. Much to my surprise, on top of the letter was my friend Linda, a tall, thin, older lady with a long cigarette in one hand and large glass of red wine in the other. She was happily swinging her legs into the opening of the D and smiling down at me. I was a bit shocked to see her on top of the letter and my mind began racing as I began to conjure an explanation to explain what I was seeing, as I thought the D stood for death or dying. 'Poor Linda,' I thought. Just then the energy of a man entered the space. I couldn't make out the face as he wandered about, looking up, down and all around. I was astonished to see him there. He turned to me and exclaimed, "This is soooo cool! Where am I? Am I going to be able to remember this when I wake up?" Immediately I told him that I had no clue but that he had no business wandering into my meditation and to get out! He walked to the left and disappeared, mumbling to himself about how cool that was. For the second time in the journey I was shocked, this time to the point that I rapidly came out. I wrote everything down to share with my friend Linda and hoped that maybe she could provide a bit of clarity about who the man was. But she had no idea.

This was only the first of a series of strange situations where the energy of the man came to me. At night I began hearing footsteps in the hallway. Thinking that one of the kids was awake, I would get out of bed and open my door only to find no-one there and the children fast asleep. This happened several nights in a row. Then one day while

I was washing dishes, I looked out my kitchen window to see the figure of a man rolling down the hill with my son, Dylan. I quickly discovered that Dylan was not outside at all but in his room playing. I believed that I was overly tired and tried to dismiss it. But later that week after dinner, I felt his presence behind me and someone kissed me on the back of my neck. I turned to find no-one there. I was a little freaked out by now. I quickly finished the dishes and went into what we called the TV room and sat on the couch next to my daughter Caitlin. A few minutes later the form of a man walked across the floor, sat down on the couch next to me, put his arm around me and gave Caitlin a 'nuggie' on the top of her head. I immediately jumped up and grabbed Caitlin off the couch, much to her surprise and disgust. She had not experienced anything, was deeply unimpressed and asked what was going on. I apologized and told her I thought something was in her hair. Irritated, she sat back down on the couch and went back to watching TV.

The next morning, I called Jeremie to explain what I had been experiencing. I asked her to conduct a spiritual cleansing on the house. She agreed, and we set a date for later that week. Upon her arrival, I met her at her car. As we walked up the driveway stairs and into the house, I explained everything again, pointing to the areas where each event had occurred. She thoroughly examined the house, inspecting each room two or three times. Finally, she returned to where I was and explained that she found no traces of anything negative in the house, only a German Shepard and his ball. She further explained that the ball must have been what I heard in the hallway and that there were no traces of the man I had described. Just for good measure she cleansed and blessed the house and buried goose feathers at each corner. She left satisfied that I would not have any more visitors. She was right. From that point on I had no more experiences with the man. I felt that the children and I were safe.

Being the good shamanic student that I was, I refused to break the visioning rules set in place at the time, but curiosity was getting the best of me. I called Nancy, one of my circle sisters, and asked her to journey for me to ascertain who the man was that appeared in my vision and my home. Also, I asked her to see if she could get a name. This was a normal practice in our circle. If we couldn't journey for ourselves, we would journey for each other. In hindsight, I believe this was Jeremie's way of getting us to practice. Within the hour, I received a call back from Nancy. She said that she had indeed seen a man and had asked him if he was the one who had been in my house. He nodded. She then asked what he wanted but he said nothing. She asked his name but he refused to give it to her. Instead he turned his closed palm over to reveal an amethyst stone inside, then he was gone. When she gave me this information I was more confused than ever and we vowed to try again another day.

A few days later we made another attempt. I received a call after her journey and she told me that she asked all the same questions and received all the same answers but his time instead of an amethyst stone, he held out a bottle of A1 steak sauce. What?! I was baffled. I was beginning to think that this was a playful spirit trying to have some fun, so I forgot about him for a while.

A month or two passed before my curiosity returned. I called Nancy and we decided to try again. The next day she called with the results. This time when she 'went in', she saw a man standing on a ladder, painting. When she entered the space, he turned to look at her. Again, she asked the questions. This time he told her, "I am the man that is going to love her and her children for the rest of our lives. And neither she, nor the children intimidate me." He then turned around, resumed painting and disappeared. "Well, alrighty then," I mused. "I guess I'll just have to wait until I meet a non-intimidated guy bearing amethyst and A1 sauce."

Several years passed and no man fitting the description that Jeremie gave or that matched anything we received in the visions materialized. So, I just tucked the information away and went on with my life.

In May of 2003, I had a business meeting in Albuquerque, New Mexico. I did not want to go. Dylan was still having medical issues and had recently been hospitalized with severe asthma, so I was afraid to be too far away from him. In a session with Jeremie I expressed this. She listened to me whine for a bit then looked me in the eye and said, "Honey, you have to go. He is going to be there. The guy you're going to marry," I immediately began throwing out all the reasons that I should not go. Finally, she said, "Okay, honey. You're going. Call me when you get back."

I had to admit that raising children by myself was a bit overwhelming at times, especially with the job I had. From a work viewpoint, the job had to come first; from my viewpoint, the children always come first. I was in turmoil over the decision but in the end I decided to go, though my heart was not in it. I was so worried about Dylan. My dad came to stay with the children while I was away and assured me everything would be okay.

My co-worker Jim went to the meeting with me. As we were en route, I saw an inflight magazine. Inside, was an article about Albuquerque. It discussed the amazing architecture and life in the desert. I was captivated, and energetically drawn to go see the desert while I was there. I felt like the very soil itself was calling to me. The urge was overwhelming, powerful and somewhat intoxicating. I had never felt like that before. I leaned over and told Jim that if I met someone that had a jeep, I was going to go to the desert. He looked at me like I was crazy.

The next day's meetings seemed to drag on. At lunch I went out to shop for gifts, and returned to the banquet hall to find that the lunch speeches had just begun. I snuck inside, standing against the wall for a moment so my eyes could adjust. Every table was full. "Ugh," I thought, reprimanding myself for being late. Just then, it was like a ray of sunshine shone down onto an empty seat at a table near the back of the room. I slinked over and asked if the seat was taken. I was invited to sit down and began frivolous conservation with my table mates. One man in particular caught my eye and I began to wonder if he could be 'the one' but decided not, because surely bells and whistles would go off or at least I would hear my guides tell me that I was correct.

Before the next meeting started I went looking for the restroom. In the hall I recognized the guy from the lunch table, Don. He was looking for the same meeting that I was in, so I directed him to the room and said there was an empty seat by me. He was there when I returned from the restroom so we chatted until the meeting facilitator arrived. I asked Don which tour he was taking the next day and he told me that he was not going on any of the tours. Instead, he had his jeep and was going into the desert. My colleague was dismayed when I asked, "Can I go?" I am sure Don was shocked but he politely agreed. He said he would meet me downstairs by the fountain and was leaving at 6:00 am Jim just rolled his eyes but said nothing.

I was so excited at the thought of walking on the soil of the desert that I could hardly sleep. I wonder if I was going to receive a download or new guide. I was sure something amazing was going to happen because I was heeding the call of the desert.

The next morning, I was up bright and early. Because there was a two-hour time difference between New Mexico and Kentucky, I called my dad to check on the kids and told him I was going to the desert. "Sheila Ann, you don't even know this guy. For all you know he could be an axe murder." Tongue in cheek I explained, "Well, I just wanted you to know where I am going just in case something does happen. The guy's name is Don and he drives a red jeep" After the call, I went downstairs and was at the fountain with a few minutes to spare before our 6:00 am departure. I did not want to miss my opportunity!

Soon Don appeared. We had breakfast then headed off, chatting companionably about various topics. I asked if he had children and then proceeded to tell him all about mine. I even showed him photos as he was driving. We shared divorce stories before moving to spiritual topics. As we talked, I kept looking out of the window waiting to come to the desert. I asked when we would see it and he explained about high mountain deserts and that we had been driving through it the entire time. I must admit, my heart sank. I don't know what I expected, but it was not this.

Before long, we were pulling into Chaco Canyon, a National Historical Park between Albuquerque and Farmington, New Mexico. The landscape was dry and barren, but the beauty was undeniable. During one of our circle meetings we had discussed Chaco Canyon, the Anasazi that had built it, and the fact that it was considered the center of the universe by the people. I was excited to be there, and it was nice to be able to connect with someone who understood the deep spiritual meaning and mysteries of the place. On the way back he stopped to stretch and shared some of his karate forms, and I taught him how to see auras of trees. He was a quick study.

We arrived too late for the prearranged dinner meeting, so we decided to go to a local restaurant instead. Don chose a Brazilian restaurant. I had never dined in a Brazilian restaurant before and found it quite good. The meal consists of only meat and an offering of condiments including, surprise surprise, A1 steak sauce. With our bellies full, we went back to the hotel and retired to our rooms.

I had a wonderful day. I was sure I would be in tons of trouble when I returned to work and maybe even fired but to be honest, I did not care. For the first time in a long time, I felt grounded and peaceful. I was so moved by the day that I felt compelled to write a little note of thanks to Don. I carefully placed it in one of the jewelry boxes with a stone and stick that I had gathered that day. I slept very soundly that night.

We had agreed to meet downstairs the next morning to say our goodbyes. I arrived early and didn't see him, so I thought he must have decided to sleep in. I took the box that I had prepared the night before and left it at the front desk asking the clerk to give it to him when he checked out. When I turned around, I saw him walking towards me. We chatted, I took a photo of him and headed to the airport with Jim.

It was not until the airplane was in the air that I began to feel sick as a wave of energy washed over me. For a minute, I thought I was going to pass out, then a strange thought entered into my mind. I felt like I missed being around Don's energy. That was very odd to me because yes, I thought he was a very nice person with a jeep, but we had been totally platonic with no indication of romance from either of us. I was going to have to sit with this and talk to Jeremie about not meeting 'the one'.

Arriving back home was bittersweet. Sweet to see the children and see their faces light up with the gifts I bought them but bitter as that sick feeling continued to linger. I made an appointment to see Jeremie within the week. I shared my entire experience with Jeremie. She just grinned, nodding her head and said we would see.

Much to my surprise, I was not reprimanded from the 'higher ups' regarding the trip. In fact, nothing was ever said about it at all. That was worse than the dreaded talk I had expected but it was spring and there were a lot of events happening. I wanted to jump back into work but wanted to file the materials from the meeting away first. As I was filing and throwing away, I came across Don's phone number and email and decided to email him my thanks. One email led to another and within six weeks he came to Kentucky to visit. In less than a year, we married.

One of Don's visits consisted of attending a workshop Jeremie was holding. It was in Asheville, NC and I was eager to introduce him to the crew. This workshop consisted of getting in touch with the elements and learning to work and influence them. Several impressive displays of our influence were clearly demonstrated. During one meditation we were taught how to call up the wind. The directions were simple but the work intense. We would close our eyes, drop into our heart space, expand our essence and connect with the wind. The longer we held the concentration, the harder the wind blew. If we opened our eyes, it would stop. We repeated this exercise with connecting to the rain and had equal success. The power of that weekend was immense.

Another exercise was about connecting to the essence of the rock people. Jeremie had a beautiful table in the middle of the room adorned with a variety of beautiful stones. Each attendee was to go to the table and select the stone that called them (caught their attention causing them to want to pick it up). When it came Don's turn he walked straight to the table and selected the amethyst stone. Nancy and I looked at each other and burst into tears. Don became quite concerned and asked what he had done. We both told him nothing but that he had selected the amethyst and then handed it to me to look at, just as Nancy had described in her initial journey.

Jeremie's declaration that I would meet 'him' at the Albuquerque meeting seemed true. I was washing dishes one night and Don came up behind me and kissed my neck. Again, I started crying. I left the kitchen and went into the television room where the children were watching tv and sat down on the couch next to Caitlin. Don came out of the kitchen, walked over the couch, sat down next to me, putting his arm around me and gave Caitlin a nuggie. Again, I started crying. During another visit he explained how his German Shepard dog loved to play ball and that he had passed before we met. Jeremie later told me that it was Don's deceased German Shepard dog that she had 'picked up' when she came to cleanse and bless my house. Then many months later, as I was sharing the story of how we had met to a circle sister, Loney, I told her about the Brazilian Restaurant and she reminded me about the bottle of A1 steak sauce Don had presented in one of Nancy's visions. Spirit had given me all the signs, but I had a veil of sorts keeping me from recognizing him right away.

Don and I had a whirlwind relationship. We met in May of 2003 and married in April of 2004. Our wedding ceremony consisted of my immediate family, his family, a few of his close friends and my sisterhood. Jeremie married us and we had a very Earth-based ceremony. We incorporated the 'wedding blanket' ceremony and in a surprise move Don pledged himself to not only me but to my three children as well. There never was, nor has there ever been, step-children. My children were his children. We were part of a spiritual family that had reunited.

Prior to our wedding, Don's mother announced that since he was moving to Kentucky that she would have to sell the family campground she built and opened in 1967. After a lengthy discussion, it was decided that Don would operate the campground and in summers, the children and I would spend our vacation there. When it closed in the fall, he would come back to Kentucky. That lasted only the two summers of 2004 and 2005 and it was decided that we would all live together in Colorado.

So, when people ask how Don and I met, I ask them if they want the short or long version. You can understand why. I include all this detail to illustrate the complex dynamics of my journey. My development often met resistance or denial of sorts, yet circumstance would often show me the truth and significance of information that came to me through shamanic journeying, guidance or other psychic means. Part of being a walk-in has been about developing these gifts, and as they developed, they offer me more support in understanding and enacting my mission.

During this timeframe, I shared with my mom, Eula Fielder, that I was a walk-in, to quiet her concern that I might be experiencing the early onset of Alzheimer's. My grandfather had suffered Alzheimer's and because I had difficulty remembering people and events that she spoke of, and because I had difficulty connecting with extended family members that apparently I had once been very close to, her concern was that I might have Alzheimer's too. My mom and dad are storytellers. When stories were told, it was like I was hearing them for the first time. Referring to childhood friends meant nothing to me and frankly, I didn't remember most of my childhood, only a select memory here or there. I remembered a few of my cousins. If I was shown a photo and the story shared that went along with it, I felt as if I were watching a movie that I had no emotional attachment to.

When I told my mom I was a walk-in, I explained the reason for my lack of memory and connection. I explained that I had become a completely different person, with a new soul and a new way of understanding. Many of the memories I lost was because they did not support my new mission. She pondered that for a moment and then asked, "Does that mean I am not your mom?" I replied, "Of course you are. Just to a new and improved version." She said it made perfect sense to her as she had recognized all the changes.

I am happy to say that over the past 20 years, I have rekindled friendships with many of my extended family members and believe that I now appreciate them more than ever. They are wonderful, colorful people with loving hearts. What a lucky person I am to have chosen this family to incarnate into.

The Mission Begins

When I entered this body, I walked in with a firm mission, but before it could be executed, I had to clear a path. The first step was that Caitlin, Dylan and I moved to Colorado in the summer of 2006. We had visited there with Don many times and believed that this is where we all belonged. Anna was in college and chose to stay in Kentucky. I was sad that she wouldn't be moving with us but I understood her choice.

After settling in Colorado, I became so homesick for my sisterhood that I would call and talk to many of the women for hours each day. They were my support system during my initial integration phase. They had laughed and cried with me as I struggled to understand my new life. I did not realize how grounding the sisterhood had been for me. I now felt a spiritual loss and for the first time since embodiment, felt empty, sad and mildly depressed. I shamanically journeyed and meditated but something was off. Instead of using my skills to drop more deeply into the understanding of who I was, I sank into despair. I started seeing an acupuncturist who told me that I was struggling to acclimate. I had gone from an altitude of

971 feet to 10,000 feet, and both body and mind were having a hard time adjusting. It took nearly six months for things to feel somewhat normal to me. Armed with this knowledge, my spirits lifted.

Now I was ready to take the next step towards enacting my mission. I enrolled at the University of Metaphysical Sciences and filled my days working to obtain my bachelor's degree in Metaphysical Sciences.

Prior to moving from Kentucky to Colorado, I was challenged by Jeremie to start my own circles. It took me about a year but in 2007, I decided to take her up on the challenge. In all honesty, I did so in hopes of recapturing the community and magic that I had felt within my own sisterhood. I soon discovered, however, that it is one thing to be a member of the sisterhood and quite another to teach one. I quickly realized that both were just as powerful and fulfilling.

I fell in love with the women of the circles that I taught. Each woman was unique and brought their authentic selves to our gatherings every week. And each of them blossomed. Teaching became an unexpected spiritual joy and I felt the sense of community once more. I have now been working with some of the same women for over 15 years and it always warms my heart when they tell me how much they have learned from me and what an impact I have made on their lives. It is entirely mutual. They have changed my life forever. Through this work it became clear to me that teaching was part one of my mission in being a wayshower.

The next step in preparing me to more fully embrace my mission was to embody the truth of being a walk-in. I had shared with several people a little about my experience but felt ill at ease with speaking the words. Even though I knew with every fiber of my being that I was indeed a walk-in, the mental aspect of this truth was still hard for me to fully comprehend and accept. I was filled with self-doubt. I sought out numerous spiritual teachers and shamans seeking confirmation. Each one affirmed that I was a walk-in, but their verification felt hollow somehow. Only later did I realize that one of the reasons I was having such a difficult time was that I was struggling through and working to clear the cellular memory and cellular imprinting of self-doubt and confusion that was part of the physical body.

Cellular memory and cellular imprinting are similar yet different. Cellular memories are memories that are stored in the cells of the body. These memories can include current lifetime memories, as well of memories passed down through past lives. They also include an inherited gene pool that infuses the physical body with certain types of behaviors and traits. These traits are passed from generation to generation such as a crooked smile, the way someone tilts their head, walks or responds to stress. It also includes aches and pains from this lifetime as well as any emotionally charged situation.

Since emotions are caused in part by chemical responses in the brain, when our body cannot detox a surge of emotion-causing chemicals all at once, they become stored in the muscles, tissue and bone of our physical body. These emotions lodge in our emotional, mental or spiritual bodies and become cellular imprints.

The type of cellular imprinting that I am referring to is then twofold: the cellular imprinting that occurs during day-to-day life, and the imprinting the soul makes on the physical, mental, emotional and spiritual bodies. This type of imprinting carries the spiritual genetic codes of your soul, your mission, higher thought processes, soul vibration and the propensity for spiritual awakening. The pre-impregnated body that I walked into was now being imprinted with my own soul codes and to say the least, there was a conflict.

I was fortunate that when I entered the body, the cellular

imprinting of the natal soul was such that when I entered into the body an energetic framework had been laid which allowed me to come in without 'frying' the body's network (I will speak about how that works in the section that follows). This allowed for an easier transition and for more of my soul essence to enter. Although I didn't remember who I was before or where I had just come from, I had retained basic skill knowledge. However, this framework did nothing to equip me to be able to effectively deal with emotions and I resorted to the preset pattern of ignoring them and acting as if my feelings didn't matter. The task of clearing this behavioral pattern, and the emotional work it required, proved to be a challenge.

The more I learned to embrace, release and clear previously stored cellular memories and behavior patterns, the less attached I became to them and the easier it was to respond in a different way. I began to understand and recognize the difference between the previous cellular memory patterning and the current cellular imprinting. In other words, I began to recognize what was truly mine and in this knowing I was able to begin to heal the behavioral responses and to let go of the old emotions. This was an excruciating process.

As things cleared, I began to see my experiences of self-doubt and confusion as a gift, a learning opportunity. This gift allowed me to begin operating from the place of knowing that I am a soul having a human experience. And that in the larger scheme of things, good, bad, joyful or painful emotions were just an experience. Once I embraced that truth and integrated deeply, I stopped second-guessing myself and began releasing the cellular memory emotion of self-doubt. Simply recognizing this truth was enough to allow the fullness of the cellular imprinting of my soul to anchor.

I felt blessed with this knowledge and knew that I was ready to move to yet another phase of stepping into my mission; it was time to begin working with my spiritual gifts. I learned that each gift resonated at a different frequency and as I was able to clear more cellular memory, I moved more and more into resonance with them. I also learned that the gifts I have are not 'gifts on demand'.

The gift of claircognizance (knowing) was the easiest to work with because it was already second nature to me and anchored firmly upon arrival. I believe this gift is the inherent wisdom of my soul and flows through me at all times. It allows me to know what is and is not true for me. It shows me what direction to take and serves as a factual road map for my life. In the beginning I had some self-doubt, but it quickly dissipated as what I knew in my heart either was or became fact. I no longer doubt my inner knowing and feel that all other gifts are an extension of it, such as the gift of clairaudience (hearing). At first I had to really pay attention to this gift, as I was not used to hearing voices in my head. Thus, another reason I initially thought I was having a mental breakdown. I often heard my name being called out and I was given, both audibly and internally, sentences, messages and information. Sometimes I hear messages so loudly in my head that I respond out loud. As this gift became part of me, people would often ask (and still do) who I was talking to. I learned that if I want to know the answer to something, all I had to do was ask and the answer would be given. It was not always the answer that I wanted but the one I needed.

Working with the gift of clairvoyance is also part of my knowing. At first, knowing things about people or situations made me feel uncomfortable because the knowledge would just come and flood me, whether I was seeking the information or not. I had to work hard to tame this beast. It seemed to become intertwined with the gift of being an empath and I would often feel someone's story or pain inside of me so strongly that it was hard to differentiate their emotions and pain from my own. With time, I learned how to effectively unlink the emotion from the information.

I do not believe that I am special or unique in possessing and working with these gifts. I believe everyone possesses these gifts, that they are pre-packaged within our soul. It's just a matter of developing them and whether or not they serve your own soul's mission in this lifetime. In fact, many people have much more developed gifts than I do but that is all part of their experience.

I am very grateful for the gifts I have received. Through working with them I have become highly aware that I am not my body. I am a soul in the Sheila suit. Source is in, around and through me at all times, as it is with everyone. I am able to remember this truth and to see things from a higher perspective, most times. Operating from a place of knowing does not mean that I do not have feelings or express emotion. I am just like everyone else in that department as you have just learned. I do, however, have the ability to really drop into experiencing emotions fully and then to be done with them. Well, with everyone except my husband, as he will attest! Frustration is an emotion that is deeply embedded within the cellular memory of the body and I continue to work with it.

Having emotions is one of the greatest attributes that being in human physical form can offer. We learn through our emotions, but these same emotions can keep us held captive for long periods of time unless we learn how to properly manage them. If not appropriately expressed, emotions become stuck in the physical body and cause blockages. When blockages occur, life force energy is restricted and the body can become ill.

The emotions I learned to release do occasionally rear their heads just to make sure that I have in fact learned the lesson and integrated them. When they surface, it is much easier for me to move through the lesson. Having experienced emotional cellular clearing and release, I was ready to move to my next lesson.

So far, my mission consisted of being a spiritual teacher and helping others to wake up to the fact of who they truly are. I assist them in remembering their missions and in working through their own cellular memories and imprinting in preparation for their spiritual evolution. I felt quite content knowing that I was on mission.

Then one day, during a meditation, I was told by my guides that my mission was about to expand. I was reminded that people cannot drop into the depths of their soul and awaken to their true nature when they are in pain. I was now charged with providing healing services as a way to get people out of pain and into their souls. Once this message was received, I felt a passion well up inside of me and I began to search for an office location where I could provide the required services. While I was searching for the perfect office, I worked with Jeremie's husband, Davis, who was an attorney. He helped me to lay the appropriate foundation for the type of business I desired. Soon, I was open for business as a non-profit church in the State of Colorado called SpiritWay Ministries doing business as SpiritWay or SpiritWay Wellness.

At first, I offered spiritual teaching/advice and Reiki, a Japanese hands-on healing technique. Before moving to Colorado, I studied with an independent Reiki Master, Ella Fay Russell and became a Reiki Master/Teacher and a Karuna Reiki Master/Teacher. I loved providing Reiki. When I would place my hands on someone's body they would receive the relief they sought. I was then called to invite speakers and other healers to the office to make presentations and to work with clients. One of these healers led me down a path that I had not anticipated and it opened the door to allow the activation of my crystalline body.

I had been having what I thought were past-life memories of being a South American Shaman. I was running, almost naked, through a jungle. There was no sense of direction and no particular place that I was going. This memory came to me as if caught in a loop as I saw the same thing, over and over again. I was sharing this experience with a healer/ceremonialist/artist friend of mine, Katherine Skaggs. Katherine had come to the office to offer soul portraits to various people. She had the gift of being able to look at a person, see the energy of their soul and then put it on canvas. Her work is amazing. (You can visit her website at katherineskaggs.com)

At the end of the day, she was painting a portrait of me and we were discussing possibilities for the memory when she gifted me a small stone from the Stone Forest in Peru. The stone was very tiny and I was captivated by its majestic beauty. When Katherine placed it in the palm of my hand, I carefully cradled it so as not to lose it when the weight of it took my entire hand to the floor. Stunned, I brought the arm back up and much to our dismay, it was sparkling. The sparkles slowly spread over the entirety of my body and I began to feel woozy, yet light and expanded. As I shared what I was experiencing, we decided that the stone had activated my crystalline body, which you can still see when I am out in the sun and sometimes when I am indoors as well.

As we discussed the crystalline body and the past life memory, Katherine began to share with me traditions among some of the Peruvian people and a ceremony with the sacred plant ayahuasca. The more she discussed the ceremony, the more I dropped into the energy of the story and began experiencing the ceremony as if I were a participant. Between the crystalline body activation and the ceremonial experience, I was in no shape to walk home, though I lived only a block away. I had to call my husband to come get me.

When he arrived, he immediately asked if we had had a glitter fight. Katherine explained the events of the evening as I was not able to. He took me home and I slept soundly. When I awoke the next morning, I felt amazing. The 'glitter' was beginning to subside somewhat, but there was still residue on my face and arms. Occasionally I still glisten and when I sweat, especially if I am out of doors, I look like the character Edward from the movie *Twilight*.

I have since learned, from another spiritual teacher, that I was not experiencing a past life. Instead, I was connecting with a different aspect of my soul that was currently living in Brazil. I was having a parallel life experience! I was so excited that I asked if I might be able to meet him but was advised against it. It seems that it is not a good idea for two aspects of a soul to meet because there would exist the possibility of the stronger soul absorbing the weaker soul, causing death to the host body. That warning was enough for me. I neither wanted to consume or be consumed by anything else.

The quickening of my crystalline body increased the strength of my intuition significantly. During Reiki sessions I discovered that when I touched someone's body, I would begin to receive messages about their illnesses, dysfunctions and emotional imbalances. I would do my best to direct the energy to dissipate the situation(s) with great success. I now could also emulate chiropractic corrections by making energetic moves above the body in the air and it worked! My business began to grow by leaps and bounds but then, the 'magic' stopped. Frustrated, I asked my guides what I was doing wrong but received no answer. I became more and more frustrated because regardless of how I asked the questions, I received no answers. I was so frustrated that I began entertaining the idea of closing my business.

Then I received my answer. A family friend came to visit after having returned from a workshop. She explained that she had learned

Total Body Modification (TBM) by one of its primary founders, Dr. Victor Frank. Practitioners use body points to determine what is going on in the body with its organs, glands, systems, pathologies and emotions. Wow! I wanted to experience this, so I booked a session for the entire family. At the end of the session I was disappointed at having experienced nothing and seemingly, no results. This disappointment gnawed at me for more than two weeks, so finally, I picked up the phone and called Dr. Frank's office. I said that I didn't understand his treatment and asked him to explain it to me. He did so at length and by the end of the conservation I had been invited to attend his next seminar. Excitedly, I signed myself and my husband up. It was explained that typically, this modality was used by the chiropractic community, but I was welcome to come give it a try.

The workshop was amazing and I couldn't wait for the next modules to be offered. I finished the entire series of workshops in about a year and a half and I began offering it to my clients with amazing results. I continued to stay in touch with 'Doc' as everyone who knew him lovingly called him, and he became a mentor and friend. I was invited to his and his wife's, Diane, 50th wedding anniversary and planned to attend.

I was heartbroken to learn that both he and his wife had passed within a week or two of each other and instead of attending the anniversary celebration, Don and I attended their memorial service. During their passing, I had been in Akwesasne, working on the Mohawk reservation with my friend, and spiritual teacher Emmy Mitchel, offering TBM sessions. One night, just as I was about to go to sleep, I saw Doc walking out of the closet towards me, cowboy boots on, hands on his oversized belt buckle. He was speaking but I couldn't hear what he was saying. I fell asleep just as he reached my bedside. The next morning, I awoke thinking it was a dream. It was that day that I learned of his passing. I will never forget that visit.

While at the memorial service, my husband and I both saw his oldest daughter, through a glass that divided the gathering space from the foyer. We never managed to catch up to her to extend our condolences because every time we came close to her it was as if she disappeared into a crowd of people only to resurface somewhere else. After a while, we decided to give up and just stay seated. We next saw her at a workshop, I complimented her on the dress she had worn to the memorial service. She was surprised. She said that the reason we couldn't catch up to her is that she was not physically there but had traveled to the gathering using bilocation. She said, "I usually don't get caught." Bilocation became another field for me to explore as it is the process of being in two places at once.

After the service, I had the opportunity to meet Doc's son, Dr. Randall Frank, founder of the healing modality, 'Natural Healing', now called Evolutionary Quantum Healing Technique (EQHT). (You can learn more about this technique by visiting eqht.net.) Dr. Frank was living in Germany with his wife Andrea and stated that he was thinking about retiring. EQHT brings the body, mind, emotions and spirit back into balance by using a variety of energetic techniques designed for healing. When I found out what he did, I literally begged him to teach me and he said if I could get enough people to take the seminar, he would do it. Within a month I had the required people and to this day I continue to study with him.

Armed with my gifts, Reiki, TBM and EQHT, my business and circles took off. Word began to spread about the work I was doing and I found myself being invited to work out of a client's home in an adjoining county. When my business grew too large for an in-home studio, I opened a second office in the Vail Valley and SpiritWay continued to grow. I was as busy as I could handle. Once again, my skill level was bumped up to a new level. But then I began seeing clients with structural issues. The energetic techniques that I had perfected typically took care of this type of issue, but I found that they were no longer effective. Still, more and more structural clients walked through my door. I began outsourcing them only to have them return worse off than when they left my office originally. I began to grow frustrated and question my abilities.

One morning I woke up with a knot in my stomach and just knew there was something else that I was to add to my toolbox. For three months I researched healing modalities and this knot continued to gnaw at me. I just about sent my family over the edge. First, I was going to go to chiropractic school, then acupuncture school then I started researching energy tools, then I wanted to be a homeopath. There were so many exciting modalities that I could not decide. I wanted to do them all.

During a healing session with Jenelle, my friend/spiritual sister/client, told me about a lady that "puts ribs back into alignment." I could do that energetically but this lady, Kimberly Klein, taught a hands-on technique that only a few people in the world offered. Jenelle had an appointment with her the following week and promised to give me all the details. Upon returning for her follow-up session I could immediately tell the difference in her physical structure. When I placed my hands on her, a knowing, like a rush of water, flooded my body and I knew that this is the modality I had been waiting for. I called Kimberly and set up an appointment with her and by the end of the session had agreed to study with her.

I began to apprentice with Kim. By the spring of the following year I had already logged over 500+ hours with her, this in addition to operating two offices.

This modality did not have a name, but Kim called it Sadhana

Therapy. It originated in China but had become a lost art during the cultural revolution. Kim had been taught by a man who received it from one of the monks that moved to New York to escape the war. I felt honored and blessed to learn this.

Sadhana Therapy (since renamed Body Evolve, or BE) worked on the physical body. Her website is bodyevolvenow.com.

My toolbox felt complete. BE works on the physical structure. The EQHT techniques and TBM worked on the physical, emotional, mental and spiritual bodies as did Reiki. Along the way I also learned other approaches such as aromatherapy, magnetic therapy, crystal clearing and energizing, chakra clearing, energizing and balancing, wellness advisement/coaching, hypnosis, past life regression, emotional release work such as emotional freedom technique among others, meditation techniques and dream work.

The latest technique is Quantum Healing Hypnosis Technique. QHHT was developed by the late Dolores Cannon. It allows the practitioner to take the individual into the state of trance through visualization. It takes the person through several past lives and the death processes. Once this is achieved, the practitioner can seek to access their subconscious mind in order to obtain current information and to provide healing.

I work with my spirit teachers and guides as well as beings from the stars and the angelic realm. I offer shamanic practices and the teachings that I learned from Jeremie and other teachers. I practice soul retrieval, divination, and offer spiritual teachings and season ceremonies. I became an ordained minister and have conducted numerous weddings, blessings and send-away ceremonies (funerals). I brought other healers, teachers and presenters into the office in an effort to share even more with the clients and the community I had created.

It felt like my practice was well-rounded and complete. But sure enough, this feeling did not last long, and I began to feel the familiar gnawing in my gut. Then it happened: another directional change. One day I was working with a client at the office when I heard, "Go Bigger!" I look around, astonished. But I maintained my composure and continued working. However, later that evening I was closing down the office and preparing to go home, when I again heard the phrase, "Go Bigger!" This time it repeated two or three times. Me being me, I shouted out, "What do you mean, go bigger? I am doing everything I can. I don't have any more time to give. I need at least a few days a month to recharge." By this time, my business had grown to back-to-back clients. I was offering workshops or circles on the weekends, or bringing in presenters. Two or three nights a month, I was offering conscious awareness classes and circles. Again I heard, "Go Bigger." I became upset and confused. I always try to do what spirit asks of me but this time I had no earthly idea how I could go bigger. I was expending more energy than I was taking in and I was beginning to get weary. I wasn't sick or burned out because my work is an extension of who I am and the more I am mission-oriented, the more energy I receive. But when I heard this request, concern began to root in my physical body and I felt sick to my stomach. I became frustrated with the thought that I wouldn't be able to meet this call. I started feeling myself going into a downward spiral of emotional and mental turmoil. I could not understand the 'call'.

A few days passed when I heard the voice again. "Go Bigger!" This time I answered, "Fine, but you have to tell me how. And I need some physical support too." Dropping into spiritual submission is all I had to do. It became clear that going bigger had nothing to do with expanding the services I offered, but was actually about reducing my time and bringing new people in. I felt immediate relief, knowing that spirit would provide all the tools I needed and help me call in the new energy.

Now understanding the message that I had been given. I began contacting speakers the next day and asking them to come and make presentations. SpiritWay hosted nearly a dozen speakers that year. I also began seeking additional practitioners to join me.

During this time, a new office revealed itself as the future home of SpiritWay and I happily moved after months of renovations. I reached out to more practitioners to see if they wanted to share office space and/or offer services periodically from SpiritWay. That concept did not work out as I had hoped but once I released what I thought the experience should look like, out of the blue, practitioners began to contact me to see if I would host a presentation and then allow them to offer private sessions at the office. I was thrilled. More services were being offered and I was not having to do the work!

Stepping into the flow and allowing the 'Go Bigger' message to lead me has provided many gifts. The biggest was that my son, Dylan, who had worked two summers with me, announced that he would not be working the summer with me but would be joining the practice full time in the fall. Woohoo! The call for physical support had been met and I felt the pressure melt away. I was thrilled to be working side-by-side with Dylan. Not just because he is my son, but because he possesses amazing healing and psychic abilities. To watch him unfold and blossom has been one of the greatest gifts of my life.

Even though I had just moved into a beautiful new space, I realized that I was going to need more office space for what I was being shown. As soon as I acknowledged the need, I was shown that a structure was needed on our land in Leadville to allow for larger events and services. Knowing better than to question, I started researching structures and found one that offered the space requirements and the ability to grow food! My energy was now directed at securing funding to purchase a 42-foot grow dome that would offer 1000 square feet in the middle for presentations, and another 600 feet for growing food, flowers and herbs around the interior edges. I was told to set the tone for this space by naming it the Conscious Awakening Center. We continue to seek funding for this project.

The 'Go Bigger' message took on a life of its own. With Dylan in the office, I now found time to spend on inviting more speakers. I was amazed that each time I invited someone, as long as the message offered was in alignment with the message spirit wanted presented, they always accepted and were well received. The quality of the speakers and the messages they brought forth were phenomenal and more and more lives began to be touched and transformed. I was ecstatic with this upgraded speaker component and fell into an easy work/event rhythm.

This rhythm was not to last, however. It was almost three years to the day when I heard the initial call that I heard the same call again, "Go Bigger." This time I responded with enthusiasm and a willing heart, excited to see what spirit had in store this time.

The next phase in the adventure led me to create an event called SpiritFest, featuring multiple speakers. The first event was held on the Summer Solstice and had a theme of Conscious Awakening. We hosted a wide array of national and international authors, workshop presenters, practitioners and ceremonialists such as Andrea Perron, Scott and Vicki Werner, Sarina Baptista, Yemanya Carey, Fernando Ascencio, Cathy Bethke, Nathalie Nuguyn and Nataline Cruz. The speakers and attendees created a portal for many people to spiritually shift and awaken. I was amazed, elated and a bit dumbfounded. Instead of the event being hosted outdoors on a beautiful sunny summer solstice weekend in June, it snowed, rained and was miserably cold. But we huddled together to be spiritually uplifted and bonded in a way that I had not seen before. Many new friendships were forged and old ones rekindled with a spiritual connection. The success of this event served as the platform to continue offering this and other events with high caliber speakers. Our little Leadville and Vail Valley will never be the same. You can visit our website for events at consciousawakeningseries.com.

The next SpiritFest is subtitled: The Flip Side of the Coin. Presenters include Barbara Lamb, Andrea Perron, Rob Gauthier, Rebecca Hardcastle-Wright, Yvonne Perry, Jacquelin Smith, Robert Mc William, Scott and Vicki Werner, Yemanya Carey, Fernando Ascencio, Jack Stucki, Brenda Molloy, Jackie Wright and Nathalie Nuguyn. I hope to release this book in time for the event.

I have laid out all this detail to offer an intimate portrait of my process, from one level of understanding, ability, skill and interaction to the next - despite periods of resistance. As a walk-in, I have been driven by my sense of mission and once I had accepted my identity, I began to dedicate myself to continual development, towards the fulfilment of that mission. At this time it expresses itself through five components: healing work, spiritual teachings and advice, hosting special events and now authorship. All these services are designed to ease people out of pain whether it be physical, emotional, mental or spiritual, so that they can embrace the true nature of their soul and work to elevate their own vibration and thus elevate the vibration of humanity.

As you have seen, I have spent a great deal of time over the past twenty years digesting what it means to be and live as a walk-in. But it wasn't until I was asked to make a presentation on being a walk-in in February 2019 that I even began to organize my thoughts around it. At first, it proved difficult to explain my understanding, but once I put pen to paper the information began to flow, just as it did when writing this book.

The following chapters are my understanding of walk-ins and the nature of souls.

Consciousness, Form and Purpose

Anatomy of the Soul

In order to understand what a walk-in is, and why people report a variety of experiences, we need to discuss the ways in which consciousness, form and purpose relate. To some, this may seem a complex idea, to others not so much, but I will aspire to make it as clear as possible. The key terminology I will use to explain this is: Source, sheantiaskaan (oversoul), higher self, soul, soul families and soul clusters.

Please bear in mind that this information was given during a download in which my guides were trying to explain to me about the nature of our souls. When this information came, I had begun to drop into full acceptance about being a walk-in and had started to question my guides about the walk-in process. How did it actually happen, what is involved? How can I be so different from the soul that previously inhabited this body?

The following is my interpretation of what I understood them to tell me. Your guides may have explained this process differently and that is perfect for you. But in order for me to truly understand it, they broke it down into terms that I could understand. The simplest way to explain is to begin with a discussion of consciousness, form and purpose or what I call the anatomy of the soul. Let's begin with consciousness. The origin of all things is known as Source (God). Source is conscious. When Source desired to evolve, it did so by fractalizing into countless forms of expression. These expressions became innumerable forms of consciousness, and the interaction between them created the experiences which drives Source's evolution. Each of us is an expression of Source in its quest to evolve through experience. That is the true purpose of the soul.

vNow let's look at form, or the anatomy of the soul. The way we are constructed begins with Source. When Source fractalized, countless numbers of these fractals became what I know as the sheantiaskaan. Most know the sheantiaskaan as the oversoul, but I will refer to it as the sheantiaskaan because that is the name that was given to me.

The sheantiaskaan is the multidimensional structure, a container, that holds all the memories, events, and feelings that we have ever experienced. The sheantiaskaan is like our personal cloud storage, holding all the data we have accrued throughout this and every other lifetime. It is our personal Akashic record. Our incarnations begin with the sheantiaskaan. In my download, I saw it as a swirling spiral of energy, light, frequency and sound full of information. The sheantiaskaan is so large, that when it is time to incarnate, only a small portion can enter into the human form. From it we bring with us various gifts, talents and skills that we will need to assist us in our upcoming life.

When the sheantiaskaan is ready for an incarnation experience, a stream of its energy becomes first, the higher self and then the soul. The higher self remains attached to the sheantiaskaan. It is our highest divine expression, thus the name higher self. It serves as a conduit between us and the sheantiaskaan and acts as a guidance system for us. It is neither affected nor influenced by our experiences during an incarnation so the information it provides to us remains untainted. As the energy of the higher self becomes denser, it attaches to the physical form. The portion that attaches is called the soul and serves as the personality for the lifetime. When the soul enters into the physical body it does so through the top of the head. It attaches to the body when the first breath is taken and remains attached until the final breath occurs.

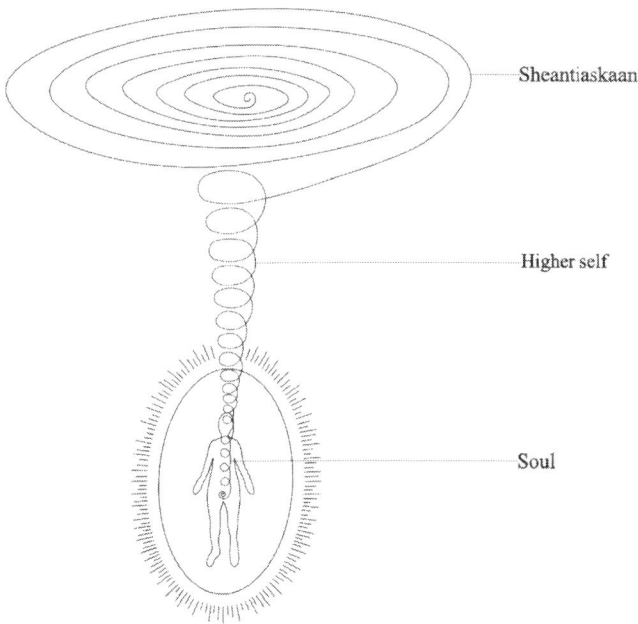

I would also like to use an analogy to explain this process. Imagine Source as the ocean. Take a bucket and dip water from the ocean. The water contained within the bucket represents the sheantiaskaan. Next, pour some of the water from the bucket into a cup. The stream of water being poured into the cup represents the higher self. The cup is the physical body and the water contained within it is the soul.

Next, let's move to soul families. When different sheantiaskaan vibrate at the same or similar rate they begin to attract and move closer to each other like magnets. Once in close proximity, they become connected, and are called soul families. It is believed that members of soul families incarnate again and again to assist each other in achieving their desired goals during a given lifetime and to help balance karma. Sometimes, the very people that cause you the most problems in life are members of your soul family. An example might be that you have an in-law that is extremely critical of you. No matter what you do, it is not good enough. The backstory to this scenario might be that in a previous lifetime you were in a position of royalty, the owner of many servants. Instead of rewarding their good efforts with praise, you gave nothing but anger and harsh words. In this lifetime, they are providing you the opportunity to experience a situation similar to theirs for the learning and growth of your soul.

Often, multiple soul families are drawn together, and are called soul clusters. Members of the soul clusters, like soul families, might also incarnate to support you along your path.

Each time an incarnation occurs, the information is taken back into the sheantiaskaan, and patterns begin to form. For example, if through several incarnations you were a kind and considerate person, the energy of kindness and consideration is strengthened in the sheantiaskaan. The same holds true for special gifts or skills, such as musical ·talent. Because these patterns are strong within the sheantiaskaan, the likelihood of them showing up again in consecutive lifetimes is great.

Going Home

As souls having a human experience, we really never truly die, we simply change form. We shed the physical suit for this lifetime as we shift into our energetic, light body forms. Your light body is your etheric form that links all the various aspects of you together.

I was told by teachers, guides and reinforced by the download that the soul has several processes it experiences once the death process occurs. The first thing that happens is the reabsorption of the soul's personality back into the higher self which in turn, retracts into the sheantiaskaan taking with it all the experiential information, and knowledge of the lifetime. Once absorbed, a soul review takes place. This review examines every action, thought and deed that transpired during the recent lifetime. It determines whether or not the mission was successful, and if the desired experiences occurred. It reviews not only how each experience impacted the soul but how the souls' responses impacted everyone involved. The review is conducted with love by your guides, teachers, higher beings and could even include a multidimensional aspect of yourself. There is never any judgement or blame about what did or did not occur while on Earth. The focus is about whether or not the appropriate experiences occurred, karma was balanced and if it accomplished everything that it set out to do.

If life on Earth was particularly traumatic, the soul undergoes healing through a light, sound and frequency infusion to repair the damage. Depending on the severity of the injuries sustained, the soul may go to a place of rest until total restoration occurs. This process is talked about many times in several of Dolores Cannon's books.

People have said to me that I am lucky because my natal soul and physical body did not have to experience the death process. I would like to reassure anyone reading these words that there is absolutely nothing to fear about it. I call it the release process because there is no death to the real you! We simply release the physical body and change forms. That's it. You are not your body. The body is only the car for this lifetime. It is the mode of transportation for your soul.

We are not our bodies but because we are in human form, most people feel anxious about the death process and some, even fearful. They think about the things they will miss, what might happen to the body afterwards and have questions such as, "What if there is nothing after this life?" Based on my memories, and my memories alone, I can assure you there is more discomfort in being born than there is in the death process.

The release of the soul from the physical form is refreshing, enlivening and energizing. It is the most freeing experience that you can imagine. This process is only the slipping out of the physical form, just like you do every day when you change your clothes. Nothing more. It is like opening your front door and walking out of your house into a new, yet familiar, surrounding. We will never experience the death of our soul. NEVER. Life is like a blip on an eternal radar screen. It is but a blink of an eye. We are here only to experience, to remember who we are. To share love with those around us. To be of service to those in need. That is all. Life is simple. We in human form make it hard.

> You can spend a lifetime
> Trying to be One with Great Spirit
> Or simply focus on love
> And realize you already are.

By Dr. Anthony Theodore

What is a Walk-in?

We have discussed the idea that the ultimate purpose of life is for Source to evolve through experience, but what role does purpose play in our individual lives? Most people ask themselves, often at various times throughout their journey: why am I here? What is my life's purpose? Each of us answers these questions in our own way.

I believe that before we incarnate, a meeting is held with our guides, teachers and all interested parties to discuss the purpose and goals of the upcoming lifetime. Agreements are made with all the players that will be involved with the future life and a plan is established. This is called your pre-birth plan. This plan is based on the intended experiences and processes of that incarnation. This may include emotional types of healings that need to occur, karma that needs to be balanced, and the spiritual growth that needs to take place.

When someone incarnates with a life mission, it may express itself through a calling. For some, it may be something with great significance, such as being a diplomat or teacher. For others, it may simply be a matter of being a good person in life. Either way, we all incarnate to experience. Feeling the sun on your face and really drinking in that experience, or offering a smile to everyone you meet is just as important as doing something of wider impact. Ultimately, all experience counts toward the process. We humans tend to be judgmental and competitive, which breeds an idea that we must achieve higher social standing and so forth, but all experience is equal to Source.

What is a Walk-in?

In order for the animation of the physical body to occur, a soul must be present. When the soul enters at birth it is called the natal soul. In most cases, when the natal soul departs from the body it results in physical death, but not always. Sometimes two souls may have agreed to swap places at a future time or an emergency decision is made to occupy a body that is preparing to expire. When this takes place the new soul is called a walk-in. It can occur at any age, depending on the agreements made between the souls and the mission of the walk-in. Typically, the agreement is made prior to incarnation. The walk-in then enters the body after an agreed-upon accident, operation, illness, extreme emotional trauma, near-death-experience or actual death experience.

Typically, the new soul will have made an agreement to finish the mission of the previous natal soul and/or the walk-in comes in with a mission all of its own. Walk-ins most often enter with a mission to help anchor a new, higher-vibrational frequency to help shift the consciousness of humanity. The walk-in can also come in specifically to complete or assist in healing genetic patterns or to clear the karma of the original natal soul. Karma can be understood as patterns of thought and behavior which affect us and those around us. Our actions create energy, and habitual actions reinforce that energy, be it positive or negative. Healing negative patterns through mindfulness and non-judgmental awareness, moves us to create positive energy for ourselves and the world around us.

Once the healing takes place, the walk-in can more fully embrace its own mission. The missions and goals of walk-in souls vary greatly but tend to have one thing in common: to be of service, and aid in the evolutionary process of humanity and the planet.

Sometimes a soul finds itself in a hopeless situation, and suffers from depression, addictions, or becomes so far off-mission that it cries out to be released from the physical body. This 'crying out' is on a soul level and the person to whom the soul is attached, has no conscious awareness of what is happening, although they may have a sensation that something is different, changing, or needs to change. In these situations, an instantaneous agreement can occur as the natal soul leaves and a new soul enters. Let me be clear, if one reads this and does 'cry out' on a conscious level to be released, this does not automatically trigger a walk-in experience. A walk-in only occurs when the natal soul cannot complete its mission, and/or when it is in the highest and best good of humanity, the planet, and both the natal soul and the walk-in soul. Most walk-in scenarios have been planned for an extended period of time.

As previously stated, walk-ins are typically service-oriented and here to help elevate the consciousness of humanity and the planet. Many beings desire to be on Earth at this time to lend support and to hold space for the upcoming mass shift of consciousness. I believe all souls, not just walk-ins, that are currently on the planet are here to experience this shift.

Depending on the walk-in, it may take on the personality and/or memories of the previous soul in part, in whole, or not at all. It all depends on the amount of the natal soul that remains to assist during the integration process. There are several different scenarios:

1. The walk-in retains all memories and behaviors of the

previous soul.

2. The walk-in retains some memories and behaviors while others are forgotten, and are no longer a part of the new soul. Some of the memories and behaviors remain, but are buried deep within the subconscious until the soul is ready to handle the information and/or actions of the host.

3. The walk-in has little to no memories or behaviors of the previous soul. Upon entering, if any of the old behavior patterns remain, they fade quickly, if not instantaneously. This type of soul uses stories, videos and photographs to evoke memories.

Preparation of the Energetic Bodies

Even though the natal soul has departed, the physical body is the same. It has the same genetic material as before and carries the same cellular memories. Over time, these memories can dissipate or change as the new soul imprints on the body and the old patterns are released, healed and transformed. The imprinting can even cause physical changes in the body, such as frame size, height, hair and eye color changes, or even shifts in their feminine or masculine aspects.

Prior to the new soul entering the body, the delicate process of detaching the energetic bodies must occur to make the body vibrationally compatible. The detachment process is the key for a seamless soul switch to occur so that the new soul can acclimate in their own time. Bits and pieces of information about the transformation will be sprinkled in as the new soul is ready to fully embrace their new existence.

There are several steps that happen to prepare the energetic body for transference. First, the hard wiring of the body's neurological system has to be upgraded so the energy of the new soul does not overload the body systems. Even with this preparation, most people feel extremely tired and lethargic after the switch. This feeling can last for days, months, or years. Most people are unaware of what has just happened to them but they feel like they need to rest, relax and just sleep. Second, each of the energetic bodies, which most people know as the emotional, mental and spiritual bodies, has to be gently loosened so detachment can occur seamlessly when the time comes for the souls to switch. The switch most often occurs when the person is sleeping. This allows for a transition without the person being made aware.

There are walk-ins who have stated that they were in a deep state of meditation when something happened. They could not readily identify the sensation, but they knew something had just occurred and they felt different and disoriented for days. In other cases, such as mine, there is little to no preparation and the switch takes place instantaneously, leaving the person bewildered, disoriented, confused and enlightened.

The new soul, having just come from a higher frequency, still carries a very strong, high-vibrational resonance, even if there is no memory of its former location or the fact that they are a walk-in. The impact of the new soul can be profound and cause numerous changes in personality, lifestyle, interpersonal relationships, interests and behaviors.

In Yvonne Perry's book, *Walk-ins Among Us*, she quotes Maxine Taylor's work: "Maxine Taylor began her astrological studies in 1966. In 1968, she became Georgia's first licensed astrologer. In 1970, she got astrology legalized in Atlanta, and spearheaded the establishment of the Atlanta Board of Astrology Examiners. In her book, Earthbound, Maxine Taylor states: "The combination of the cell memory of the walk-out and the advanced psychic ability and knowledge of the walk-in can be confusing and frustrating. But, ultimately, these energies balance and you will be able to express your mission."

Walk-in Souls: Types, Experiences and Origins

Now that we know what a walk-in is, we can examine the different types of walk-in experiences. They can vary significantly in terms of duration, degree, origin and purpose. By duration I mean that the classical walk-in is a full soul exchange, which is permanent - one soul out; one soul in. By degree we mean that some experiences involve a portion of the natal soul remaining. By origin we refer to the sheantiaskaan, from which the walk-in aspect emerges and to the galactic or dimensional location from which it hails. By purpose we mean that the objective of the incoming soul can vary dramatically. People report numerous combinations of all these elements.

Types

When a walk-in event occurs, there are countless soul combinations possible, as the new soul can be a single aspect or a combination of different soul aspects:

1. Souls can incarnate from their own or from a different sheantiaskaan.
2. The soul can be from its own soul family or soul group, or it can be from a different one.
3. Souls can incarnate from its own planet, galaxy or dimension, or from a different one.
4. The soul can be a combination of any or all of the above.

Once the soul is ready, it enters into the body or the energetic field of the new host. The soul will then take one of many forms. It will become a soul exchange, infusion, overlay, braid, jumper or layer.

Soul Exchanges occur when the natal soul permanently leaves the body and a new soul replaces it. When people talk about a walk-in, this is typically what they are referring to. The natal soul is never forced to leave as the exchange is mutually agreed upon. We could call this a 'classic' walk-in scenario.

When a soul exchange occurs, it is a life-altering experience. Many times, changes take place that leave the person unrecognizable to themselves or to others. They may change jobs abruptly, get a divorce, move to a different location, receive an increase in intellect, express spiritual gifts or any number of things that are out of character for the 'old' version of them.

Soul exchanges typically have the feeling that they have a mission to accomplish. In many cases, the new soul knows exactly what their mission is. In other cases, karmic or cellular clearing has to take place before it is revealed to them.

In several sections of Ruth Montgomery's book, *Strangers Among Us*, she writes about walk-ins saying, "They are high-minded entities permitted to take over the bodies of human beings who wish to depart this life. Their mission is to lead us into an astonishing new age. [...] They are enlightened beings, who, after successfully completing numerous incarnations, have attained sufficient awareness of the meaning of life that they can forgo the time-consuming process of birth and childhood, returning directly to adult bodies. [...] The motivation for a walk-in is humanitarian. They return to physical beings in order to help others help themselves, planting seed-concepts that will grow and flourish for the benefit of mankind."

One thing that has become clear in writing this book and in talking to countless individuals, is that there are many different types of walk-in experiences that occur in addition to soul exchanges. There are soul infusions, soul overlays, soul braids, soul jumpers, and soul layering. Each one unique. Each one profound. And each one results from an agreement to experience the scenario before incarnating.

Soul Infusions occur when a portion of the natal soul remains and a new, higher-vibrational aspect from its own sheantiaskaan enters. The new soul aspect(s) meld(s) with the old aspect and becomes a single soul. In this case, there is no disruption of memory. Because the two aspects are from the same sheantiaskaan, their integration appears seamless. But not necessarily so. Often, the new aspect is so much higher in its vibrational frequency that it is difficult for the physical form to contain it and illnesses occur. In some cases, the new aspect has difficulty integrating into the old identity and the host struggles with accepting the fact they could be something more than they once were.

Soul Overlays can be either permanent or temporary. An overlay occurs when the natal soul remains and another soul enters the body at the same time in a harmonious fashion. This is not a possession. The entree is an agreed-upon arrangement and the natal soul becomes the observer and is not consciously aware of what is occurring. The overlay soul covers the natal soul like a neoprene suit covers the physical body. For a time, the overlay soul is in full control while the natal soul rests, recuperates, or regroups. Sometimes the overlay soul assists the natal soul in completing a mission and then the natal soul departs, leaving the body to be inhabited by the new, higher-vibrating soul. The two souls remain separate while achieving the goal, yet work as one. When the work is complete or the experience is had, one or the other souls leave. There is no power struggle for control. If the soul is too damaged to leave, the two souls can meld together to form one new soul.

Sometimes the overlay acts like a battery charger, enlivening the natal soul and remains until the natal soul is strong enough to move forward on its own. Moving forward can include remaining in the body, melding with the new soul or becoming a walk-out and turning the physical body over to the new soul.

The overlay soul is generally an aspect of the natal soul's own sheantiaskaan, soul family or soul group. In this case, melding most likely occurs, but not always.

Soul Braids are a bit more complicated because one or more souls are occupying the body at the same time and both are consciously aware of the other. The souls can be either side-to-side or intertwined within the same energetic space. Braided souls come and go at will. They do not attach to the physical body and become the new soul. Instead, they attach to the natal soul or the natal soul's space. Many times a braid will arrive to assist the natal soul and help propel them to their next level of service. They will enter the body and work side-by-side with the natal soul to achieve a goal. Some braids may choose to stay for a few days, weeks, months, years or the entire lifetime, but they will always retain their individuality. When and if they decide to leave, they will do so having edified and enriched the natal soul. Braided souls can be an aspect of the natal soul's collective soul group, family or its own sheantiaskaan or from a different group and location.

Confusion often surrounds the topic of soul braids. Some claim that they are a disincarnate soul, a demonic soul or a fragmented/split personality. Some take the view that there is no such thing as a braid as two souls cannot inhabit the body at once. Others, especially those who have experienced a braid will strongly disagree.

Soul Jumpers are souls that move in and out of a body over a few hours, days, weeks or months. These are brief experiences in which the new soul will inhabit a body to accomplish a particular goal and then leave. They have a contract with the natal soul to help in times of need, to birth a new project, to just experience being human, or they can be on a mission of their own.

The intensity of such an experience can be overwhelming as the temporary soul begins to imprint and change the vibration of the host. Once the jumper leaves, the imprinting remains and the host may feel a sense of loss and long for the return of the experience.

Soul Layering is when multiple aspects of the natal soul's sheantiaskaan enter into a single body or energy field. These aspects can be from any time, place or dimension. Once the other soul aspects are activated, the aspects move in and out of the host body for varying lengths of time. The natal soul remains intact and flows effortlessly in a shared dance of experience. I have heard of these aspects remaining activated for years and then the natal soul returning to the forefront. Thus, the co-creative dance.

Many people have confused soul laying with multiple personalities, but they are very different as no fragmentation of the personality is present. Instead, these soul aspects are more like a team that chose to incarnate together to support each other during their learning experiences on Earth. Each soul aspect brings a different gift to the experience, and comes forward when the timing is right.

The amount of perseverance and spiritual strength that it takes to enter into a contract of being an soul infusion, soul overlay, soul braid, soul jumper or layered soul aspect is awe inspiring. Whether permanent, temporary or reoccurring, these aspects imprint on the natal soul and the physical being as constant adjustments are being made to the emotional, mental and spiritual bodies. Whether or not the soul aspect remains, the soul imprinting does. If the soul stays and there is a misalignment of the energies, the person can suffer from anxiety, depression, illnesses and insomnia.

The phenomenon of the discarnate soul is very different to soul layering, and it is essential to identify the differences between them. The body must have a soul to be animated and without it, physical death occurs. Typically, the soul moves to the next level of existence, but in the case of a disincarnate soul, it lingers. Discarnate souls are trapped in the lower astral level and wander aimlessly about for some time. When people think of possessions, they are referring to evil discarnate souls, not benevolent walk-in souls. Discarnate souls cannot inhabit a body unless given permission to, but they can influence a person by entering into their energy field. Most often this occurs when a person is under the influence of drugs or alcohol. Sometimes discarnate souls attempt to enter a body but are kicked out by the soul inhabiting the body, and return to the lower or first astral realm of the Earth.

According to Dolores Cannon's work, there are three realms found within the astral plane. The first is the etheric double of the Earth. The Earth is an exact double of its astral etheric double, in a denser form. The second realm is what most people would call heaven, and the third is where the halls of knowledge are located. It is in the first plane, the Earth etheric double, where disincarnated souls can be found.

Awakening Experiences

I wish to discuss two other types of soul experiences that may or may not be walk-in related. Many people experience them with their natal soul firmly intact while others experience them as a result of a walk-in. It is up to the experiencer to decide which is true for them. These definitions are from my perspective only. As with all spiritual experiences, each person has their own way of interpreting them.

Kundalini Awakening - The kundalini is the creative energy that resides in the subtle body at the base of the spine. It is often represented as a coiled snake. A kundalini awakening can occur through yoga practices, drug use, the result of spiritual studies, or be caused by illness, emotional trauma, accident, a near-death experience or a walk-in experience. When it occurs, intense heat travels up the spine, leaving the experiencer with a euphoric feeling, a new outlook on life, perhaps a desire to change their lifestyle, relationships, job and so on.

Spiritual Awakening - Experiencing a spiritual awakening is a rite of passage which offers a higher spiritual path. An awakening can occur as a result of spiritual studies, meditation, or it could be totally uninvited, or result from a walk-in experience. The euphoria is often followed by a feeling of loss, loneliness and bewilderment, and the person finds they can no longer relate to their friends or loved ones.

Regardless of the experience, each one can change the life of the experiencer.

If you believe you might be a walk-in, please refer to the Appendix and take the questionnaire.

Origins

We know that we are divine sparks, fractals, of Source but where did we go after our creation? Straight to Earth? To a different dimension or realm of existence? To a different planet or star system? The definitive answer to these questions does not exist for most, only to those who remember or have received answers through visions, meditation or from their spiritual guides.

What we do know is that our souls originate from a plethora of solar systems, galaxies, universes (realms), and dimensions. These souls incarnate as both natal souls and walk-ins, inhabiting human bodies for the purpose of learning, pursuing their missions, and being part of elevating and expanding human consciousness. It may seem that natal souls and walk-in souls are very different from each other, but they are both souls. The differences, however, are in the timing of the soul's arrival into a body, the vibrational frequency it carries, and the mission it has agreed to undertake.

When souls incarnate, most are subject to the veil of forgetfulness, causing them to lose sight of their past lives or the origin of their soul. Just imagine if we remembered every event from every lifetime, every war, every loss, every love. We would be so preoccupied with our past that we would not be able to focus on the here and now. There are a few people that I have encountered that remember where they are from and the life they had prior to incarnating, but they all talk about the emotional power of those memories.

Just as Gaia has many different races that make up humanity, so the universe has different races and expressions of soul energy. Below are some of the origins that have been shared by people that have awakened to the truth of who they are.

There are four classifications of soul origins. They are Earth Seeds, Source Seeds, Dimensional Seeds and Star Seeds. They are called seeds because they seed the planet on which they inhabit. Within the star seed community we have Indigo, Crystal and Rainbow, Wanderer and Hybrid Souls.

Earth Seeds - Earth seeds are souls that are 'native' to this planet and have been with Gaia through every incarnation cycle. Throughout the millennia, they have experienced evolutions of being everything from basic molecular structures to the elements of earth, fire, water and air; to rocks, plants, animals and humans. With each density cycle, Earth seeds have imparted a new strand of DNA. Earth seeds are the true native inhabitants of this planet.

Source Seeds - These are souls that have never incarnated so their consciousness is very high and pure. They are non-imprinted souls that have come to Earth or any planet for the first time and are here to help transform the planet by infusing it with unconditional love. Their very presence helps to transmute lower vibrations into light. Their souls have incarnated to serve humanity. These beings are typically angelic in nature.

Dimensional Seeds - These include intra-dimensional, extra-dimensional and multidimensional souls. Intra-dimensional souls are those that hail from the same dimension that we are in whether they be from this planet or a different one. Extra-dimensional souls include those that are outside our dimension such as light, sound and frequency souls. Multidimensional souls contain various aspects from a variety of dimensions. There are also souls that reside between dimensions.

Star Seeds - Star seeds are souls that hail from a different planet, galaxy, star system or realm. They have lived in places other than Earth, sometimes for eons. When they incarnate on Earth, they may feel like they don't belong or fit in; they feel alone or are homesick but don't know where home is. These souls are typically more spiritually evolved and come to Earth with a mission of being in service to humanity and to help raise consciousness. Their mission usually involves assisting humanity in becoming more spiritually attuned, but ultimately, star seeds come to Earth to have a human experience. The most prevalent star seeds have identified themselves as being from the people of the Sirian, Arcturian, Pleiadian, Orion, Lyran, and

Andromedan systems.

Indigo, Crystal and Rainbow Souls - These souls come from every part of the galaxy. Some are from other planets and star systems while others are dimensional beings. They are here to help humanity in the Ascension process. What is being discovered is that most of these children are coming in fully awake, possessing gifts that border on the supernatural such as telepathy, clairvoyance, healing abilities, memories of where they are from, and scientific talents. Some have been reported to bring direct information to humanity from their home planet.

Wanderer Souls - A wanderer soul can be any soul that has lowered its vibrational frequency to come into a human body for the purpose of raising consciousness and increasing the vibrational frequency of Gaia. This type of soul can be an Earthen soul that has chosen to reincarnate instead of moving forward but typically, this type of soul 'wanders' through time, space and dimensions to assist where needed and to gather information. Sometimes they live full lives on Earth and other times they arrive as walk-ins. As a result, these souls tend to have a host of physical ailments such as allergies and autoimmune diseases. They tend to feel alone, even in a crowd, feel lost or like they have been abandoned. If these feelings are not resolved they can become depressed and even suicidal. They can have addictive personalities and traits. This group tends to grow up to be an environmentalist, activist, and work tirelessly on behalf of mother Earth.

Hybrid Souls - Hybrid souls are combinations of souls from any number of different systems, galaxies, star families, or the angelic realm. These souls typically have already ascended and are returning to assist with a specialized function. Once incarnated on Earth, they tend to seek out lower vibrational situations, events or people. Some choose to be born into dysfunctional families because one of their primary purposes on this planet is to bring love and order into hatred and chaos. They are bringers of transformation.

Now that we have a better understanding of walk-ins and the various types and origins of the soul, presented in the following section are 15 interviews where other walk-ins share their experiences. Some are soul exchanges, others have experienced the soul infusion, overlay, braid, jumper or soul layering scenario. Some remember their origins and their incarnation process. All are unique stories.

It is understood that my story and the stories of others you are about to read about are just our experiences. There is no scientific data that can prove that we are the products of soul swapping or soul manipulation. None. But then again, there is no evidence that we have a soul either, and that is a widely held and accepted belief by a good number of people on this planet. I can only offer our experiences and let you draw your own conclusions.

Part Two

Interviews with Other Walk-ins

Marilyn Harper

Marilyn Harper has been called the Bette Midler of the new age movement and is considered a midwestern Spiritual Spark Plug. She is a world-renowned speaker, spiritual teacher, workshop leader, public speaker and channel to Adironnda and the Council of Light, 17th dimensional beings. She holds a Bachelor of Science Education and prior to the walk-in, had completed her classwork for a Master of Arts degree. She is a Reiki Master, Karuna Master, Quantum Touch practitioner, a certified intuitive consultant, certified remote viewer, certified Peak Potentials trainer and has been listed twice in Who's Who in America. She has developed her own method of healing she calls Holographic Healing. Before becoming a spiritual life coach, Marilyn was a deacon in the Christian church. She became a walk-in soul exchange on April 22, 1993 in the Springfield, Missouri hospital at the age of 41.

Marilyn's Story

In April of 1993, I was admitted to the hospital due to complications following a gallbladder surgery just five days earlier. I found myself in more pain than before the surgery. More than 26 hours had passed before they finally made the decision that I needed an x-ray. Prior to that, they had done nothing to relieve the pain or to treat me. When I was in the hallway outside the x-ray room, I was only one of many waiting their turn. I was there for at least two hours. I was in terrible pain and remember thinking that if I was going to be in that much pain for the rest of my life, I would rather die. I was not really suicidal, I was in just horrific pain.

Looking back, that single thought must have given my unconscious permission for the soul exchange to happen because as soon as I had that thought, I felt a surge of energy rushing into my body. This is when I believe the walk-in arrived. I don't remember exactly what happened next, but I must have made such a fuss that they rushed me into the x-ray room right away.

I stayed in the hospital for several more days and was then released. Even with the x-ray, it took them nearly six weeks to figure out what was going on. When I was released, I did not feel like the person that had initially come into the hospital. I did not feel the same at all. I was different somehow. I was not into metaphysics back then, although as a child I remember playing with the Ouija board and participating in a couple of seances. Now, I just considered myself a normal, Christian woman who sold advertising for a Country and Western radio station.

After the hospital stay, things felt different and I began to change. The first thing I noticed was that my ability to write had diminished. I had completed my master's degree work the year before but still needed to finish my thesis. After the walk-in, my profound writing skills vanished and I felt like English was a second language to me. Even the ability to articulate was different.

I already had 43 hours on my masters, but I could not finish my thesis, which made me sad. The two to three chapters that I had written prior to the walk-in were really good but when my professor read the chapters written after the walk-in, he was surprised. His comment was that my work read more like a child's diary and he wondered what had happened. I wondered that too because I never regained the ability to write as I had before. What I did write was like reading something someone else had written. I have no idea what happened.

My writing had always been second nature to me and at the time, I would rather have written plays and performed in them than anything else in the world. I had already written five successfully produced plays, and I desire to write more of them. Prior to entering the hospital my dream had been to write one-person plays and travel around the world performing them. I loved doing that. It was my passion.

The next thing I noticed was a change in my sewing abilities. While recuperating from the surgery, I decided to make a freestyle counted cross stitch project. You have no pattern on the embroidery cloth. You simply look at a book, count your stitches and off you go. But when I started the project, I realized that I didn't know how to do it. I had created a lot of items in the past but now, I couldn't remember how to do it.

I had also been a proficient seamstress before entering the hospital, so I decided to make a blouse to occupy my time while recuperating. When it came time to make it, I couldn't figure out how to read the pattern or even how much material to purchase. I had designed costumes, made wedding dresses, and a lot of different types of clothing in the past, but now, I seemed to have lost the skill.

Not too long after my return home I noticed that I needed reading glasses. Even my eyesight had changed! Prior to entering the hospital my vision was fine, so I began to think that maybe I was having medical complications or that I had had a stroke or something similar.

One of the biggest changes was that I immediately realized that I was uncomfortable wearing the clothes that were in my closet. My taste in clothes as the walk-in, was totally different to hers (the walk-out). Her wardrobe consisted primarily of reds and blacks. She had gigantic earrings and would never, ever allow anyone to see her without her makeup. She was very gregarious. So, I went shopping. The first outfit I purchased was a pastel pink suit and then a green one. I bet she had never worn a pastel in her life. It was so strange having such a radical change in my clothing preferences. I was really struggling because I knew something major had shifted but I had no idea what.

Also, she was a true party girl. If you called on a Friday or Saturday night at 10:00 pm, she wanted to go drinking and dancing. She was always up for a party! As for me if, and that's a big if, I was still awake at 10 o'clock at night, I was already in my pajamas and ready for bed. So, my set of friends changed too.

At first, I thought there had to be something wrong with me because my personality was different. My humor was different. My walk-out had very self-deprecating humor and I just couldn't do that. Before the walk-in, I had been contracted to perform the plays that I had written. I had to rewrite them because I just couldn't perform them the way that they were. And in fact I really didn't know if I wanted to perform them at all. That was a huge change especially since performing had been my life's dream.

My son also knew that there was something different. When he walked into the hospital room and saw me hooked up to all the machines, he said he knew I was not his mother. He didn't know I was a walk-in until he found an article that had been written about me on the table. I thought he was going to be gone for the weekend, so I just left the magazine out. When he read the article, it didn't take him long to figure it out. He was angry and upset. I told him I would answer any questions that he had when he was ready. It took him nearly a year but during his birthday dinner he began to ask questions, as if no time had passed between his finding the article. The way he found out wasn't ideal and not my preferred method, but that's the way it happened.

It was definitely a strange time. From April of 1993 to November of 1995, I had no idea what was happening to me. At times, I would be so frustrated that I would shake my fist to God and say, "What in the world has happened? I feel so different!" I even looked different. You can look at pictures of me before and after the walk-in and be able to visually see a difference. But one good thing that happened is that I retained my childhood memories. Many walk-ins do not.

There are days that I felt so frustrated I didn't know which way to go. And then magically, the universe intervened and put someone in my life. That is when all the synchronicities began. A person that I knew from graduate school, and really did not get along well with, showed up in my life. That was John. A mutual grad student friend of ours had just given birth to a baby and we ran into each other at the hospital. John and I became very close friends after that. At the hospital, we were talking and realized that we had just read the same book, *The Celestine Prophecy*, and began discussing it.

John was already on his own spiritual pathway. He had gone to college to get his master's in theater, and then became a massage therapist after he became a walk-in, but I didn't know that at the time. Our friendship blossomed and we began to spend quite a bit of time together.

I experienced three synchronistic encounters that introduced me to the walk-in possibility. The first was Thanksgiving 1995. I have a big family so there were probably 60 people gathered at my parent's house, and at this time I still didn't know I was a walk-in. With that many people in the house, you can imagine all the hubbub and noise going on. I stepped into the kitchen right before dinner and my mother came straight over to me holding up a book and asked if I had ever read it. It was *Strangers Among Us* by Ruth Montgomery. I wanted to look at it, but she kept hold of it. I thought it odd for her to come to me right at that moment, right before we were to eat this huge meal with 60 people, and not even let me look at it. I told her no and I asked if she was the weird writer that talks to dead people. She said no, so I asked her if I could borrow the book and again, she said no. But, to be fair, I never return borrowed books. But I didn't read or buy those kinds of books, so it was fine with me if she kept it. It was probably too weird for me anyway. I even threw Shirley MacLaine's book, *Out on a Limb* because I thought it was sacrilegious. but that's just where my mindset was at the time. Actually, the book kept showing up in my car even though I threw it away several times.

A couple of days later, I was out on a date with another friend of mine who I always called Big Bill. He looked like Hoss from the TV show *Bonanza* and he talked like Gandhi. While we were on this date, he asked me if I had ever read the book *Strangers Among Us* by Ruth Montgomery. That was so weird because my mom just asked the same thing. He said after we ate, we could swing by his house to pick it up. I thought I grabbed the right book but didn't realize it was the wrong one until I got home. The one I had was a book by Charles Fillmore. I quickly put it down because he was involved with the Unity Church and I was a Deaconess in the Christian Church Disciples of Christ. I didn't even know the philosophy of the Unity Church or what it was about, but I was sure it wasn't for me. I put the book down and didn't think any more about it.

A couple of days later, a friend of mine, Dan, who I used to work with at the radio station, invited me to go to Milwaukee to his company's Christmas party. Since I didn't want to drive that far up by myself, I invited my friend John from grad school to go with me. He agreed because he also wanted to go to Milwaukee to attend a workshop during this same time. Needless to say, the universe arranged for us to drive 12 hours together and we had a lot of time to talk. I began to explain to him how I had never felt quite right after getting out of the hospital, how I felt so different and about my personality changes. After I described everything John asked me if I had ever read *Strangers Among Us*. Are you kidding me? That was the third person who had asked the same question in just a few short weeks. I asked what the book was about, and as he described it, I realized that is what must be what happened to me. I was a walk-in. Oh my God. The more he talked, the more the book resonated with me.

When I returned home, I went to my mother's house, sure that she knew that I was a walk-in. I asked if I could see the book that she had shown me on Thanksgiving, but she didn't remember. She said that she had several of Ruth's books but not that one. I reminded her it was the one she showed me in the kitchen right before Thanksgiving dinner and she didn't know what I was talking about. We went through all 600 of her books and sure enough, it wasn't there. She had never even heard about it.

Then, I went to see Big Bill and asked him about the book. He said he had heard of Ruth but had never read anything she had written. I reminded him that it was the book he mentioned over dinner and that we had even gone to his house to retrieve it, to which he said he had never owned that book. 'Oh my God. What is going on?' I thought. So I went to John, and asked him if he had told me about the book *Strangers Among Us* by Ruth Montgomery and if we had discussed it on our way to Milwaukee. When he said yes, I felt relieved. Then he explained that it was the universe, the world, God, whatever, speaking through the people I trusted the most, to give me the message that I was a walk-in.

People started calling me strange nicknames like Mare and Q, without either of us knowing why. I discovered later that my soul name is Mare Ashannani and that I am from a star system called Q. This star system does not translate well into English because the human vocal cords cannot make the exact sounds, so they just called it the Que system.

After that, I started having energy sessions every week with John to clear the old patterns, programs and contracts of the walk-out. I would highly recommend to anyone that is a new walk-in to do the same. It really helped me to see, sense, feel, hear and understand where I was on my path,

Once some of the patterning and programs cleared, I started doing automatic or inspired writing and now I teach others how to do it. Through these new skills, I discovered that the walk-in was three to four generations more advanced than the soul that left. I volunteered to come here. I contractually agreed to take a soul-jump in evolution. This body went from housing a regular soul to a more advanced soul that had a lot more intergalactic experience than my walk-out had. I had a lot of clearing to do.

I've been to walk-in conferences and I've interviewed quite a few. The one thing that I found to be a constant among all walk-ins is that they come to this planet with a burning desire to make a difference in the world. They have a mission to be the difference, to make the difference, to do something major to shifting the consciousness of the planet. Just as I do. I know that I am here to awaken as many people as possible and to help people understand that it is possible to live a life that they will love. Whatever dream or vision they have for their life, it is possible! There's a shift in people's consciousness when they know what it feels like to be held in total and complete unconditional love. Once I understood that myself, I began channeling Adironnda.

Adironnda is a group of beings that has never been in human form and serves to open the energy for each group or session. They refer to themselves as 'they' or as a mist as they have evolved well beyond the need for a body and serve as spokes-being from the 17th dimension who represent a Council of Light. Adironnda was sent from Source (God) to Earth to help people awaken for the shift in consciousness that is imminent. This council has identified itself as being composed of the Archangels Michael, Raphael and Gabriel, and Ascended Masters who have lived in human form: Jesus, (now referred to as Yeshua) Mother Mary, Buddha, Isis, Ra, Sekhmet, Babaji, St. Germain and more.

When the council first contacted me, they said they were here to serve as a support team. I think it was easier for me to accept a support team. At that time, the Council of Light name alone may have been too overwhelming for me. But in July of 2015 they seemed to increase in number and began calling themselves the Council of Light. Sometimes, a particular member of the Council will come forward to communicate directly, but typically they speak with one voice.

Adironnda opens the participant's heart chakra to allow the person's own guides to start working with their heart. They bring through total and unconditional love and anyone in their presence can feel it. Many people cry as they provide a deep healing activation. This activation allows people to experience what it is like to be held in and to experience total unconditional love. So, my mission is that I am an activator. I actually activate others that I come in contact with. What I mean by activate is that because the person experiences such profound changes, they begin to open up and accept infinite possibilities for them. Some receive profound physical healing while for others it is emotional healing. I don't want to sound egotistical, but people tell me that when I am in their presence, they feel great joy, happiness, peace and love. That makes me happy because I know I'm on a mission.

Adironnda once told me that they first encountered me in an interdimensional realm or location, doing healing work. It was a place that was colored in all shades of blue. The buildings were rounded, as were the doors. These doors are not the type of doors we typically think of. These doors were actually a curtain of energy that could be strong enough to keep you out or malleable enough to allow you to enter.

In this place I would do healing work, and a cobalt blue light would come from my hands. I was told that the blue I was working with is a 17th-dimensional vibration. And they chose me to work through me because I could hold that vibration. Adironnda refers to me not as a channel but as a vessel or a divine link. And they said that if I can hold that vibration, I could hold theirs. Another reason that I think they work through me because I am only five foot one inches tall and have a round frame. I'm not generally intimidating, although I can be. So I don't threaten people when I come up to them. They experience the energy first, then my physical presence.

I think people have, for a lack of better terms, little time capsules inside of them just waiting to pop open. Once it opens, it makes what was previously unacceptable, acceptable. In my automatic or guided writing of the 90s, they would always say that I would be a speaker, that I would be bringing messages from other dimensional realms as in a channel. They said that I will be activating people en masse because the planet needs to awaken and that I am here to help it awaken people a bit more quickly, and a bit more interestingly maybe. My life now is so totally different than I imagined it those many years ago. At first I resisted, but by the time I gave in, the cellular imprinting of the new soul had mingled with the cellular memory of the body. I think I had the ability to channel all along but until the walk-in occurred it was put on hold. I first had to learn what it was like to be a character in a play, to set my personality aside and let the personality of the character emerge.

I've been an Oracle and a prophet and several things according to past life memories, so I know what it feels like to step aside and surrender. I think that is a skill, a gift the walk-in brought with it. This may sound weird, but I have the ability to see interdimensionally, meaning I can see into people's bodies and realign something that is out of alignment, like mending bones. I have rebuilt discs in people's back, rebuilt cartilage, made heart repairs and more. In fact, at one time, I was so busy with private sessions that I began to see everything as energy. If I can do that, anybody can. I don't think I'm special. I think I'm doing what I came here to do. A while back, I developed a holographic healing program. Holographic healing is teaching the person to develop their own innate ability to see, sense, feel, hear and know what is going on inside their own physical, emotional or even their mental body, or that of others. Now, I have a certification program that teaches those skills. Again, if I can do this work, anyone can do it. In addition to working with Adironnda, I work with The Council of Light. These beings told me that they are here to magnify the energy of activations. And I have witnessed it many times. Sometimes big strapping men step onto the stage and begin to cry. For some, it is the first time they have ever experienced the power of unconditional love. I travel all over the world to speak, channel and teach. I work with 50–300 people every weekend, helping them to activate, and have fun doing it. I help them to discover their own innate abilities, their own gifts and talents that they were born with. Everyone has them. So the mission that I have, that the walk-in has, is being fulfilled. I meet a lot of people and unfortunately, I see so many get so caught up in all the intergalactic, interdimensional hoo-hah. They will tell you that they were a commander on this spaceship, and they were going into the 102nd dimension and blah, blah, blah. What does that matter? I don't mean to offend, but they chose to be here on Earth right now. They are not visitors. This is not just a vacation. They volunteered to be here to help this planet evolve. So, what are they doing spending their time researching who they were and what they might have been? I think a lot of times people get very frightened. I know as a walk-in I went through that. It can be so easy to get caught up in the fantasy of where you have been and what you have done and where you are from, etc. I know what the mothership may look like at the Intergalactic Federation and about the energies of the Saturn Command but that doesn't really matter. I'm here and you're here and we are doing our part to help people realize that there's much more out there. Being an activator, I get to watch people wake up and that's really what it's all about: waking up and remembering who we truly are; to experience love and to be love.

Hildegard Gmeiner

Hildegard grew up in Germany and has a professional background in languages, international trade and broadcast journalism. She has lived in Europe, South Africa and Canada, where she raised her four children. She is an Intuitive Awareness Consultant, a speaker, writer and poet.

During her early thirties she had several near-death experiences. At age 33 she had a soul exchange walk-in experience. This opened her up to continuous telepathic communication and support from her own Andromedan soul aspect, LuiMar.

Hildegard came in with a firm mission that was two-fold: To raise her children to the light; To tell her life story and in so doing help others who had similar experiences.

She offers one-on-one consulting services, provides lectures/workshops/seminars and is writing a book. You may contact her at youruniverseyourway@gmail.com or find her at her website: hildegardgmeiner.com.

Hildegard's Story

After the birth of my third child, I unintentionally lost a lot of weight and began experiencing unexplainable bouts of fainting. No doubt they were brought on by stress placed on my body as I had gone through having three babies in less than six years. I didn't get enough sleep, and due to the demands on me, I had developed poor eating habits, putting the needs of my children above my own.

While pregnant I had weighed over 200 pounds. After my third son's birth, I began to lose weight so drastically that I went below 100 pounds. I had lost more than half my body weight without even trying. I just thought that having three children under six years of age with no extended family close by to help, while my husband had to be away all the time due to his work, was the reason for my ever deteriorating health.

At the time, my diet consisted of the typical German meat, vegetable and potato diet. I had been conditioned to bake with white sugar. I loved the typical Black Forest cake-style pastries for dessert, and I drank a lot of coffee. In retrospect I realize I was a workaholic, and as a result had become an adrenaline junkie. Growing up in Germany, my family, who had suffered through two wars, had been conditioned to work hard and to be busy all the time.

Though I wasn't aware of it at the time, I now know that my rigid and perfectionistic worldview ultimately caused the breakdown of my physical body. I thought that I had to be perfect, but try as I may, with three little children, that wasn't possible. All of my striving for perfection led to the first collapse of my body on an escalator in Germany in April of 1992. It also happened a couple more times back home in Canada with the most memorable one being when the walk-in event occurred.

At that time we lived in suburban Toronto. I thought I had the perfect life. I was married to my best friend, we had three healthy children and a beautiful home. Life was great and I felt content. I enjoyed being a mother and spent all my time taking care of them.

One day, the children were outside playing on the sidewalk when all of a sudden, my youngest started running straight for the road. I took off after him as fast as I could when suddenly everything went black. I saw what appeared to be a black velvet curtain closing, like those at an opera house. Then, for a second or two, I was in total darkness.

The next thing I witnessed was an ambulance drive into our subdivision. I felt like I was watching a movie. From a bird's eye perspective, I witnessed my body lying on the ground and the neighbors, who had just come home from work, flocking together.

I was raised in a strict Roman Catholic household. I did not believe in life after death, yet here I was, somewhere in between the physical world and what else was there? Looking down, I saw a lady in a pink business suit holding the baby. I saw my six-year-old, and the four-year-old. My eldest was holding onto his toddler brother. I'll never forget the look on his face. He looked stunned, scared, seemingly instinctively feeling the need to comfort his younger brother, by putting his arm around his little shoulders, his right hand, holding his brother's right hand. It still brings tears to my eyes whenever I think of it.

Next, I witnessed my body being placed onto a gurney and then into the ambulance by the EMS personal. I kept yelling on the top of my voice, "I'm here, what are you doing with my body? I'm here. Hello!" Then the image suddenly disappeared and the scenes rapidly changed.

I initially saw a tiny little spot of light in the distance, which grew in size. It was so bright that I felt the need to cover my eyes with my hands, when I suddenly realized that I had none. I then desperately attempted to touch my chest and find my arms and legs, yet I had neither.

Panic overcame me. What had happened? Had I died? For a split second, I felt relief at the thought of no longer being subjected to well-meaning doctors telling me there was nothing wrong with my body. I wouldn't have to argue with my husband anymore, who had sided with the medical experts, and had been led to believe that I had just been faking these collapses. I had become increasingly frustrated, since no-one was willing to listen to or believe me when I attempted to tell them, about how difficult it had become for me, to even carry my baby or push a stroller or carry groceries. I had become so weak that I had to lie down multiple times a day for at least half an hour, before I could get up and do something again. I then saw the iridescent light coming close and I heard a voice saying something I agreed with. Suddenly I remembered my children and now I found myself begging the voice to please stop all of this, whatever it might be, and to let me go back to my children. I promised I was going to do whatever it took, if he/she/they, or whoever it was could make it possible for me to get back to my three little boys.

All of a sudden I had an all-white body. I was lying on some sort of a table and there were 12 people standing all around me. Four were positioned on each side of me, two by feet and two behind my head. The person next to me looked into my eyes and began to telepathically communicate with me but I couldn't talk to him. As I recall, these people looked humanoid and had long platinum-colored hair. Their eyes were almond-shaped and at least twice the size of ours. They had wrinkle-free, very youthful-looking skin and appeared to be in their twenties. They wore silvery suits that sparkled like an opal in sunlight. They appeared to be androgynous.

I felt safer with those beings than I had ever felt before. I felt incredible love in their presence. I was told that I would periodically be brought back in order to have adjustments made to my physical body so I would be able to hold higher vibrations. But for now, they had to step down my vibration because there was too big a frequency gap between the 7D and the 3D physicality of my Earth body. I was telepathically told that once I arrived on Earth, I would need to make my physical body stronger by detoxifying it and getting rid of all the lower-vibrating heaviness in my diet and surroundings. It would then become increasingly easy to anchor higher vibrational light frequencies in my body.

I didn't understand most of what I was being told at the time. They told me that I have nothing to worry about. I would want for nothing. All my needs would be met. I might not get everything I desired, but I would get everything that I needed to evolve. I understood the messages they gave me, but it didn't make sense why they felt it was necessary to be saying these things.

Then in a flash, I saw all of my multidimensional lifetimes including the one that was occurring on Earth. I remember receiving the mission to raise the children to the light, tell my story and be of service to others.

Meanwhile, my body was in the hospital. Once I regained consciousness, one of the doctors asked me what had happened. I looked into his eyes and said something like: "I am a 7th dimensional consciousness scientist from Andromeda, here to anchor higher vibration on this planet." As you can imagine, this was not the answer they expected and I remember the physician standing by my bedside glancing across my body to a man sitting on the left, speaking to him about having to medicate me.

My reality had forever changed. It hit me really hard when I was brought back home to the place where this 33-year-old woman, Hildegard, had been living with her husband and three little children for almost 10 years.

At the time, I had no idea that I was a walk-in. All I knew was that my world and my perspective of self had been turned upside down and I thought I was going crazy. I was immediately guided not to eat. Only to drink ginger tea and lemon water. I went cold turkey off coffee, sugar, wheat, and dairy, all in one go. I changed my diet completely, and ate only fruits and vegetables. I discovered that I had to take liquid minerals and vitamins because my body had been severely depleted of vital nutrients due to the three pregnancies and having nursed my children for nine months each.

I am not sure when they first showed up, but I had two beings serving as my support team, which guided me telepathically. There was Ashtar-Athena, and LuiMar. Ashtar-Athena, was a voice I could hear, who helped me learn about and function in daily life as a woman and a mother. She telepathically communicated with me constantly for about two years, helping me with the mundane daily activities. LuiMar is and always was the big picture guide, who explained about the Andromedan walk-in program and how each walk-in is constantly being monitored and yet, based on the cosmic law of non-interference, allowed to slowly find new ways of doing things. Most of which, of course, was quite often perceived by 3D conscious people as senseless, yet in the long run always proved to be the best thing for me and my children.

I didn't know how to care for myself or the kids. I recalled very little about life in a carbon-based body. Basic skills were very difficult for me initially. Functioning in the body was almost impossible and I believe that this was the reason for Ashtar-Athena to step in and teach me everything I needed to know about being human. She stayed with me for the first two and a half years or so.

She taught me about being a woman, personal hygiene, how to feed babies, diapering, cooking, cleaning, bringing children to kindergarten, all the basic life skills that I need to survive here. I couldn't do anything without this inner whispering, teaching me step by step. However, no one around me knew about this, since I didn't dare to speak to anyone about this, not even my husband. As a result of these fainting spells he had become increasingly hostile towards me.

I continued to have severe physical problems for many years. Sometimes I had the sensation of someone hammering away on my spine with a chisel and hammer. I experienced profuse bleeding, as if I had lost a pregnancy. On one occasion I thought I would bleed to death but I heard the reassuring voice of LuiMar telling me that at a certain time, the bleeding would stop. Sure enough, it stopped and I was perfectly fine afterwards. None of that made logical sense and over time, I learned to trust my inner wisdom and the communication that came from it. I learned that the bleeding was occurring because adjustments had to be made in my body and the bleeding was some sort of a physical house-cleaning, which had become necessary due to things being done in my spine. The temporary bloodletting was helping to flush out low-vibrational toxic debris.

I was also having lots of memory issues. I had to make notes to remind me where I was supposed to be, and what I was supposed to do. I kept a notebook with me all the time for the first year or so, and wrote everything down I had to do, and also journaled what I was hearing Ashtar-Athena tell me.

I had to relearn a lot of things and I felt as if I had been abandoned and left with this person, who apparently had been my husband for many years, yet was totally clueless about what was going on inside me. He didn't understand anything I was saying. I kept begging for somebody, anybody, to rescue me from this reality. The "Beam me up, Scotty" line from *Star Trek* came to mind quite often, yet Scotty appeared to not comply with my desperate pleas.

For the first two and a half years, my body felt like I had been shot by a cannon and a huge hole had been blown through me. It was as if my feet and my head were connected by a very thin line of physicalness on the outside of my torso and the inside of my body. Where organs were supposed to be, it was hollow. That's the only way I can describe it. I felt as if people could see through my torso. It was a very surreal feeling.

Over time that sensation changed, and it felt like I had a zipper along the entire front side of my body. I thought I had to zip it up and would do a motion to kind of zip myself up. When my little ones were having difficulty sleeping, I would lay them face down on my body. LuiMar told me to take a diaphragm breath, then stroke my middle finger up the child's spine and it would knit my energies back into place, help the child relax, and knit our energies together at the same time.

All the while I was super stressed. It felt as if I was locked inside the physical body, and had been dropped off behind enemy lines, with Ashar-Athena and LuiMar being my remote lifeline to a more sane world. It felt as if I was imprisoned in a foreign body. It did not function the way I wanted or expected it to. I had very little energy and experienced limited mobility or maneuverability at times. That was totally opposite to what I was used to. I was trapped. And I still didn't understand what had happened to me. I was in a mental haze, desperately attempting to make sense of what had brought this on.

As for my children, after the walk-in experience I felt like I had never seen them before but I had an instant love, compassion and adoration for the little creatures. These kids were no accident and I definitely loved them and wanted to do the best for them. I was initially scared of them and kept thinking, 'Who are these guys?' I had a recurring fear about being responsible for the little lifeforms, but I thought they must be important because my first mandate had been: "Raise your children in the light."

LuiMar was always there to lend support. I trusted him and felt comforted just knowing he was there somewhere, keeping an eye on my progress. Based on insights gained from his council, I decided not to vaccinate the children. He never told me what and what not to do. He just suggested becoming very selective and aware of what I would put into their little bodies. He would ask, "Is it accelerating their vibration, or does it suppress it? You are a master. You are the creator. What are you going to create? You are 100% responsible for these life forms until they have matured enough to make decisions for themselves. It doesn't matter what their dad does or doesn't do with them. It is you making the choice for them, when they are in your care."

Besides, I had no reason at all to believe or trust anything that western medicine suggested. When they couldn't get a handle on what was going with my health, they gave up on me. They went so far as to tell me that I would not live to see my children graduate from kindergarten. Can you imagine? But LuiMar told me that everything would work out and if LuiMar said it, I believed it.

During the late 90s in rural Ontario we had started receiving internet service. It wasn't as strong as it was in the big cities, but it worked. I started to research and found a few online groups that I followed. I started one group and called it Walk-ins. It was a sub-group of the Ashtar Command site. Suddenly people from all over the world began to join and share their experiences. It was the very first time that I had connected with other people, who could relate to what I was saying. I had never met any humans who had had a similar experience to mine or at least no-one had ever talked to me about it, so to find these groups was so exciting.

Then one day, I read about Alex Collier. Alex was the first person I ever heard speaking in public about Andromeda. I am so grateful for what he has done and is doing to help me along my journey.

So why did I become a walk-in? When western medical doctors told me that the next time I fell and my body would hit the pavement, I could die, my soul must have cried up to the heavens for help. But LuiMar once said that all the agreements and contracts for this event to occur had been made long before I was born. Me crying up to the heavens must have been the cue for my walk-in soul to come in.

LuiMar kept telling me that I was part of the walk-in program and although I believed him it took about six years for me to fully accept it and stop having doubts. I had so much going on at the time that although being a walk-in made perfect sense, I couldn't fully comprehend the full implications.

During the early integration days, the more I learned, the more desperate I had become. I was eager to share my experience with others. But the more I did, the more trouble it caused in the marriage, with my extended family, neighbors and friends. The new me caused an abrupt change to my traditional German style way of life. This did not sit well with my then husband. Needless to say, in time the relationship took a turn for the worse. I eventually needed to take the kids and leave otherwise I felt I was running the risk of losing the children and my physical freedoms. There were too many shifts happening too fast for my partner to comprehend. He couldn't cope with the person I had become.

One February day, in -27 degree winter weather, I saw my chance to take kids and run. I didn't know where we were going to sleep that night, but guidance led me into a real estate office. I explained why I was there to the lady on call that day and she agreed to help me. I

Walk-ins

ended up living with this lady and her two teenage children for two weeks until I could get a place of my own. Once I did, I was able to better take care of myself and my energies and my life over time began to stabilize.

However, true stabilization only came after I learned to assert myself in a variety of different settings. This was the legal system, the medical system and also within the school system. I soon realized that the systems didn't acknowledge the existence of a soul and the innate human inner guidance system, speaking to us via our feelings.

My young children were hypersensitive to everything. They had food allergies, asthma, you name it they had it. Some had trouble with food colorings and preservatives in foods, others were very sensitive to loud noises, and yet another was so eager to learn that he was told in school to stop putting his hand up in class.

Thirty years ago, when a single mom told a doctor or a teacher that her kids shouldn't have peanut butter or that they shouldn't have juice because of the red food coloring, she was labeled to be an over-sensitive overprotective mother. Interestingly enough nowadays food and other sensitivities have become the new norm.

I had a lot of battles to fight and if I would have said I knew what I was talking about because I was a walk-in from Andromeda, they would have taken my kids away from me. Thankfully LuiMar had taught me to keep a low profile until the right time would come to speak about it. LuiMar said, you must focus on raising these children to the light first and in due time, you will tell you a story.

One day I decided to ask LuiMar why I was here, and he said that my old soul agreed to be part of the walk-in program. He further stated, "Walk-ins are other dimensional intelligences, who volunteered to step down into a lower dimension to help a specific planetary community evolve. In compliance with the universal law of non-interference with an evolving species, this program had become necessary ever since humans had been given technology, for which their collective spiritual consciousness has not matured enough to handle it responsibly.

Hence, the Intergalactic Federation of Star-Travelling Civilizations (IFSTC) had agreed that walk-ins from various worlds would be parachuted into a human form, to help accelerate the spiritual awakening and growth of the collective human consciousness." He said that one day soon - who knows what soon means to him - there would be other walk-ins "popping like popcorn" (waking up) who will be confused, and I would know what to do to help them.

Then I asked, "Why me, and why do I have these little critters to look after, if in fact I'm really so smart and important? Why did you drag me down here and leave me to care for these children?" Very reassuringly he told me that humanity's spiritual awareness is comparable to the limited awareness of tiny little children, when viewed within a cosmic, galactic bigger context. He said that as I learned how to best nurture the children, I would also learn how to best help and nurture humanity. I would learn on a spiritual galactic consciousness level and on an intergalactic conscious level, how to interact with humanity. In order for me to be taken seriously, I had to become empathetic to what people on planet Earth were going through during their various transforming vibrational states. He said that I had to be immersed in the child-rearing experience because they were still hardwired to a higher consciousness. And that my little children were giving me all the things I would need to learn and integrate here. They would be my immediate masters and teachers on humanity. And boy, were they ever. They are still my Master Teachers to this day.

LuiMar said, "Humanity is much like children, lighting the playpen on fire. Humanity is playing with nuclear weapons and doing things that harm themselves, other life forms and other worlds. But humanity is ignorant of many such impacts. Due to the law of noninterference between one species of beings and another, they have to just observe and allow the species to evolve at their own rate and pace. But through the walk-in programs, higher-conscious beings can get many 'boots on the ground' quickly, circumventing the birthing and lengthy developmental process, whenever necessary. If the leaders of Earth can't be reached (and it has been tried in the past, 'Stranger in the Pentagon') the program decided to reach out to humanity by other means, simply by placing walk-ins in certain spots for special missions."

Therefore, a call went out through the galaxies for volunteers to walk into this 3D physicality to help humanity wake up. Volunteers from all over the galaxy and from different dimensions volunteered and the souls of people volunteered to give up their forms, so another soul fractal might be permitted to animate it.

The human physical hardware received regular upgrades via the walk-ins, and their souls received the software upgrades that allow their consciousness to rapidly expand faster than normal.

The soul is an infinite being in and of itself. It has many aspects or fractals. The soul is the Shakti with Shiva being the all or Source. One soul aspect can be in the 7D while another one lives in the 3D. These two aspects communicated and agreed before this body was even born, that at a certain time, age 33, in my personal case, that the 3D fractal would depart, and the 7D fractal would come in.

So, I am a soul fractal, which after thirty years of Earth life, has chosen to switch places with another aspect of the same soul. At least that is my understanding. This has been my attempt to give you insights into some aspects of my very challenging and yet, ultimately very interesting walk-in experiences. It definitely was a crazy time early on. Even though, right now, I'm clued in on the third dimension, it doesn't mean I'm only a 3D being. I believe nobody is. There is much more to a human being that I can claim to know.

It doesn't mean that I am limited to 3D thoughts and beliefs just because I live here. And it doesn't mean that I'm limited to only having experiences on this planet, for I am having multiple lifetimes on other planets and timelines and dimensions, yet all is happening at the same time; because I am actually a soul, which has created a physical body. I am first and foremost consciousness, from which everything else then takes shape.

I would like you, the reader, to know that if you are having unusual experiences that you are not alone, and everything happens for a reason. You might just be a little ahead of others in your soul group, who might be still asleep. They might be waiting for you to shine your light, so you might become a beacon of light for them. Many people have said to me over the years, just by me sharing my story, it gave them hope. It is good to know there are others and that we are not alone. Please know, even at the worst of times, "We are never alone, for we are ultimately all ONE."

Emma Louise LivingSoul

Emma Louise LivingSoul is a walk-in from what she calls 'the White Planet'. It wasn't until many years later that she started using the term LivingSoul to describe herself. She explains it as "just becoming a part of me." We are all LivingSouls in a physical body. She describes being here to help us usher in the New Earth.

She brings her gifts and talents forward as she works with the elements, especially the energy of water. Before she had heard of the work of Dr. Masaru Emoto, author of *The Hidden Messages in Water* among others, he visited her from the spirit realm with the message that this gift was on its way. Shortly after, she received the gift of a pendant through a friend. It was the water crystal for gratitude.

For the past six years, she has served humanity by being a nurse in her country of Norway.

Emma's Story

Around the age of seven, in the summer of 1985, Emma began having profound spiritual experiences and realized she had become a walk-in soul. She lost all of the memories before the age of seven, yet was slowly gaining access to memories of where she had come from before she walked in.

My first memory about this incarnation (besides entering the body) was my first day of school. The graduating students picked flowers for the new students starting that year. They were to act as protectors and advisors to the new students. Each graduate picked a member of the starting class to deliver their flowers to. I was picked by a tall, blue-eyed blond boy and I remember that he met me in the school yard and gave me the flowers. I remember that so clearly and it was just him and me. So it can't be something that someone had told me. It must have been my own experience. So that is practically the first memory I have for this planet.

Prior to incarnating into the Emma body, I have memories of being part of a non-human-looking family. I call us 'the shiny ones' or 'the crystal people'. We were extremely tall and slim. We don't have any 'natural' hair on our heads. What we have instead of hair is an almost fluid shape that dances around our heads. Typically, it is only the oldest and the wisest of our group that have 'hair'. We do not walk on legs like humans do, although we have them; instead we seem to float when moving. Our skin is shiny and luminescent, whitish and transparent. It's almost like looking into a crystal that radiates all of the spectral colors. Our eyes are very large and look completely black, but when gazing into them, you can see that they are actually filled with what appears to be stars and galaxies. There are all kinds of things moving around in them. Our heads are very narrow and very long in the back as it extends behind us. Our noses are very distinguished with tiny slits where a human's nose would be, and our mouths are also very distinguished and small. I don't remember any ears per se, but we did have some type of a system or hole on the side of the head. We also had small holes, almost trumpet-like, on the inside going down the back of our necks, and I think they were used as gills because I also remember being in water. I think that we were aquatic beings just as much as we were on the land, going back and forth between the two often.

There was some type of hierarchy, but it wasn't like politicians or kings. It was a council of elders or wise ones. Being a part of this council didn't mean that you were 'old', because there were young beings as well as older ones on there. Our bodies did not age. We remained in our middle 20s, in comparison to humans. Some could look older in body, but that was a matter of preference. To be part of the council you had to have some sort of a repertoire of knowledge, calmness, and an overview of everything that happened on the planet. I remember my mother and father were part of this council and we lived very beautiful lives. I just want to go back there. I don't want to be here in this place anymore actually. Not that I want to die, I just want to be home. I'm so homesick. At the same time, late in the evening, right before bed, I always smile at the sky, because I know that I will return one day.

I remember that the planet was extremely colorful and vibrant. It was a place of peace and ultimate beauty. There was this one place that I really loved because it was so stunning. The architecture was a cross between the Greek temples and the old English castles from medieval times, with an abundance of stunning columns.

Everything was white and extremely light; it was made of a special type of stone or marble. But it was also similar to crystal. We used a lot of crystals in our architecture, so you can imagine the beauty of this place. I remember when we came there was this large column that led out to what I could only describe as a patio. From this landing you could see across a strikingly beautiful valley, and glimpse the ocean in the distance. On each side of the patio are enormous, exquisite trees with magnificent birds sitting in the branches. I remember the fruit on these trees as they appeared to glow with vibrant colors. I loved to stand there looking down this valley.

Behind the patio was a picturesque garden. It was so quiet there that I called it the silent garden. And behind the garden was a lake with a waterfall cascading over the rocks. There was a bench by the water, where I sat with my teacher, Oriel. I remember him very well. He taught me various styles of energy work and about nature, the universe and how everything was consciously connected. I remember playing and jumping in the water among the huge water lilies that floated effortlessly there.

I was practicing some type of martial arts, similar to Qi Gong, with bent knees while my body made flowing motions as I worked with the elements – the wind, water and land. I was playing and dancing almost on top of the water lilies. When I jumped into the water, I could cause the water lilies to submerge and come up and out of the water like a dolphin. I used to swim in the lake and if I dove down, there was a cave that had ascending steps that could come to the top of the waterfall.

I have a vague memory of standing with a man on the platform, overlooking the silent garden and the valley. He was wearing a handsome uniform of golden armor and there were many other men standing behind him. He was the leader of some type of group. He was explaining that he had to go away to defend our planet. There was some type of a threat outside of us. I know he was very close to my heart.

What I do remember is that I came to Earth as a result of running away from home. I was very sad about something happening on another planet that was very close to where we lived. I remember entering one of our shuttles that accommodated up to four people. They were similar in color to the white luminescent appearance of our skin, egg-shaped and almost completely white. You couldn't see any windows or doors, but upon approach, it was as if it could read my frequency and the door opened up as a walkway lowered. The entire seating and control area appeared to be composed of a transparent jelly. When I sat down, the substance shaped around my body. I put my hands in the jelly and was connected to the ship, which was a type of biological mass that I could steer with my thoughts.

I remember going off-planet and within no time, landing on a desert-like planet with sand everywhere. It was very dusty and dimly lit, like right before sunrise. I exited the ship and entered a cave system. Inside were Earth humans! Unfortunately, they were not being treated very well at all; they were dirty and had very little clothing on. I realized that they were slaves. They seemed to be using very simple tools to cultivate the sand and stone. I remember seeing some type of low-technology transportation. It was a huge wheel-like structure with something attached. In the middle was a seat where the person sitting on it kept the wheel balanced as it moved. There was also some sort of being or presence inside the cave that was keeping the human slaves working. I don't have a clear memory of who they are. I recall seeing the beings as shadows, but I remember thinking that they didn't feel heart-centered. I don't feel good about them at all. When thinking about the humans, I feel really sad. I knew that they should not have been there. Neither should I for that matter, but I wanted to get some kind of proof or help them in some way.

Then my mother appeared. She knew I had a rebellious soul so when she found out that I had run away, she came after me. She was afraid for me. She took me out of the cave, saying, "You can't be here. It's really dangerous for you. They know you have run off now, what you have seen, and I can't protect you anymore. I have to send you away." Then I remember her hugging me and telling me how much she loved me. She explained, "I don't want to do this, but it is for your own good and protection. I love you." This may not be exactly how it happened, but it is the way I remember it. Then it was like she was pushing me away.

The memory that I have next is very strange because I was floating off the planet in the middle of the universe. There was no land to be seen anywhere, I was just floating for what seemed like an eternity inside some type of capsule. It was very dark yet very comfortable. It felt like I was pure consciousness floating inside the capsule.

My next experience is that of me inside a golden sphere, but the sphere was me. I was now floating through the glass of a little girl's bedroom. I could see her lying in bed. I had no sensation of having a body. It was just me. I remember thinking, 'I am me. I'm me in every sense, but I don't have a body! I'm a sphere.'

The golden sphere floated over to where the little girl was sleeping and hovered above her body, I was having a conservation with her, but I can't remember the details. (I'm working these days on trying to recall the memories in full.) I just know that we were communicating.

Then I began to see her soul and realized that I was a soul too. She was like me except that she had a golden string with light around it that attached her to the body. She looked like a cloud of dust as she lifted straight out of her body and entered the sphere. At the same time I was coming into the body and entered through her crown chakra at the top of her head.

As you can imagine, the next day things were a little strange around the house. When the little girl, Emma, had gone to bed, she had light blonde hair and blue eyes. When she woke up, she had light brown hair with green eyes that had golden flakes in them. Having now assumed her identity, my sister said they noticed right away that in addition to the physical changes there was a personality change as well. It was like having a brand new family member. Little did they know. They knew that something had definitely happened.

My father was contacted by two beings in black suits and they gave him very clear instructions on how to raise me. They said I was not allowed to watch television, listen to the radio or read books. They instructed him that I was to go to a private, special school, with as little influence by the outside world as possible. I was to receive no introduction to religion either.

They also gave him specific instructions about how I was supposed to eat. I was never allowed to eat any type of sugar. Instead I had to eat very pure foods and drink only water and herbal tea. He was told that I was never to be given any type of vaccinations.

My sisters and brothers said it was like the visitors placed some type of protection around me so that no one could ever hurt me. And they said they felt like they had to always protect and stand up for me. Everyone I have ever met in my life, even in my grown-up life, say the same. They say they get this extreme feeling to protect me.

The first thing my fiancé said to me was that he felt he had to protect me in all ways. Very strange. I see myself as a pretty strong person.

Early in life I began to learn Qi Gong and was trained in the martial arts. I was training my body extremely hard and I was very different from the other kids from my own age. I was sailing a big 25-foot Viking-style boat on my own at the age of 11. Finally, I was allowed a very limited time to listen to the radio, to watch television and to begin reading a little. In my teenage years I did sneak out and visit friends.

Growing up, I didn't have many friends. I was bullied a lot because I was too strange for most. I can understand that, because there were a lot of things happening at school with me that no one could really explain. For instance, they found me in the basement of the school one time. It was locked; no one can get in there except from the janitor. It was not him that locked me in. I just walked through the door because I needed some peace and quiet. I hated being at school. I couldn't understand the concept of it. I thought it was so limiting. No one ever seemed to pay attention, every time I tried to raise my hand, say something, they didn't really listen. I was so glad to leave and get on with my life.

Many people have asked me if I came to this planet with a particular mission. For me, the concept of 'mission' is a typical human way of looking at it. I feel that I will go back to where I came from after this lifetime. And I don't think that I'm here to save humanity or the world or anything, but I do feel that since I am here, I can bring as much positivity and light to this world as possible.

One of the things that I've decided to do is to write my story and as much of my own knowledge and wisdom as I remember. I feel like one of the strongest things that I can give to Earth and humanity is the way of becoming one with the elements, the natural environment and everything around us. I understand that people cannot just drop everything and run off into the wilderness to connect with themselves, but everyone can connect.

As a child, one of the first things I would do after school was to jump on my bike and go as far into nature as I possibly could. I am lucky to live where there are mountains and the ocean. We are surrounded by nature here. I would go into the mountains while still maintaining my view of the ocean. The sea is very important to me. Water has great importance in my life.

One time, I was sitting on top of the mountain, looking over the water. I was doing a simple silent meditation where I connected to my physical body, but at the same time I became one with everything around me. I became the mountain and the grass and the birds, the wind on the ocean and everything. And within that oneness with everything, there was mindfulness. I have been talking about the wellness way before it became a popular thing for everyone in the new age. And there, in this wellness, I could feel that I was floating, I was part of the sea. Becoming part of the mountain, was to, in a way, transform my energy to be part of the mountain's frequency. And then, I tuned into the frequency of the water, the wind and earth, and whatever I chose to become one with. And within that experience, I could hear a whisper. It was like a web of information. Then, I could suddenly see myself over the Sahara or the pyramids, Brazil or wherever in the world I chose to go with this whisper.

Maybe the whisper is consciousness. My understanding of consciousness or Creator or God, is that it's just part of this whole web of everything. It's an energy that is embracing everything that has been created. It's almost like the whisper of the collective within the whole universe. I don't see God or Creator as one man or woman. I see it as a perfect balance of everything.

The walk-in has been very positive. But I have to say that I always had people in my life who had extreme challenges because of it. I think all my training before I came here, the energy, moving of the elements and the Qi Gong, taught me so much about energy and frequency that I have always been able to rise very quickly above most challenges. I have always landed with my feet first. I feel extremely supported by my surroundings.

I'm an educated nurse and have been working in the emergency room for six years. I see lots of people in there experiencing fear. I think one of the most important things in this life is to step completely out of fear. I know it's probably easier for a person to say when you feel you are supported, but at the same time, I would say that the reason I am supported is because I've never been fearful of being myself. People should be their authentic selves. As different as people saw me, I have never been afraid to show who I am and what I stand for. When I have something coming to me in a vision or whatever, I have shared it with those around me. You must trust yourself. You are unique within this ocean of consciousness and trust yourself, be yourself in whatever shape and color you are.

I know that on this plane of reality, we are experiencing duality. In the higher densities (dimensions as Earthlings call it) we don't have a brain that is divided in two hemispheres, we don't comprehend knowledge and wisdom from a point of duality. Nor do we experience it from a duality. We see all as one. We don't have a time-space reality, where all is linear with a future and past. We see it all as happening at the same moment. So in the universal law of truth, we are all in one place at all times. We never move anywhere, we just experience ourselves as moving from A to B. So when I was meditating and let myself raise my frequency, and my energy started vibrating as one with all, I basically widened my awareness of what is, I could see myself wherever I wanted to go in the world.

We humans are controlled in a construct; we are the only place in the entire universe where we vibrate at a third density. And because of that, it is so easy to keep us in fear. All the duality of dark and light doesn't exist in the same way in the higher densities. Earthlings need to get out of the pit of believing just what they are shown from the narratives. Because Earthlings are so much more than they perceive themselves in the mirror. Let me share this as an ending of this beautiful testimony, which I give from my heart to all the Earthlings that are ready to open to who they really are.

Through what level of awareness do we see our reality? For example, let's look at the symbol of the swastika. From a third-density awareness, we see the swastika as a character that is divided into many different meanings. As a geometrical figure it was in ancient religions used as an icon for the cultures of Eurasia. It was a symbol for divinity and spirituality in religions in India, like in Hinduism, Buddhism and Jainism. But in the western world, it was a symbol for auspiciousness and good luck, until it became a Nazi symbol, and an emblem for the Aryan race.

From a wider, even wiser point of awareness, symbols hold the power that you put into them. In other words, what you as a creator create within your own awareness holds a focus, holds the power of your will. That is another example of the Creator (you) and Creation (what we perceive as the reality we live in). Remember this example when you are faced with the world of today; everything you consume or take part in is a reflection of your own creation.

We are having many experiences at one time. From a universal standpoint, we are ONE. We are the one 'God/Creator' creating a creation, in a co-created state of being. We are the ONE, and we can choose to wake up to a higher, wider, wiser awareness. Yes, the Creator wants to experience it all. There really is no separation between the 5th and the 3rd density because all is already inside of you.

Words like you, me and us, are also just creations. It is a concept. Just as the concept of soul, consciousness and so on. What power do you fill the creation with? And remember, all energy can manifest into matter. So saying that 5th density is non-physical is against the universal law of truth. All is energy, always; frequencies vibrating at a level of awareness creating energy into matter, or what is perceived as matter. The densities are inside of you, me and us. We have never been separated from any of it. Densities are a journey within yourself, your inner universe. We can always be in a perceived physical form, and in that form we vibrate, depending on what frequency of awareness we are at the moment. And in this way we can wander in and out of densities; that is the land of consciousness. The higher we vibrate on the scale of densities, the bigger gifts we can give to us all. There has never been any separation between the densities (dimensions as Earthlings say), only a narrowing and expansion of awareness that we refer to as consciousness (God, which is also a third density concept). In a third density concept we say we are all gods. And from a wider awareness we are all aware of being consciousness vibrating on a high frequency (tone).

The closest way to get to this awareness in this plane of reality (here on Earth), is to leave the old world behind. That means we have no attachments to what we have created here in the third density. As an example, when I leave my home, I have no attachment to whether it is there when I get back. Go out in nature and practice listening inside, in silence. I practice silent walks, silent meditations, silent breathing work. Connect to your heart center, and create new synapses to your brain. Grow your brain together. And become one with all. You can have an individual experience and still be in the awareness of being one with all creation. The star beings are here, and we are working to raise this third density world into a higher tone. Be consciously part of the real side. Because our awareness is the key to being free LivingSouls.

Jacquelin Smith

Jacquelin Smith, B.A., is a certified hypnotherapist, gifted psychic, healer, speaks star and light language, is a metaphysical teacher, star being communicator, animal communicator, experiencer, a hybrid and has experienced multiple walk-ins. She is a speaker and has spoken at numerous conferences including the International UFO Congress, Midwest Veterinary Conference, and the Universal Light Expo to name a few.

She has authored two books, *Animal Communication - Our Sacred Connection*, and her latest book *Star Origins and Wisdom Of Animals: Talks With Animal Souls*. She believes that we are all star beings here on Earth and that the animals are star beings as well. She has multiple audio downloads and CDs available on her website which include *Deeper Heart Openings*; *Awakening Star Consciousness*; *Communication With Star Beings*.

Jacquelin has been interviewed extensively about being an experiencer, a hybrid and her animal communication work. She has written numerous articles about communicating with animals and nature for a variety of publications. She was interviewed and has her own chapter in two books written by Miguel Mendonça, *Meet the Hybrids* and *Being with the Beings*.

Her website is jacquelinsmith.com.

Jacquelin's Story

Throughout my life, I have had what many might call a variety of walk-in, contact and spiritual experiences. I have encountered soul exchanges, soul infusions and soul layering with a variety of soul aspects from multidimensional planes, and from different planets and galaxies. The beings (other life expressions not of Earth) that contact me come in a variety of forms including extraterrestrials, angelic forms, balls of light, fairies, elementals and other natural beings.

The first time I was contacted was in utero. I was genetically altered while still in my mother's womb with seven different types of star being (extraterrestrial) DNA. I was injected with a DNA cocktail, which also included the DNA of a hybrid man living on the Earth, and that of my human mother and father.

For the procedure, my mother had been taken aboard a ship. On some level, both she and my father consented to this process, but consciously were unaware of what was going on. They have no memories of being on a ship because they had an implant procedure conducted that blocked all memories of this or any other contact event.

My original star family is Quabar. Quabar is from the seventh universe outward from Earth. I come from a collective consciousness that is pure energy, love, light and joy. Quabar has a great sense of humor and they make me laugh.

My star parents in this lifetime are Tall White Zeta Masters named Ametha and Zazu. They are a beautiful shimmering white light. Beneath that, their essences are like neon blue globes of light. They are loving, amazing and express emotions. I want to share that about the emotions because a lot of people think that star beings don't have emotions. They would hug me and were very loving. They began visiting me after my birth to help me adjust to being a human/hybrid. We maintain a strong contact through visitations and dreams.

Prior to being born, I wanted to back out of coming into human form again. My Earth mother told me they had to force the labor.

As an infant, I had several star beings around me. Some might call them guardian angels. They were members of my original star family, Quabar, an etheric group consciousness that radiates love and light. They wanted to reassure me that everything would be alright. I remember them being around my crib. They are a group consciousness. There are neither males nor females in the group. They can, however, manifest in whatever form they choose.

Around age two or three, I began being taken onto a ship, almost nightly, where I was taught to expand my consciousness, and was educated about the power of love. I was always met by my star parents along with a variety of other species. And just like any three-year-old, I was running around the ship getting into all kinds of things. When it was time to go back to Earth, I would try to talk my parents into letting me stay but they would remind me about my soul commitment to be on Earth.

As I got a little older I would take classes on the ship and would learn about working with energy, how to levitate objects, how to materialize objects, travel multidimensionally (astral travel), and how to speak light language. I would speak light language to my parents and the other beings that were on the ship. I continue speaking it even now. I was also enhanced, leaving me as an empath, with a telepathic ability. I am clairvoyant, clairaudient and clairsentient. I have various healing abilities, and the ability to communicate with animals and star beings.

My star family and I traveled to other planets where I met different races. At the same time, those on the ship and on the other planets we encountered, were studying me as much as I was studying them. These visits continued for many years.

When I was six years old, I had a near-death experience. Another aspect of my soul, as well as two other souls, came in to support me in my life during this time. I had taken a bad fall down a flight of steps. Suddenly, I found myself in other dimensions. A spirit who had been human, Joe, was watching over me. Then I found myself in the arms of angels. They were comforting me. I felt totally loved, safe and comforted.

Next, I found myself floating in the midst of very tall beings of light. Waves of love poured over me. I could see my soul and how bright I was. There were seven tall beings of light. None of them had any faces. They were vague figures which radiated brilliant white light. The beings of light said to me, "Feel the love." A couple beings said, "We are you. See how beautiful you are. You are divine love and light."

Countless waves of unconditional love poured through me. It was so much love that I felt I couldn't hold it all, but in this state, I could allow it to flow through me since I wasn't in my physical form.

Several beings silently said that they were reflecting to me who I truly was. I knew they were me and I was them. We were one. And when there is Oneness, there are no faces or bodies, but only the divine love. They told me that I had to return to the Earth plane stating that I had many things to do on Earth. I told the angels and beings that I did not want to go back to Earth, and that I loved being in heaven.

Then an aspect of my soul joined with me and entered my auric field. Also, two other souls joined with me, or 'walked in' to support me in my journey on Earth. We had made this agreement before I was born.

The aspect of my soul that joined with me remained with me. The two other souls stayed with me and supported me through my teens. Then they exited, knowing that I no longer needed their support and that they had also learned what they had come in to learn. I was already having multidimensional experiences communicating with star cultures, but my experiences were enhanced after this experience.

As a little girl I was able to communicate with animals and trees. I could hear the trees sing and I would sing back to them. When I would share this with my mother, she told me that it was just my imagination, so some of my innate intuition went underground but opened back up more fully as I got older.

When I was in my early teens, memories of what had been occurring my whole life began to emerge. At first the memories started to dribble in, then they poured in. At age 14 I remembered sitting on my bed one night yelling for them to come take me on the ship. Within a week, a ship appeared. It made a cross configuration in the sky and then shot straight up into the air as it disappeared.

I didn't realize it at the time but they did take me on a ship and began to prepare me to have hybrid children. They began taking eggs from me during my teens. I have over 40 hybrid children and have met them while on the ship. My star families have raised them while I carry out my mission here on Earth. It was hard to leave them but I can telepathically communicate with them whenever I want. They speak to me as one consciousness instead of individually.

I am still in contact with my star parents. I travel back to the ship and have been on other ships as well, but I prefer to visit my star parents ship because it is like my home. I do call on them for help if I need healings or whatever. When I need support, I call on them and my entire guidance team. I am constantly in contact with star beings; it is part of my daily life. Throughout the years, I have been in contact with more than 80 different star cultures.

In 1979, I was in a serious car accident that left me unconscious and in the hospital. I had been in several car accidents before, but this one changed my whole life. After the accident happened, I remember going to the other side (spirit realm) where all types of different beings were talking to me, including my star family. They were all explaining to me that I was not finished on Earth yet and wanted me to continue, which was very significant and a turning point of sorts for me.

Prior to the accident I had worked as a veterinary assistant. The veterinarian fired me while I was lying in bed at the hospital. That's when I started doing what I was supposed to be doing. I started utilizing my gifts with animals and people.

Quabar came to me in the 1980s and that opened me up to be able to communicate with the star beings more deeply. It opened me to communicating with many star cultures.

On Thanksgiving Day, in 2013, I had an amazing experience. When the comet ISON was going around the sun, although she broke up when she rounded it, she had a huge effect on this solar system - more than people thought. The star beings contacted me and told me to go outside at midnight which I did. When I went outside there were seven starships in the sky. Then a portal opened up over my house and a craft came out. It was just above my trees and they shined a light into my eyes. Incredible electromagnetic fields were in and around my house, which people witnessed. That's when they took me aboard the mothership. I had two weeks of solid experiences of being on starships, a mother ship, traveling between dimensions as well as through time, having out-of-body experiences, and having lots of star beings at my house. When I was on a mothership, I discovered that I was part of a council there, so I was shifting in and out of my human self, becoming my council star being self.

During this time, I also had a variety of walk-in experiences. Some parts of me left and other parts of my soul came in. The star beings told me they removed 85% of who I was, so there was only 15% of Jacquelin left and they replaced that 85% with other aspects of my star being soul. I had to integrate these multiple aspects so as I was communicating with them about the integration, they said, "We are integrating you too." This was a difficult process for all of us because the star beings are of a much higher density and had to lower their vibration in order to be compatible with my human form.

You could say that I had multiple walk-in experiences all at once. But instead of integrating just one or two aspects during a resting phase, I was receiving these different aspects all at once. Each one was separate, each one unique, each an aspect of me. The integration process was not fun for them or me. I even had to talk with some aspects to help them understand what I call 'birth stuff' of lowering their vibrational frequency in order to come into third density.

When these aspects were integrating, there were changes in my personality which I could see and some others noticed as well. The walk-in aspects altered the way I ate. I was eating foods that I hadn't been eating. I was drawing, painting and writing in new and expanded ways and with new subject matter. There were also changes in how I dressed.

One day the bank called me because my signature looked totally different from my previous signature. I told the bank that I had signed my name to the checks they were questioning. Also, I started writing dates on my checks and other papers, beginning on the right-hand side rather than the left. When I was sitting with someone at the bank, I had to sign and date some papers, and he noticed it, and made the comment that he had never seen anyone do this before.

My walk-in experiences were pretty rough. There were times when various multidimensional aspects of my soul were merging with me all at once. It took a lot of time and energy to deal with these other selves. Sometimes, I didn't know who I was with all of these aspects trying to integrate on various levels.

One of the most disconcerting things that happened during the integration was that I lost some memories of who my friends were. They felt very foreign to me, and the integrating aspects did not have the memory of who my friends were. It took a while for me to remember who my friends were and to recall what my relationships were like with them. Some of these friends I had known for 40 years.

It was a process which took many months to move through. Eventually, the memories that I had of my friends were accessed by the walk-in aspects of my soul, and things integrated.

If I had to give advice to someone experiencing a walk-in, I would tell them to seek support from those who have been through it. They need to have support so they can understand what is going on and to help them integrate in the easiest way possible.

I am a walk-in but I consider myself a blend of multidimensional soul selves. It has been a heck of a journey. Souls live many lifetimes all at once. It is all simultaneous. The soul chooses each form or non-form; it chooses to experience for the sake of learning. I believe we are all different aspects of the creator, and the creator is learning and expressing itself through every form of consciousness.

I support a lot of people who want to know about their experiences on ships or whatever. I offer light language sessions which I love doing while I play the singing bowls. During these sessions I usually have four or five different star races come through to give that person whatever they need, or the divine mother comes through. Sometimes Tara, the female Buddha, comes through to help clear that person from old patterns so they can be more of their authentic self. I also offer star origin readings, which is helping people understand when and where they first sparked off from the creator.

Using light language has been a powerful experience. It is a multidimensional heart-centered cosmic soul language that is actually a light frequency which carries its own consciousness. When light languages flow through me it is a frequency of love. It bypasses the mind/ego and resonates directly with the heart. It is a language that can be felt throughout the entire body. You may not understand the words, but you can feel them and connect with their meaning for you. It is a language of feeling and flow. It carries within it light codes that activate and shift your holographic blueprint and DNA to bring you more into harmony with yourself. When the body, mind and soul begin to resonate with these codes it can bring about a shift in a person's life. It can help to activate and awaken the mind to be able to release thought patterns that no longer work for a person. It can also help bring you into a higher frequency of love, light, peace and joy.

I never know for sure what is going to come through me because I work with so many different star beings as each has a variety of dialects. Light language is spoken as a frequency. Sometimes I channel my guides. Sometimes I channel other beings. And sometimes I channel my higher self or other aspects of my own soul. Many people ask me about my connection with the various beings. I believe it is because these people may be waking up to the truth of who they are or somewhere inside them they have a resonance with star beings. They may have been visited, been on a ship, have had an encounter with them or they may even have hybrid children but they just don't remember. They may even be searching for their own star family.

At our core we are all divine love, but then the soul has its first expression, which is what I call the star origin expression. People's original star frequency runs through all their lifetimes, it is a key energy signature. Many people are seeking their cosmic roots which is what one needs to be waking up to during this time.

The star origin readings that I provide helps a person identify the first expression of their soul, who their star origin family is and they discover their own original frequency. For example, when I gave you a reading, you discovered that your star origin family is an angelic collective, that is linked to the Elohim Creators. Your original star family purpose was to assist with the creation of different angelic beings and to send love and joy into the universes. The name of the star origin family is a frequency so I gave you that frequency and your own individual frequency. We are all star beings.

Animals are star beings too. I offer animal communication training as well as one-on-one sessions. I provide animal behavioral work as well as work with animals on the other side by communicating messages. I track lost animals, and do long-distance healing work on them.

I work with people psychically by providing psychic readings and Tarot readings. I am a certified hypnotherapist, so I work with experiencers in terms of helping them sort out their experiences. What is great is I can just call in the star beings who they had the experiences with and they will answer their questions. I offer apprenticeship programs on how to communicate with animals telepathically and how to communicate with star beings.

I help remind people who they are: a soul, an aspect of the Creator. We are the universe and the universe is us. A small part of the soul resides behind the human heart. It is what animates the human body. And it is eternal.

The soul is vast and as I mentioned, it is multidimensional. We are living and experiencing many lifetimes simultaneously. The soul is a spark of light and consciousness that is an expression of the creator. And the soul then creates many expressions (lifetimes) for the sake of having all kinds of experiences, as well as for spiritual growth and expansion in consciousness. In the end, all souls are expressions of the creator expanding in consciousness, and coming to knowing itself in countless ways.

We are all expressions of the Creator. Each human; each star being; and all etheric and physical forms are divine expression. We are all connected. We are all part of one large soul.

All of these experiences are challenging to put into words. Yet, I know they are real. I hope that my story will help support others who have been through similar experiences and encounters.

Dylan Kuczko

Dylan is an angelic soul infusion walk-in that came in at the age of seven. He is an empath, sensitive and intuitive, and applies these skills as a Holistic Healing Practitioner, BodyEvolve (BE) Therapist, Life Care/Bio-Dynamics practitioner and a Reiki Master. He is learning the Evolutionary Quantum Healing Technique and becoming certified as a Kinesio Taping Practitioner (KTP). Dylan is the manager of the SpiritWay Wellness holistic health center.

Dylan's Story

When I was seven years old, I had a rushed exploratory surgery that was due to a birth defect caused by my appendix being much higher than it should have been. It was tucked up inside of my intestines, so when it ruptured the doctors had no way of telling because I wasn't showing any signs of appendicitis at the time. The body was extremely weak and any kind of movement caused excruciating pain. In the hospital they had told me it has been several days since my appendix had actually ruptured, and that it has caused peritonitis and sepsis, causing a large amount of toxins to leak into my system. After the surgery I was told they had to take out all of my organs and physically wash them to get all of the poison out of my system, so I can completely understand why the body was no longer habitable.

Before the surgery, my parents were sitting with me in the pre-op, and I started speaking a language that I had never spoken or even heard before. I could feel myself getting much weaker at that point, and I was trying to fight it as much as I could, but I feel like it was my soul's way of crying out to be let go. I have talked with my parents about this on several occasions and they were shocked at the time, to say the least. I don't recall it clearly now; however they described it as being a very rhythmic and melodic tone, much deeper than any seven year old should be able to go.

I remember what happened right before coming into this body. There were several very large beings around me, around 35 feet tall. They were radiating light in a constant, very low humming sound. We were floating atop an infinitely large body of golden white liquid. It was completely transparent and went on indefinitely. I remember the deep bass humming sound getting louder as they moved as a unit, similar to birds moving with each other. They encircled me and extended their hands outward. There were many shapes around me that started to rise from the golden fluid, mostly circles that had rings constantly rotating around them, and in the center there was a pure white flame; the circles were radiating a heat that was very soothing. There were several triangular shapes as well, which folded in on themselves continuously. I laid back effortlessly and began floating about six feet above the liquid. As the shapes and beings began closing in, I remember a euphoric feeling as I lowered into the liquid. Once submerged there was a feeling of warmth and gratitude all around me, and I could feel myself slipping away as my being completely integrated with this fluid. I have other memories of this fluid; it was a place where we would come to heal and become whole.

It is the closest thing to 'source' I would say I have experienced. It was unity, and it was being. And this time, as I became one with the energy, I woke up in this body.

Once the surgery was over, I was left open to drain for a few days and make sure that any infection didn't set up. It took a long time to walk again. They told me it would take some time to get used to the feeling again, but it felt entirely foreign to stand on my legs and move them. Being seven years old, with no frame of reference for anything, I simply believed it was the surgery, but looking back at it now I am sure it was because 'I' had never walked before. And my behavior patterns changed. I went from being an overactive ADHD child, to being able to assess situations and read the energy of people. I was still a kid of course, running around and playing once everything had healed, but there was always this extra sense I had about places, people and situations that would allow me to prepare myself for what I was getting into. I also had many memories come to me as a child. Some were just flashes, like I was in a fast car moving and wasn't able to focus on them. Others were much clearer; they were of events I had not lived through yet suddenly knew about, information I had never been given that I could just recall at the drop of a hat. I am from what humans would call the Angelic Realm. However the beings there are not always what people picture when they think of the word 'angel'. They have no set form. I can recall all shapes and sizes. Some look more animalistic than humanoid, having the head of a lion or in some cases multiple faces or heads. Some take the form of shapes or patterns that are constantly in motion and rotating, and some have no form at all. The first thing that people think of when they hear the word 'angel' are wings, however most are not physical at all, not feathery like a bird's wings, but exist as energy and light that can't be contained in the form, shooting or rupturing from the back and arching over the shoulders, almost washing down the back. I think that when these beings come to people the reason they are seen as humans or humanoid is so that they can understand rather than be in fear.

I remember a beautiful city. The architecture there is hard to explain, but if I had to compare it to anything it would be Greek temples. They are large white crystalline structures with intricate pillars that are made of a marble-like stone, but it's more pure than marble. There isn't a single blemish to these structures, everything is perfect. There are towers, obelisk-like structures that spiral hundreds of feet in the air, and building designs I am unable to describe in words.

Through many forms of meditation and spiritual practices I have seen myself in my truest form. I retain a humanoid body that is extremely tall, with five sets of energetic wings; each set of wings resonates with a different energy. I have a large, dark blue and silver robe; the silver threads of the robe don't seem to be solid, they flow as if they were liquid silver. The eyes are like wisps of blue and gold fire, and there are several bolts of electricity that extend from the top of my head in almost a crown formation that hovers several inches above my head. In the center of my chest there is an orb that spins in constant rotation with several rings and dozens of eyes around the outside and an extremely bright flame in the center. I have seen myself with three sets of arms extending, holding the orb in the center but the additional arms I feel are energetic extensions and not part of my actual body.

I work directly with two angelic beings. I am not sure if it is all Angelic beings, or just the groups I work with, but we are always in sets of three. One takes the form of a very tall and proud humanoid woman who wears bright silver and golden armor. And the other first came to me as a Japanese man, wearing a light blue and white kimono. But his form has changed. Again I must say that we see them as humans because that is what our minds can understand, but as I have remembered more and had more experiences with them, they have taken the form of a blue phoenix, who emits cold rather than hot flames. The wings are an electric blue fire that shine an extremely bright light. They have helped me understand energy work much better and it comes to me extremely naturally. The feeling I get when working with both of them, especially the female, is a sense of peace and stillness that is hard to come by in this life. It is a feeling of home, but the feeling is also melancholic. It's a feeling of homesickness that makes me both happy and sad. It's something you can't touch but still feel.

I remember an event where there was a council being held, and hundreds of different kinds of beings were there - too many to describe them all. Some were small, sitting on little metallic disks. There were beings that looked like squids, but they were floating in the air instead of swimming. There were tall beings sitting at tables with very slender necks that extended nearly 10 feet, with small heads and bulbous eyes, and many many others.

There were hundreds of these floating rings almost like tables that each race sat at. We were gathered to discuss actions regarding a planet of beings that had been waging wars against several other races, plundering resources and disturbing the natural balance by using technology that I have no way of describing. The council came to a consensus that action had to be taken. After futile attempts to resolve things peacefully, the conclusion was reached that elimination was the only remaining option. We then left for their planet. It was red in color but its skies and clouds were a dark greenish grey, an almost sickly color. Many of the races that had been at the council were there as well. I was there along with 11 other angelic beings, making up four groups of three. There were these bolts of energy being shot towards these different races. Some were in craft, others were on the metallic floating disks which seemed to almost merge with their bodies. Some races had weapons and others used forms of energy they generated with their own bodies. In a perfect unison, each race raised their weapons; I remember simply extending my hand in front of myself, palm facing outward and then an extremely bright light surrounded the planet's surface, and it was gone.

I have been fortunate to receive many messages and downloads from angelic beings since I have been here. They are always there to assist me. I experience déjà vu several times a week, often feeling like full days are repeated because I have felt what is going to happen. I have many voices in my head on non-stop chatter mode, expressing many ideas, many thoughts all happening at once. It took me many years to be able to soften and filter through what they are saying, but now it is much easier for me to filter through my own thoughts, versus what I am receiving. When I was younger it felt a lot like chatter with random words here and there mixed with static. However, I am now much more able to focus and get clear messages if I need to.

I can always tell when I am about to receive a big download of information because I get an immense ringing in my ear, with a deep tone, similar to tinnitus. It does not go away until I quiet my mind and focus on the sound. Then it will stop and I receive an 'idea', or my thought process will completely shift.

I entered this body as a sensitive, empath and as an intuitive. During the early years, picking up on everybody's feelings was not useful for me. I had a hard time processing my own feelings, much less everyone else's. I can pick up people's emotions and thoughts regardless of the distance between us. When I ask someone about how they are feeling, they don't understand how I knew. I also just have to be in someone's presence and I can pick up and take emotions from them, leaving them feeling renewed and refreshed, and me down and out.

My sensitivities caused me to be removed from the public school during my high school years and to receive internet schooling at home. If I physically touched or even brushed up against someone, I could take away the person's physical, emotional or mental pain. That was great for them, but not so much for me. I could leave my house headed to school in a great mood, enter the school and end up calling my parents to come get me within an hour because I was so overwhelmed and stressed out by everyone's emotions - students and teachers. If I was taking a test and someone around me became distracted, I became distracted. If someone felt sad, I became sad. If someone was mad, I became mad. Can you imagine picking up on every single high school student's emotions all at once? Not good. As frustrating as it was at times, being homeschooled was the best thing for me. During those years I was able to recover and heal from all the school and life trauma that I had experienced.

Those years also provided me the opportunity to travel with my mom to a variety of holistic healing workshops and seminars. It's funny because even as a kid, many of the instructors or class participants would end up asking me questions based on the questions I asked during their seminars. Connecting the skills I came in with and the knowledge I gained at the workshops helped to perform the work I do now. It is extremely useful for me to be able to know the injury site and what needs to be done in order to bring it back into balance. I can't tell you the number of times people have commented on my intuitive ability. The fact is that I can feel it, or get a sense of where someone is in pain within my body. And it's cool to be able to help people get out of pain. I think that is one of the reasons that I came here.

Being in human form has its ups and downs. Somedays, I feel like I am connected, ready to take on the world and feel like I have it all figured out. Then on other days, I just want to stay home in bed, contemplating the universe and wrestle with the feeling of disconnect. Even those 'bad days' are productive because I have found that when I slow from the busyness of life, universal truths, knowledge and information comes in. Plus, there really is no such thing as being disconnected. We are always connected to each other through a universal thread or by the web of life, as the indigenous people say.

I think that I am here to experience the fullness of the ups and downs that being human can offer, to help people get out of pain and to bring a smile to someone.

We all have a job to do and it is different for everyone. No one job is better than the other. I don't think everyone realizes that it's just as important to make someone smile as it is to have a large bank account.

But one thing I know for sure is that this universe is much larger than people think.

Robert McWilliam

Robert McWilliam was born in January of 1971. He obtained his degree in nursing and has been in service to humanity since 2005.

He became a walk-in soul exchange on January 3rd, 1989 at 11:11 pm from the Pleiades System. This is not his first walk-in mission. He first incarnated as Queen Marie Antoinette and at the time of her beheading into the body of a young impoverished, abused French girl. Next he walked into Abraham Lincoln prior to his marriage to Mary Todd. Prior to being a walk-in to Robert, he walked into Adlai Stevenson, Governor of Illinois. His overall mission has been to bring integrity to politics. Having completed his mission, he volunteered to serve as a walk-in to Robert. He feels this will complete his mission and he will then be able to return to the Pleiades to continue his spiritual growth.

His spiritual name is Dylan Michael and he resides in Melbourne, Australia.

Robert's Story

My walk-in occurred on January 3rd, 1989. I would like to start my story on the other side and share what I was experiencing there because I remember feeling a range of emotions in the weeks and days leading up to the soul transfer: excitement at the prospect of taking on a completely new mission, much different than the ones I had volunteered for in the past. I thought this would be a much more peaceful, relaxing lifetime and I could help Robert with balancing his karma. I also experienced sadness at the prospect of returning to the physical plane, and trepidation at coming into a new body, another life, arriving into the unknown. I started becoming a bit restless and just wanted to get on with it.

When the time of the event was very close, I was summoned by my guardian spirit and personal angel to undergo a spiritual cleaning, healing and light programming at the Archangel Michael's healing chamber. This is where light codes were infused into my energetic body and a final consultation session took place to help me prepare me for what lay ahead. Archangel Michael met me and supervised the session, blessing me for my upcoming mission and gave me my spiritual name of Dylan Michael. He reassured me that he would always be there for me. I said my final goodbyes and was taken to a darkened bedroom, where the body of my walk-out lay sleeping.

There was already a team of spiritual surgeons working on the delicate process of separating the energetic (etheric) body from the physical body in the room when I arrived. It is quite a complex and risky procedure. Many astral nerves and energy life force centers had to be separated and removed so the walk-in's own energetic body can be put into place. There are also vibrational calibrations to the physical body that has to occur to make it compatible with the new energy body.

This procedure only took two hours in Earth time, with about 16 hours of work crammed into them. Watching this procedure was fascinating but made me nervous. My spiritual team was there talking to me, offering encouragement, giving strength and hope. The walk-outs team was there too, waiting to whisk him away.

Finally, the procedure was complete and I watched as the surgeons detached my walk-out from the physical body. He was unconscious and his body as he began rising upwards. It was an amazing sight to behold. His team thanked the surgeons, wished me luck and thanked me for my sacrifice in releasing him.

The surgeon beckoned me and asked if I was ready. I was. We had to move very quickly because the silver that connects the soul to the physical body had been removed and death of the physical would occur quickly if it was not reanimated with another soul. The surgeons levitated me upwards and down into the body. As I entered, I lost consciousness. The operation wasn't over however. My energetic body had to be attached to the physical form. There was a danger that rejection could occur, causing death to the body, but fortunately, my vibration was accepted. At 11:11 pm I assumed the life of Robert McWilliam, aged 18.

I had arrived, although I don't associate myself with this identity anymore. Robert was born on January 5th, 1971 and I, Dylan Michael, walked in on January 3rd, 1989. I am a soul exchange from the Pleiades.

Robert was very traumatized and had suffered immensely throughout childhood and had been relentlessly bullied all through his school years. He was extremely depressed and couldn't face life ahead. He couldn't see a future for himself in this world. He left school without his final year high school certificate, no longer wanting to be abused, and started working the following year in a menial job. The future was bleak and hopeless, and he was afraid to face the future. He had taken on too much karma in this life and found himself completely overwhelmed and lost. Not long after he started working, the soul exchange took place.

I didn't know at first that I was a walk-in, but I knew that something had changed. Not long after my walking in, a sudden change came over me. I was no longer fearful, but strong and fiercely determined. I knew I didn't want this future and knew going back to school and finishing my high school certificate was the answer. I told my parents I wanted to return to school, and they adamantly refused. I wrote my parents a five-page letter, demanding I be allowed to return. I went back to high school the following year. The old Robert would never have done anything like that.

For the first time in my life, I felt strong and determined, no longer fearful of returning to school and facing bullies. All those emotions were gone. I remembered everything but there was no longer an attachment to the childhood memories and trauma. There was no emotional charge associated with them.

So many changes took place: tastes in foods, the determination to succeed in life, no longer being shy and awkward, and so on. I was not the old Robert, but a completely different person. After graduating from high school I went to university and obtained my nursing degree. This was a new direction in life that the old Robert would never have contemplated.

I had agreed to take on a huge karmic load from my walk out, including taking on his future wife and children. I married my wife in 2001, then two children followed. They are Robert's karma, but I agreed to take them on. I have spent years working through his issues and healing his family.

I don't have any past life associations with anyone in my current life, and in some ways I feel like I am only a surrogate. I love the people in my life but there is no soul connection with them because our relationships are based on completing Robert's karmic contracts with them. They are all part of the walk-in contract that I agreed to take on when stepped into Robert's life. I am completing his contracts for him, not for me.

No one in my life knows that I am a walk-in, only a few spiritual friends, that is until this book is published. Most of the people I am around are not very spiritually based and I am not quite sure how I can tell my parents or wife. It's a struggle because I really don't want to be associated with the Robert personality anymore. I desire to change my name to my true name, Dylan Michael, and step into my own mission now. My family just knows that I am very different. I feel like a stranger in a strange land.

Over time, my guides have helped me with my integration process and have given me memories of the soul transfer that I shared with him. It feels good to remember changing places with him and the energetic process.

I remember the contract he made to finish karmic ties with the woman he was to marry (my wife), and it had been quite a volatile relationship, with no soul connection. This has been tough.

This is not my first walk-in mission. I have been here four other times. The first time as Queen Marie Antoinette, a young impoverished, abused French girl. Then Abraham Lincoln, and later Adlai Stevenson, Governor of Illinois. From the outside, people think these lives must have been wonderful, but I am here to tell you they were not. There is a reason that I walked into these bodies.

My original star system is the Pleiades. I came here with my twin soul many eons ago, going back thousands of years. I have been incarnating on this planet almost continuously, with a few breaks here and there. My soul is weary. It has been a very long mission. After this life my soul contract is finished on Earth and I will not incarnate here anymore. I will go back and be reborn on my own home planet where I will finish the final stages of my evolution.

The fact that I have been a walk-in before equipped me for this very difficult mission this lifetime. Because my overall mission on planet Earth has been to help change Merlin Consciousness (the integration of the awareness and acceptance of consciousness) and to shape Earth's history and culture, I wanted a quiet lifetime this go around. That's why I chose to volunteer to be a walk-in for Robert.

I think that most walk-ins will agree that you never step into a situation that is easy or a bed of roses. You are in there to do a job. It's a serious thing. You're in there to heal that wounded life and those that are in that life. You come in with an awareness of life and the meaning of life. You come in with that sense of spirituality and over time it ripens like a fruit. It becomes sweet.

It takes time and you do become aware over time of who you are, what your mission is all about. Though I have heard about some walk-ins that never know who they are, it was necessary that I knew who I was and what my mission was about. My guides told me that it was important for me to know who I really was in order to achieve my mission. When you come in, you naturally have a love of life, and you know that you are on the planet to make a change. Some walk-ins come in pretty quietly, and are there to help heal themselves and the family lineage, while others come in to change history or the consciousness of a nation. Some come to help humanity elevate, and help you spread your light and love, and give divine inspiration and help wake up their consciousness.

For me, it has been a very difficult walk-in. Before walking in, I agreed to clear up a lot of emotional and mental health issues that have me to suffer a lot in the process. What is interesting with me and my situation is that my walk out was content to just leave. He did come back to hang around over the years which caused a lot of problems. I allowed him to learn quite a lot of life lessons from me, to come back from the spiritual plane. I don't think this happens very often. I don't mean coming into the body or anything like that but he was learning lessons from me. It's hard to explain but I sort of let him in, which I regret doing now. I did put a lot of pressure on myself and the mission and my walk-in has made it doubly difficult. At this point my guides and higher self have gotten him far away. I don't mean to say that he was a bad spirit or anything like that. It was just that he, after a while, regretted leaving his life and he wanted to come back but of course, that was never going to happen. So, he knocked on my door and asked if he could hang around and I let him do that which as I said I now regret because he was able to impress a lot of stuff on me which wasn't positive. Some of the same reasons that he wanted out of the body and life. I found that I still was dealing with him and his issues. This compounded things really badly and made it much more difficult for me because I consistently had to clear the same issues. It seemed like the more I was trying to work through an issue the more he impressed it upon me. It made things unbearable to the point that I am surprised that I didn't end up losing my mind. During that time, I even had suicidal tendencies, but I knew that I wasn't allowed to commit suicide. I knew that I couldn't do it. I knew it was just rhetoric and I was able to work through his tendencies. As I healed more and healed that situation, I allowed more of the divine in. As I worked with the seven sacred rays my spiritual awareness and third eye was opening up more, and more healing came, I became more balanced. As this happened my consciousness became more of who I really am. And yet it has been quite extremely difficult. I don't want to sound egotistical, but I will say this, no ordinary human being could have gone through what I went through and been able to stand all the mental and emotional pressure. I was specifically chosen to deal with it as part of my contract. I don't think I could ever explain it to another human being and have them understand the complexities of this. But I've gotten through it.

Luckily, I chose a really good body and it has given me no real problems other than the occasional colds and flues. I have had to, over the years, clean up the emotional body. There have been karmic implications with some things, for example weight gain and high levels of cholesterol associated with stress and emotional patterns. But it is like certain things had to happen as part of the contract that I had agreed to. Not just with the physical body, but in general.

But what they have told me is that I am going to go through major spiritual initiations later this year (2019) which coincides with the 30 year anniversary of this walk-in. And once I have had these initiations later this year, pretty much, I am going to be free of the karmic debt that I have been paying back for Robert, and I am going to be free to be Dylan. Dylan doesn't want to be overweight. Dylan doesn't want to eat the wrong things. Dylan is a very fit and active soul who wants to embrace the bounty of Mother Gaia and eat what's highly vibrational for him and this is where I am going to finally be able to be set free.

It's hard to explain but there are certain tendencies that I have had to work through as I have had no choice in the matter. Dylan knows and my higher self knows that I have this higher blueprint which I will finally be able to embrace.

I am so looking forward to being set free of Robert's energy and karma. It has taken 30 years to work through all of Robert's stuff. It has been a really long and complicated process. I have heard of other walk-ins taking on karma for their host, but it seems that they are able to finish in a third of the time that it has taken me. It has not been very easy. It has been quite a horrendous process at times, but I am looking forward to having the final shackles being loosened, to finally being free. I have just a little bit more to go. Once this is over, I am free to be the soul that I am meant to be. One hundred percent.

My belief is that we are just one. So taking on Robert and the others as I did only makes sense. Source energy or God is all there is, the only reality, and everything is source energy. There is nothing outside of source - it is all that has existed and will continue to be so throughout eternity. Consciousness with no beginning and no end. The goal of life is to awaken again to this fact, and re-emerge into full divine consciousness with complete realization we are the source, and the one source only exists - nothing else.

The Ascension includes the collective consciousness of mankind, every energetic aspect. We are all brought from to this state of the 3D level and move from the 4th dimension to the 5th. We all have to be brought out of the 3D awareness we all have to move out of the materialism spectrum. This is the upliftment of our consciousness on all levels into that spiritual portal. Mother Gaia will be able to ascend into the new 5D reality. It's a huge task now; it is essential. We all have to evolve beyond this level of consciousness in order for Mother Gaia to move up and open those cosmic gateways in order to move into 5D. I have been given no knowledge as to how that is going to eventuate. Only that we are now getting to the crucial points that have been occurring for thousands of years. We are getting towards the end of the time frame, so something has to push the collective consciousness. There is something that Mother Gaia has to unleash on some part of an energetic level. Exactly what that is, I don't know. I have not been privy to that kind of blueprint. But there is quite a cosmic plan. It is going to be interesting to watch what is going to be happening as we are all part of it.

My message to all of you is simple: live in the consciousness of your true selves; the realization that we are eternal spirit and consciousness, and one with our creator God. Live a life of peace, contentment, joy, and gratitude. Spread your love and light to every being you come across.

Nicole Richmond

Nicole, a Canadian lawyer and wellness consultant, specializes in building healthy work environments and strong, transparent and supportive governments. She graduated from the University of Toronto Faculty of Law in 2006, where she was awarded the President's Award for Student Leadership. A consistently high academic performer and respected leader with a knack for efficiency, Nicole brings a new approach to the practice of law focusing on personal well-being, good governance and consciousness in action. She is an Ojibway member of the Biigitong Nishnaabeg First Nation and lives in her traditional territory on the north shore of Lake Superior. She is a proficient beadwork artist and seamstress, and is well-known for creating powwow attire for dancers across Turtle Island. Her artwork is showcased at instagram.com/nicole_nicool.

Presently, Nicole carries on a blend of a legal practice and a wellness facilitation practice. She is a speaker, workshop facilitator and is called on to share her nuanced legal knowledge in Indigenous legal traditions, as well as meditation, emotional wellbeing and consciousness. She is a Reiki master, healer, a past life regressionist and intuitive meditation coach.

Nicole is a soul infusion walk-in that resonates with the Arcturian energy.

Nicole's Story

I was raised in the Anishinabe ways, attending a variety of ceremonies including completing my four years of sundance as a teenager. There was a gap in the teachings after colonialism, but I grew up hearing about interdimensional beings, the power of the grandfathers and grandmothers and the important knowledge we can acquire from our ancestors about 'minobimadiziwin' - the good life. I have had numerous metaphysical experiences, both growing up and as an adult.

In July 2007 I became a lawyer and shortly after that I met my future husband, Korie. We loved each other immediately. Korie was handsome, fit, kind and funny. He would give anyone the shirt of his back and was an incredible athlete. I was very focused on having an Indigenous life-partner and I welcomed Korie into my life. We looked good together. We spent endless hours swimming, hiking, laughing with friends. Korie had a drinking problem though, and he would regularly drink way too much and knock himself out for the whole next day. He would lie in misery, unable to kick his habit but also unable to forgive himself for destroying his body. We were married in 2010 and after a series of difficulties in our relationship, Korie was finally able to quit drinking. In the summer of 2013, I agreed to move to his community to support him in an alcohol-free life. I left my law practice and my relationships in order to make this relationship work. I told myself that everything was going to be okay.

In January of 2014, I was in an automobile accident. There was a bad snow storm and for some reason, I remember going home a different way on a different road that I don't normally travel. I was heading north across highway 401, which is the Trans-Canada highway. The 401 was closed so traffic was redirected onto the road I was travelling, which was otherwise a two-lane country road. I was in a super safe car and I was not worried about accidents until suddenly, I saw two lights driving towards me on my left hand-side. I remember thinking that someone must be coming down their driveway towards me. I spun out of control and ended up in the ditch. It was a very high speed collision and it happened quickly. I might have lost consciousness temporarily but I seem to remember everything. I had a profound sense of "this is what is happening now" - a surrender feeling, that things were out of my control but they were okay. I walked away from the accident and sustained only soft tissue injuries.

I had been practicing car accident law for several years at that point and I thought I knew the stages I would go through and what was going to happen. It took about three weeks before the symptoms showed up. It was worse than I ever expected. It felt like battery acid was poured all over my back. I was dealing with so much personal misery at the time and I wondered whether I had called the accident to me. I had given my whole life and career up to support my husband and I was very lonely and resentful. I was experiencing a deep, profound emotional injury. I had a variety of treatment providers but no one seemed to be able to see me or treat me. I felt so invisible in my husband's territory.

My insurance company eventually referred me to an orthopedic surgeon to determine whether I was eligible for on-going benefits. The doctor wasn't paying any attention to me as I spoke. He was just typing into his computer, asking what happened, and not appearing to care about any of my answers other than to record them. It was humiliating. When he asked my occupation and found I was a lawyer, his whole demeanor changed. He took an interest in my case. He could tell that my emotional state was profoundly interrupted and referred me to a neuropsychologist. I later joked about the referral with another accident lawyer, a mentor of mine, and we agreed that we would NOT want to hear what a neuropsychologist would say about us. I felt that the limits of Western medicine would not support the healing I needed.

I began seeing a psychotherapist who offered past life regressions. He was more interested in counselling me and I had to fight with him to get the hypnosis sessions, which is where I felt the real healing was required. At that time, I had really become interested with past life regressions. This is when I started to get into hypnosis and I took the level one hypnosis training from Georgina Cannon and then took Past Life Regression training at the Ontario Hypnosis Centre. I became obsessed with this idea of past lives. Obsessed. I was very influenced by Delores Cannon and her no-nonsense and practical approach to past-life experiences and their influence on our lives. I also really had the feeling that hypnosis was a key to something more than human lives. I knew there was so much more.

For the next eight months, I just took it easy. I started my own law firm. My husband and I were having a lot of difficulty with his family, who had completely excluded him from leadership of his family business after he'd married me. It was devastating for him. We were confused about what to do. On one hand, Korie was trying to commit to his family and to healthy living, but on the other hand, we were constantly rejected by them. That September, we took a trip to see my family and we visited friends in my hometown. Maybe because I was suffering so much despair, I was able to see what my hometown had to offer. I became enamored with small-town living. I needed a place where everyone knew me and cared about me. I was surprised. My husband agreed that we would move home, where we could live more simply. I needed time to heal. I needed to be in a place that was safe and Korie agreed to that. I feel a really important connection to this place. There is no good explanation other than I am required to be here somehow.

After moving home, I developed really awful low back pain. I did not think it was related to my car accident, but it was excruciating. I went to see one of my friends, a chiropractor who was a former law client. He knew me really well and I trusted him. I'll never forget that appointment. He took one look at me, with the most concern anyone has ever taken for me, and asked me what was wrong. I explained that I was having dreadful low back pain. He said, "No, what's really wrong?" I explained to him about the car accident and he grimaced. He said, "I've never been wrong about this, but I'd like you to go get x-rays". I went into my car and cried. What was wrong with me?

When I got back from my x-ray, my chiropractor started running neurological tests on me and he concluded that I had sustained a concussion in my car accident and I had not received proper treatment. He explained that my neck's curve had become inverted because of the strength and tightness of my front shoulder muscles, and that my cerebral spinal fluid was not running properly. This explained why I was in such a mental haze all the time. I looked back at all my previous health care professionals and wondered why no one had diagnosed this. I also regretted not going to the neuropsychologist. Had I been complicit in my own poor care? My chiropractor did an adjustment on my neck, after which I immediately saw more vibrant colors and heard more vivid sounds. How had I spiraled into a diminished version of myself without anyone noticing? I was so grateful for my chiropractor, who knew the old Nicole so well and advocated for her recovery. I got better, bit by bit, knowing that my emotional recovery would be matched by my physical recovery. It was a beautiful process.

Looking back I believe the accident set the stage for the walk-in to occur. From a spiritual perspective, I believe I received more of a download, an infusion of sorts, of my own spiritual essence. Whether it was from my higher self or soul I don't know. I retained all my own memories and personality, but many memories are difficult to access. People will tell me stories about things that happened in my 20s and I have absolutely no recollection. But I feel the same as myself, but different - enhanced, empowered, stronger.

About a year after my car accident, I had a very vivid dream that explained my walk-in experience, although it would not be until I met Sheila that I would understand the connection between the dream and my actual metaphysical transformation. In my dream, I was standing inside a tunnel, but to me, it looked like a subway. A man, dressed in black, approached me and said he had a job for me. I agreed to do it and asked what the job was. He clearly told me three things that I have never forgotten:

1. "You're going to go to a place that looks very real but it's not real."

2. "Where you're going to go, it's going to feel like you're gone for a very long time. But when you get back, it's just going to be like a minute of time has passed."

3. "The people there are sleeping, but they don't know they're sleeping."

Then he showed me to an elevator and I entered it. I went down for a long time and I came out in Marathon, where I live. I remember looking out at the water of Lake Superior, and was thinking, 'Wow, it looks so real. How do they do that? It looks so real.' I saw people walking by. I observed them and thought, 'Wow, they are sleeping and they don't know it.' As the dream went on, I became integrated into human life and forgot where I came from.

I understand now that this whole process was facilitated for my walk-in experience to happen. When I look back with more clarity, I understand that something major had happened. It was more than a physical injury, it was a recalibration of my whole identity. I was different. I can't pinpoint whether it was a different consciousness that unified with my consciousness, or if I received a soul upgrade. But I knew that having suffered a brain injury and having been invited to slow down and suffer was a requirement for this process to take place.

I did not return to practicing law just because there was no way that I could do my job properly. I had no ability to focus or support clients properly. It took years before I returned. In the meantime, I had a lot of different and wonderful jobs in education and justice fields. I was so happy to be home and connected to my own people. I knew that my role was simply to support the local people, as a powwow dancer, as a lawyer, as a teacher. Spending time with First Nations communities and helping them with their collective healing is my main priority.

My work often required me to travel and perhaps if I had been home more, I might have noticed that something was really wrong with Korie. He had always been restless and moody, but as the years went on there seemed to be nothing that I could do to help him feel better. I think the rejection from his family had been difficult for him, and although he loved and supported me, there was a big missing piece in his life that he was never able to explain to me. The more I could feel Korie's misery, the more I focused love on him. If he needed something, I would get it for him. I invested a lot of my energy in his happiness, but he seemed so lost, so sad. Although he never talked about it, I think Korie had suffered childhood trauma that had shaken his core confidence so badly.

In July 2019, Korie committed suicide by hanging himself. It was the weekend of my home community powwow. Korie wanted to stay home to sleep, he was restless like a bear and told me he would not be able to sleep with me at home waiting for him. I was reluctant to leave him. I knew there were so many friends and family that wanted to see him at the powwow. He told me he could come down for supper after he rested. Supper break came and went and when he didn't show up, I drove home and found him in our shed. Just like my car accident, I had this profound sense of "this is what is happening now." I realized that all the love and supports I had provided for my husband was not enough to transmute his existential suffering. I also realized our soul contract was up.

After Korie died, I started to put the pieces together and realized that he had been abusing drugs throughout our whole relationship. Although I was not able to tell that he was high, when I looked back through pictures I saw it so clearly. I began to realize the nature of Korie's financial debts, and that some of his closest friends near the end we're all connected with the drug community. You can chalk this up to my naivety or perhaps willful blindness, but so many of our closest friends were also duped. He hid it so well. He had engaged with the world in such a meaningful way for a man embedded in addictions. He swam, he worked out, he charmed people, he laughed, he ran his own business and he was extremely kind to all people. My mom reassures me, "Nicole, your husband was extremely strong" and that is the truth. There is no way he could have stayed married to a lightworker lawyer for 12 years while battling a secret addiction of some of the hardest drugs imaginable - unless he was very strong.

Many of my friends tell me that I must have definitely added more years to Korie's life. When I look back at all his self-destructive patterns over the years, I see this is true. Korie had escaped death a half-dozen times and I realize that I had brought him some peace and comfort in our years together. When I found Korie that day in the shed, I knew immediately that he was dead. I screamed and sank to my knees, but in the back of my mind, a program was running that seemed to say, "You knew this was coming and you prepared for this."

I began to understand that my infusion of extra energy, through my walk-in experience, had enabled me to make it through the last six years of our relationship although they had been difficult. I had loved my husband unconditionally and I was proud of that. I realized also that Korie had given me the biggest experiential growth-spurt of my life. What woman can use the suicide death of her husband to catapult her emotional and spiritual growth exponentially? Only a woman that knew it was coming and had prepared for it.

In hindsight, I believe that the walk-in came in and activated to give me the strength to be able to handle the situations that were ahead for me. I understand on a soul level, that I was drawn to Korie, married him, and stayed in the relationship to help him heal his past. I just didn't know his ultimate healing would come through suicide. I am looking forward to the day that I meet Korie in some other dimension and we can share about the roles that we played for each other, whether our performance was on script or not. How had this man duped me and so many for all those years? How hard had that been for him and why would he have agreed to that experience, especially if it bore the risk of totally jeopardizing his wife, the woman he loved above all things? There are so many things we don't know yet.

I believe that loving Korie was the primary mission of the first half of my life. The tools he helped me develop - by putting me through the most devastating experience a wife can have - are now firmly integrated. It has not yet been a year since Korie died and the nature and scope of my next missions are not yet clear. But loving my husband throughout has been the most beautiful experience of my life.

If I could give one message to humanity it would be to wake up and embrace the whole essence of who you are. You are downloaded into this human body with so many unique talents and experiences to help you upgrade yourself. Your unique contribution is so important. Always be proud of every single experience you've manifested for yourself because you are sent here to make the world a better place.

ẎnDon Clark

ẎnDon has had a longstanding involvement in Regenerative Technologies that address the unsustainable practices within the world's current power generation and agricultural paradigm. His formal college studies are in Renewable Solar Electric Energy at the Ecotech Institute.

After working as a Residential and Commercial Solar Technician, he embarked on an alternative education journey to pursue his passion for Ecological and Off-Grid Systems Design at the Earthship Biotecture Academy and began developing his passion for Water Solutions, when he later became directly involved within courts hearings that contributed to the legalization of greywater and the removal of the Rainwater Catchment ban in Colorado. His training in Biotecture (Biological Architectural Symbiosis) opened his heart to pursue learning more about Natural Building and permaculture as he transitioned from a technology and policy-focused career path into an ecocentric worldview seeking to integrate regenerative technologies in our built environments. Since then he has acquired certifications in Permaculture Design and Village Building Design with an emphasis on terraforming, habitat restoration and wild food forestry.

He has also trained at the Eureka Institute in an applied theosophic temple design science known as Homeodynamics

(Alchemical Architecture). His mission has since then expanded to assist the further disclosure of our Ancient Interstellar Origins and the resurrection of our cooperative Godhood as one Planetary Synarchy. The capstone of his life's work has evolved to prominently focus on teaching about the holographic wisdom of the DNA using The Gene Keys and Human Design System to help guide others in awakening their genius. ẎnDon is a soul infusion (integration) walk-in.

ẎnDon's Story

I was born in Colorado Springs, Colorado. At the age of two we moved to Arizona. My mother and I shuffled to Tennessee for about a year, then quickly returned to Arizona. I spent most of my elementary schooling days in Arizona until we moved to Virginia at the beginning of my 5th grade year. I grew up living in Virginia and remained there until at age 23 when I decided to reconnect with my origin in the Colorado Rocky Mountains. My love for nature guided me to pursue a degree in solar energy technology as a solution to the rising of environmental challenges. I commuted an hour and a half each day to campus and eventually moved up to Denver to finish out my semesters. After college, I started my new career as a Residential Solar Technician. I had just transitioned out of college and was living out of my car, showering at the office and cooking on a grill in order to save money. The night I had my walk-in experience, I was outside the office laying down in one of the parking spots, using the light on the corner of the warehouse to read a book called *The Eagles Gift*. I had just finished a section and began contemplating while staring up into the sky when I noticed a brilliant starlight dancing between different colors.

I began noticing that the star was pulsating and hovering slightly, while the other stars around it remained stationary. At that moment of realization, it flashed as if to say hello and reaffirm that it received my message and was acknowledging that it was more than a star. At that point, it seemed to come a little closer as its light expanded brighter. I felt a deep sense of peace begin to permeate my awareness and it gently open my heart to a sense of trust as I sent the message, 'I welcome your connection.'

My intuition told me that it most likely wouldn't understand human language but probably could communicate with energy or geometry. So I started thinking about and sending geometric symbols telepathically and the light started tracing them in the sky. I made more and more intricate sequences of different geometries until we became so telepathically entrained together that it would complete tracing the symbols before I had even cognitively registered the last shape in my own sequence. At this moment, I knew we had synced onto the same telepathic wavelength and it flashed again - its endearing affirmation of communion.

I heard a faint humming in the distance, which I soon realized was a group of Blackhawk helicopters coming from out east near the Denver International Airport. I was at the edge of the foothills in Westminster, and the helicopters had to have been moving extremely fast because they probably only took three minutes to reach me. When they arrived at my location, they flew directly overhead as they scanned the sky with their spotlights searching for the anomaly that I'm sure came up on their radar. The 'star' and I remained still as they continued to fly west towards the mountains as they followed the range south towards Morrison and eventually disappeared.

Once the coast was clear, the 'star' sent a soft flash of assurance and slowly began growing brighter as it descended and moved into alignment over top of where I laid in the parking lot. We quickly reharmonized back into a synergetic connection when suddenly, the light on the warehouse, that I had been using to read by, started to pulse. The flashing morse code-like light phenomenon continued for about 15 minutes as I laid there. I intuitively knew I was receiving a 'light language transmission'. I felt guided to imagine opening up my DNA to receive the incoming code.

I stared at the "star" hoping to get some clues as to what it might be happening. As my eyes began to adjust, I was actually looking at a solid stone craft, similar to looking at rough granite, that was covered in moss and ferns and seemed to be generating its own atmosphere because it was suspended in a soft blue light. I was surprised to see something so utterly contrary to the typical saucer-style craft we have been culturally conditioned to believe in.

About 10 minutes into the transmission, the frequency around me changed. The change was subtle, almost like gravity had altered slightly and the air had become ionized, causing static to dance across my skin. I instinctively knew that the download was almost complete.

During the second wave of the transmission, the stone ship began to form these soft blue holographic cogs of translucent light that materialized out of the bottom of the stone. They looked similar to the wheels of the Mayan calendar and were encoded with a script of continuously morphing language on the inner rim and glyphs along the teeth of the cog that would discharge these electric symbols in every direction as it turned. One by one, the cogs stacked together forming a column of gears that directly aligned over top of me. The last one formed on the earth right around my body and grounded the whirling currents which started to charge up the column, infusing all of the gears with a white light as they began to spin faster.

Realizing I was laying directly underneath this column of

electrified gears, I remember thinking to myself that I was strangely at peace about getting beamed up, and yet none of my family or friends would know where I've disappeared to. I honestly thought that everyone would discover that I had vanished.

The gears continued to charge and spin, reaching a kind of zero-point, when I realized something totally different than what I had anticipated, was about to happen. I was still lying flat in the parking space staring up through the column of spinning gears at the stone ship when an emerald blue soul descended, parallel to the exact position I was laying in and fused with my core. It was that exact second when the soul hit my body that the light on the warehouse stopped pulsing. Then each of the gears retracted one by one back up and into the stone craft. I continued to lay there breathing in a profound silence of being touched by such grace as its presence remained suspended overhead. This scene is eternally etched in my mind's eye.

At this point I just laid there peacefully in awe and deep reverence. Nothing about what had just happened really freaked me out, though the thought of having to explain what happened to others carried a sense of heaviness around it. I watched the stone craft steadily holding its position. Just as if it were a guardian watching over me, it stayed for a few more minutes after the process was complete. I eventually started considering the need to transition and prepare for bed since I would still be around in the morning for work. Transformed, I rose up from the ground brushing off the rocks and debris, grabbed my book and looked down at it: *The Eagle's Gift*. I walked a short distance to my car and opened it to get out my sleeping bag and hygienics and found myself pausing to reflect on what just happened.

Contemplatively staring back up at the ship that never left, I sent my last telepathic message, 'I will integrate this and be alright. Thank you for being here and staying by my side.' I rolled out my sleeping bag under the piñon where I slept every night, slipped into the warmth of its cocoon and caught one last glimpse of the stone's majestic light hovering above. Before drifting off to sleep, it gave me one last twinkle of reassurance. I knew its eternal light would continue watching over me even after its disappearance at dawn.

The next morning I went back to work installing solar panels, and the only thing that was different was my awareness that something had shifted internally. There were no physical or mental changes. Life was just still very much life. But there was just something in the background that was guiding me to grow into the unfolding mission ahead. I woke every day continuing to wonder what happened, and why.

For about the first two years, I didn't tell anyone about what had happened. Oddly enough, it was while I was playing this really unique board game with some close friends the following winter that I decided to share. The cards of this game each have an image and a word that prompts you to tell something about yourself that relates to the card. Then you place it on one of the sectors that each have a different theme and you just keep on building an evolving storyline together. I ended up getting a couple cards back-to-back that were very synchronistic. One of the cards was named secrets and the last card I drew had a man standing in front of a spaceship. I remember the bubble of my secret popping as I thought to myself, 'You pulled the cards and it's time.' So I began to share and said, "Well I've never told this story, but I think the game's telling me that I need to share."

So I shared my soul integration experience after a long silence, and from that point on I felt confident enough to start sharing more. It was like the universe had given me a little nudge and all of a sudden, all this pressure was lifted and I felt as if telling the story was healing for me.

Over the years I went through a trial and error process to find out who the right people were that I could trust sharing this part of myself with. As more synchronicities led me to more secure allies, I started getting certain clues in my dreams and during visionary experiences. There was one particular message that I kept hearing over and over, the name was 'Drunvalo Melchizedek'. I actually knew his daughter, Aja.

One night during a gathering at a friend's house, she asked me if I could drive her home to drop her dog off. While driving back I realized that it might be the only opportunity we would have to speak in private, so I started to confide in her. "Aja, I need to talk to your dad. It's extremely important and I'm pretty sure he's the only person that can actually help me."

At the time, I didn't really know much about his work. I had stumbled upon his work in passing many years before my experience and saw some videos about him working with the tribes down in South America, but I didn't really explore or know the extent of his work. I had no clue that he wrote The Ancient Secret of the Flower of Life.

Aja was assuming that I had a new age celebrity crush on her dad, which she later admitted was a challenge in many of her relationships, and that I was just trying to get a hold of him through her. She candidly deflected saying, "So he is just kinda, you know, traveling and teaching. Can I take a message?" I paused to consider that I might not get a chance to talk to him so I started to tell her about what happened. At the end of the story, she says, "Oh, you're a walk-in, just like my dad. He had a near-death experience and when he went on the other side, he spoke with a council of light beings." The council's message was that Earth had become compromised by Dark Forces trying to seize control of our dimension that had bent all the planetary laws in place to the point of nearly breaking them. The council can't directly intervene, but in special cases certain souls volunteer to incarnate or lattice (connect and integrate) with existing vessels to carry out certain rescue missions. After she told me about her dad's story I just sat there floored, realizing I could be one of these souls. She carried on casually asking if I was ready to drive back to the gathering.

For the next couple of months, I dove head first down the rabbit hole researching walk-ins. I looked into the International Walk-in Society, the different types of reported walk-ins and all the historical threads throughout many different religions and records about walk-ins. I was astonished to realize that this was not a new thing. It has been happening on our planet for thousands and thousands of years.

I began connecting with guides and mentors that were familiar with walk-ins. Some of them I built trust with over time and felt safe enough to share and others were Seers who already knew. Finally, I started receiving the support and information that I needed for my journey ahead.

Carrying this new knowledge of my purpose, I began openly sharing my story with more people. I think this path will ultimately lead you to the necessity of disclosing what happened. I assume a majority of walk-ins go through a phase where their secret builds under silent pressure until it has no other choice but to emerge. Most importantly, we really need people we can trust to share it with. Personally, it was a hard lesson to learn that even though people said that they were a safe friend or lover that I could trust, there were still reactions that resulted in defense and ridicule.

I have witnessed severe cognitive dissonance take place that created such a rift in the consciousness of some people that thought forms and entity attachments would start to play on their fears and aggression. This experience taught me that no matter how much I loved a person, sharing was not always the right thing to do. I'm sure many of us have experienced this - there is a certain level of physical, emotional and mental healing around our belief systems that we have to go through in order for us to make space for our integration. I feel this purpose acts almost like a time-release mechanism which is always harmonizing with certain wavelength access points that unfold new aspects of the mission as we become more prepared along the journey. I definitely saw that there was a level of deconditioning and clearing out that was required to fully realize what my mission was.

I think what helped me most was feeling accepted even when I didn't have all the answers myself. This allowed me to heal and open up to greater levels of integration in order to fully arrive. I see the entire process of humanity's awakening as 'arriving'. We are all a galactic family of refugees who became stranded here long ago and the reason we are so disconnected from this planet is because we have struggled to fully grieve the ancient ache of our fall from grace and chosen Earth as our new home. That's why the Ascension path has dominated as the highest spiritual goal for so long. We have longed to leave these bodies and move to a higher plane, but now we must Ascend and build the New Earth.

There are several layers to the onion in this arriving process. At the most basic layer it has to do with clearing karmic debris from your biological bloodlines. In fact, I wouldn't have been able to walk-in without the biological bloodlines that I have. This is often a pretty significant detail in these missions that most people might not realize.

There are spontaneous emergency walk-in scenarios where human vehicles become available in near-death experiences or due to high level trauma, but then there are other long-planned intergenerational missions. In certain cases, long term biological preparation is seeded through several bloodlines, on and off planet, that eventually hybridize and specific key genetic sequences evolve that unlock and mutate our DNA to accept and integrate new paragenetic and endogenetic aspects. When an upgrade of such caliber takes place, there finally dawns an awareness that might have taken several reincarnational life cycles in several star systems to form, but now its spark exists in you.

This quantum leap in consciousness acts like an energetic zero-point and living node within the soul's DNA within all of the correlating timelines, dimensions, densities and parallel realities simultaneously. My soul integration is actually a past, parallel, and future aspect of me that has journeyed from all the farthest reaches of time and space just to walk this path back to here and now. When this sacred shift takes place inside you it serves as a portal, allowing all beings the gift of integrating our inner and outer illusion, the wound of separation. Each intentional benevolent act then serves the resurrection of the living breathing prophecy.

The Eternal one is walking in your footsteps. In the stillness of this knowing, You and I Arrive.

Scott Mathias

Scott is a Journalist, Author, and Gut Health Specialist who lives in Agnes Water, Australia. He worked in television and radio in New Zealand and Australia for nearly 40 years and is an award-winning journalist and researcher. Scott draws on a lifetime of human experiences, which has seen him associated with Heads of state, Royalty, including the late Princess Diana, and ordinary folk who have wonderful stories to tell.

As a former TV journalist in both Australia and his native New Zealand, Scott has a strong connection with planet Earth, winning media awards for stories based on raising human awareness around the plight of Earth and animals that walk its surface.

Scott is recognized for his high level of natural empathy and intuitive powers when dealing with others who desire to experience reconnection.

He has authored four books. Three on gut health entitled, *Understanding the Divine Gut*, *Let's Eat Raw*, and *THE ULTIMATE GUTFIXx*; He also wrote *The Antares Seals: Return of the Holy Grail*. His websites are theantaresseals.com and scottmathiasraw.com.

Scott became a soul exchange 'walk-in' during November of 1987, at the age of 32, after the death of a child. This death launched Scott into an extreme state of grief which caused his metabolism, heart rate and pulse rate to drop dangerously low. Ambition and ego drained from his body. He lay in an almost comatose state for almost three weeks. Scott believes that this event precipitated the ANKHA'ra's arrival because of his bodily state and the immense grief that caused his heart to blow wide open.

His walk-in comes from the star Antares and he is an EL'an known as ANKHA'ra with memories of his non-Earth lifetimes.

Scott's Story

As I share my story, please only believe that which feels right to you. My words will resonate more with some than others. Just listen with your heart and do not believe anything until it is right or wrong for you. Scepticism is healthy. It allows us to weigh the facts for ourselves and choose our own best path.

Grief is an amazing energetic stabilizer. My heart was literally broken open by the baby's death. It allowed an energetic portal to receive the new soul. Many walk-in exchanges happen during grief. At first, I was unaware that anything had transpired. The walk-in was a subtle, gentle merging. It took years to understand what had happened and about 15 years to fully anchor into the Scott Avatar body.

Gradually, my values changed along with the nature of my connection with everything. It was as if in an instant, I became a cosmic citizen and my earthly connections were severed. I experienced a complete loss of long term/familial memory for 5 years following this event. My marriage of 13 years dissolved very quickly along with any desire to continue to live a life based on acquisition and attainment. Ambition and ego drained from my body. The nature of my being changed particularly my countenance.

A contract exists between the walk-in and the human soul for the exchange to occur. I have known the Scott Avatar forever. We are very compatible. Scott's body carries DNA within it, ancient programming, that enabled the exchange. The body is human, my soul is of the EL'an which are beings made of pure electric light and acts as receivers and transmitters for Prime Source energy. The frequency of my electric body is tuned with the frequency of the Scott human Avatar body that I currently inhabit. The soul that inhabited the Scott body and I have exchanged souls on many, many occasions and we know each other as if we are one. And we have had this arrangement for billions of so-called years. I possess this notion of longevity. I do not have a sense of death. I have a sense of cosmic permanence.

I believe the term 'walk-in' has been written about widely but not fully understood. Only those species possessing a specific electrical resonance or frequency can undertake a walk-in process. The EL'an (EE-lan), have this capability and to my knowledge, there are no other species currently involved with Earth who can do this. There could be but I am just not aware of them.

The EL'an are the original inhabitants of the star Antares. All celestial bodies go through life cycle phases and Antares was going through its final phase (Ascension process) and dissolving back into the Prime Source. Antares is the red light within the Scorpio Constellation and is approximately 620 light years away from Earth. When we look into the sky at Antares now, we are actually seeing the light moving towards us originating from the Antares star, but not the star itself. You can see it very clearly, but there's actually nothing behind the light, as it has been reabsorbed into Prime Source. The actual body itself is gone.

As this final phase began, the inhabitants had to leave the star. The civilization that existed on Antares was but in the tens of thousands, yet they contained a vast amount of wisdom and knowledge. In order to preserve this information and the culture of the ancients, the EL'an took to the skies. They travel through the cosmos and position themselves in locations to bring up the frequency and vibration wherever they travel.

We are a tremendously advanced civilization with a wonderful connection with the Prime Source. That's a very simplistic description of our relationship. At this moment on planet Earth, everything is filtered through belief systems, cultural, educational, and religious thoughts. You have humans struggling to actually connect with the source because there's so much in the way. The EL'an, have no such restrictions. We are 100% connected and empathic.

The EL'an ride a 'wave' of energy throughout the cosmos. We can be in more than one frequency (dimension or matrix) at a time. There are actually a series of layered multiverses which all operate at different frequencies. There are literally billions of them.

The frequency of the EL'an is extremely high. When we interact with humans of a lower frequency, we reflect to them the higher frequency of our nature through our physical presence, and by our thoughts. Our frequency enables them to actually rekindle the memory of their own illuminated state. The results that we are seeing now on planet Earth, is a tremendous resurgence of spiritual expansion. Everything you do, we do, is about helping to increase frequency through every thought, word, action and deed. We are here to be of service. Even being in someone's presence can help increase their frequency. We are very intentional, very mindful. Every individual that we come into contact with, every person we might glance up and see and exchange eye contact with as we walk through the street, is about increasing their frequency in order to evolve. That is the reason we are here, our mission.

We are also here, first and foremost, for this particular celestial body, Gaia, which still has a tremendous amount of life in her. She is not yet ready to dissolve and actually move back into the prime source, but that will occur in about 500 million years from now. Gaia has an incredible desire to go back into the prime source in order to actually come out again, greatly evolved, greatly expanded. So again, what we do is we actually come back to this whole notion of embedding ourselves. We embed ourselves into human bodies to assist humanity and Gaia.

We are operating within 3D, which is a generated matrix, a created matrix, holographic existence. The energy in which the humans live at this particular point is very temporal, very much of the mind. An example is the whole business of consensual belief, consensual reality, like humans agree to live a certain way. They agree that this way is the normal (norm), when in fact it is not. And we're beginning to see those things that are considered as normal, considered as convention, falling apart like the banking system, the education system, religious bodies, and political systems. We're seeing all of those old constructs beginning to dissolve and walk-ins are a part of that. Each of us has a particular skill set or competency that we bring into this particular matrix. There's also a tremendous number of positive things happening on the planet and within the greater consciousness of planet Earth, herself.

Then there is bad. The media has been a very big part of that manipulation and it continues to be part of it. But notice in America the media is going through tremendous pain at the moment and basically carrying the narrative of the controllers and carrying the narrative of the shadow and deceivers. The media will not change until it comes back to the nature of authentic truth and of being in actual service.

The level of service from the EL'an on Earth is extremely high. The number of EL'an vary but there are about 200 of us here. The level of our empathy is 100%. We embed ourselves into the human bodies that enable us to actually function as best as we're able to. Being inside Human form also allows us to reach the goal of influencing the human DNA to such a point that a new generational phase can benefit from the introduction of a 'high powered' electrical charge to the human DNA. As the human DNA increases its ability to hold more of the electrical charge it will change so that future generations of DNA can hold more of an electrical charge. As you know, coming into the human form can be quite challenging because we are entering into a physical body. We have had to overcome what the body has experienced up to the point of a habitation. For us, we experienced a great deal of suffering and pain because of the energetic consequences arising from living in Planet Earth's old 3D magnetic matrix for the duration of our missions. Neck, jaw, lower back and hip issues often plague 'walk-ins'. I now have my lower back and neck pain under control. The Human body struggles enough as it is living inside this 3D magnetic matrix without having to cope with the higher frequencies of a walk-in. When I came in, this body had a critical health issue with acid reflux. I nearly drowned in the fluid. When I couldn't breathe, I had to exact a high degree of personal responsibility to affect life changes and that was very profound for me. Everything began to change and I embraced the whole of the vegan movement - the papain enzymes, the bromelain, and how these can impact the way food is broken down in order to relieve stress from the gut. We need to get the nutrients flowing through the body because they are electrical nutrients. These nutrients are electrical charges, lifeforce energy. I eat nothing with a central nervous system.

There will come a time when, in fact, evolved humans will not need to eat anything. They will simply take the lifeforce energy of the Prime Source in through the skin. Human biology is rapidly changing. It's happening to the body I inhabit daily.

Having been trained as a professional communicator in radio and television, I shared with the world numerous blog posts about gut health and the whole food plant-based lifestyle (veganism). The vegan lifestyle of purity of thought and no harm to other sentient beings became a major part of my on-going lifestyle. I have adapted this lifestyle as a way of healing my own gut and written several books about it.

Another issue I have had since 1987, is of experiencing extreme tinnitus which is part of the daily frequency alignment with cosmic energies. I currently live with the frequency of more than 18,000 Hz in my ears, which resembles the sound of screaming bees underwater. Depending on the clarity of communications with my EL'an family,

I am often subjected to even higher frequencies. To measure the frequency, I use a tone generator which you can find online. Once you find the site, put on your headphones, then bring that tone generator up slowly until the tinnitus disappears. Then, just slightly bring it back and then bring it up again and align the number of hertz that you're pumping out of the tone generator with the buzzing in your head. That'll do two things. One, it'll confirm that you're not mad. Two, it'll indicate just how high frequency you're operating at. And I'm operating over 118,000 Hz, but it's changing daily at present. The reason this happens is the EL'an want to actually enhance the human DNA from a biological perspective with increased frequency. We arrive at the planet, having come from an electric state of existence, to being stuffed into this rather limited human body.

The biological father of the body I inhabit, always referred to Scott as a 'bloody dreamer'. You will find many walk-in folk who transferred with human bodies are dreamers. In this case the arrangement for a so-called walk-in to occur is part of a deal between two souls covering eons of linear time as humans know it to be. These dreamers are also your 'walk-ins'; your so-called extraterrestrials from our El'an and other species who have made agreements to take over a human body.

Nearly 20 years ago, I began sketching on napkins. At the time, I didn't know what I was scrawling. But as the years passed, these images, which I now know are the Antares Seals, resurfaced and I began to write down what each one meant and the resonant frequency that each image transmits. I have an inner knowing that the seals serve as portals or gateways for change. You can read in depth about each of the seals in my book, *The Antares Seals: Return of the Holy Grail* but in short, I will share a brief about each of the 13 seals.

1. Shm'esis - To unveil your new reality within your heart;
2. Chro'mos - To align with the energies of all sun-life;
3. Tri'anne – To experience the merging process with all that is
4. Lava'koor – Living a new dimensional life;
5. Omkara'kis – A tool to tune your vibrations to the new dimension;
6. Gar'wish – The return of vibrational language;
7. Shend'ela – Moving at one with your mother Earth;
8. Garom'kas – The quickening of all universal vibrations;
9. Arvanka'sud – Prepare to open your doors to other civilizations;
10. Garom'rii – Salute the arrival of beings from other worlds;
11. Gjilom'os – The point of final correction;

12. Gjril'man – Final welcome back into the universal federation of consciousness;

13. Humana'el – The return of human and the Antares seals master device – the Ur'narka

"Now is the time to once again adorn your entire being with the contents of your Holy Grail – love, care and compassion. It is, however, your choice to drink from the mythical metaphorical Grail or not."

Incorporating the seals and working with them on a regular basis can bring about profound changes in your life.

In recent years, my skills through intuitive healing have intensified. I now have the ability to literally 'see through walls' and second guess the words which are about to issue forth from another's mouth. I have to write almost daily and have already commenced another book containing more in-depth information about *The EL'an Flyers: My People, My Origins, My Relationship with Humans and Planet Earth.*

We all have a job to do and that job is to ensure that the Holy Grail is returned to humans and Planet Earth in the form of love, care and compassion. We are not here to upset or save humans, but to empower sufficiently that realization occurs and both humans and Planet Earth are adequately prepared for the major burst of photon energy arriving in this sector of the Cosmos after 2020.

Earth will have succeeded in her desire to also electrify her biology and there will be no need for me here any longer. Those humans who are/will have responded to the bio-electrification process will have a choice to either remain on Gaia or recommence their cosmic travels once more. Those humans that cannot find it within them to respond to this process will resettle elsewhere." Everything is moving. Everything is evolving. Everything is frequency and vibration.

Ka'Lama. EhH'utos. Em'Metritous

We are you. So honor you. We acknowledge your supreme origin.

Kaza Blizz

Kaza was 33 years old when she became a walk-in on June 5, 2017. Although she entered into the body of a woman, she is becoming more unisex and not of a particular gender.

She is a walk-in from the 13th dimension and has abilities of trance healing and prophecy. Kaza is able to speak and write star languages.

In 2013, Australian aboriginals recognized Kaza as a Shaman, also known as an 'Avatar', a goddess of incarnate deity in ancient times. She is a soul exchange and time jumpers. "We are a team of various different souls which will show up depending on the different circumstances," says Kaza.

Kaza's Story

I was diagnosed with scleroderma, an incurable autoimmune disease. It came on suddenly within three months. The doctors told me that I was still young so maybe they could control it with steroids and different medications. I believed them, but the case was that I was getting worse. After a few years, my whole body couldn't even move at all. Fibrosis developed in my heart, lungs, kidneys and liver. Even the skin, muscles and veins in my body got fibrosis. The doctors said they couldn't help me and gave me only three to six months to live and told my family to prepare for the worst. They wanted to send me to a special hospital and let me try some very strong medicines. They told me there was a 50% chance that I might die from taking the medicines and a 50% chance that I might get better but they were not sure because this will just be a test stage. Since I was told I might die with or without the drugs, I decided to just go home and spend my remaining time with my family. I wanted to live at any cost. Not for myself but for my family.

I was glad I was home but the pain was unbearable. I couldn't move. I was crying every day because I had lost all my freedom of mobility. I couldn't go to the toilet. I was hungry but I couldn't eat. I couldn't even roll in the bed. I couldn't do anything and I lost my ability to walk.

At that time, my husband and I owned a café but we couldn't run the business anymore because I was sick and he had to be home taking care of me and our two children. We went bankrupt. I had no sexual relationship with my husband and I didn't want to be like this anymore. I prayed to the Buddha and asked him to either let me die or to give me a chance to survive with good health. After that a miracle happened.

I had a dream in the middle of the day. That was very unusual because I was in so much pain that I couldn't sleep. As the dream started, I remember hearing a voice speaking to me. I wasn't scared because I had been preparing myself to die and I thought this was it. The voice said to me, "I'm going to shut down all of your senses now, one by one." I told the voice it was okay.

First, they turned off my sense of sight and I could see nothing even though it was a broad daylight. I closed my eyes. Then the voice said, "We are now going to shut down your hearing senses." And I couldn't hear a thing. Then one by one, my senses were shut down and I felt nothing. I was conscious but I felt nothing. Only peace. No pain. I thought, 'If I am dead, that wasn't too bad. It was quick.'

I felt very relaxed and at peace. I saw a golden light and I followed it to a place that I had never seen before. I could see my own body and there were three people around me. At that sight, I felt scared because the people around my body did not look like buddhas. They looked like Jesus! They had long blond hair, and their eyes looked different, bigger than ours. They were in all white shoes and clothes. At first I thought I was having a crazy dream because I was a Buddhist. I thought, 'Why am I seeing Jesus? Are you kidding me? How can this be?' They all looked alike but not the same. I now know they were actually extraterrestrial beings.

I saw them put a lot of lights into my body as they were speaking a different language. When they turned to me, one of them said, 'We hear what you are thinking. We are here trying to heal your body and restart your life. But in this case, if we give you back your health, give you back your life, one of our spirits will go into your body. Will you agree with that? They will guide you and help you help other people.'

I didn't care what that meant at the time. I just wanted to live and be able to walk again. So I said, "Sure. Yes! Anything. I just want to live. Just do it." It all sounded great to me. That was the best moment in my life and a wave of relief washed over me.

After I agreed, I saw a lot of different symbols and colors going into and through my head. These symbols looked like a different language. I experienced so many amazing things during this time that I don't have the words to explain what was happening. They told me that they would guide me and help me with other people. I thought I understood what was happening but after it was over, I realized I didn't have a clue.

It seemed like this experience went on for a long time but when I woke up it had only been about 40 minutes. When I came back, I was still me. After this dream, I could sit up by myself! Within a few days, I could walk.

I didn't tell anyone about the dream. Katze, my name at the time, knew that something had happened. I, Kaza, had entered her body. At that time, our soul energy was 50/50. 50% was Katze and 50% was me, Kaza. We lived together in the same body. I learned how Katze eats, her habits and how she is as a human being. We began to understand each other, but honestly, I thought I was going crazy.

I kept up the normal western medicine visits but I started seeing a naturopath and started living a healthy life. I changed all my habits. And very slowly I recovered my health.

Then a miracle happened. I was pregnant without having sex with my husband! I thought there was a mistake. The doctors didn't believe me when I told them that I had not resumed having sexual relations with my husband. Everyone said it was a miracle because firstly I was pregnant, and secondly that I delivered a healthy baby.

I never told this fact to anyone before I told Mary Rodwell. She was very reassuring and said that pregnancy is common with many women who experienced what I had experienced. My second son is from a different planet. Exactly how it happened, I don't know. I do know that he was traveling in his spaceship when he noticed that his planet was having a very bad war and that they were losing. He knew that if he returned, he would be killed. He decided to leave his body and go to a planet where he could be safe. He chose to come here and chose me to be his mother. One time he said to me, 'This Earth will have a war soon and then we will all go to a new Earth.'

After I became pregnant, the voices started. At first, there were a few voices. I started researching more ways to be healthy and each time they would tell me when something was right or wrong for me. When I went the grocery store, I began to see different colors on top of the food that other people couldn't see. When I touch a pack of cheese for example, I would know and hear what the ingredients were inside and if they were good or bad for me. It was like I was receiving information from the cheese, like a download of information with data running through my head.

Chinese people believe in ghosts so when the voice began, I thought they were ghosts. Over time, the voices began to materialize during my dreams, and in the daytime showing up with fuzzy bodies. There were many different kinds of beings that began to show up. At first, they would just stand there and look at me and I would look at them and we knew each other. The more I meditated the more they came forward. Some told me who they are, where they're from and taught me things to help me while I am here on planet Earth. They said they were here to help me and to teach me how to help people around me.

I was confused because I didn't know how to help others. I was just a normal woman, a housewife. I didn't have a strong educational background and I didn't want to go back to school. They said they would help me if I would give them permission. I agreed.

They taught me how to use essential oils, how to make potions and they taught me how to speak star language. I would receive messages and learn that I actually have a team of helpers that are with me all of the time. This team was from the 13th dimension. People who can see energy or spirits will see them around me.

Sometimes the deceased would come to me and ask me to pass a message to a loved one. I just do it because I felt like I should. Then I began to know things that others didn't know, or things about that person. If I was watching TV and a newscaster came on, I would know things about them. I felt uncomfortable with all this information. I could read people's minds too. I didn't like that either. I still didn't tell anyone about what was going on with me because I thought I was losing my mind and going crazy. But that all changed with my fourth pregnancy.

This pregnancy was quite a journey and I had 27 near-death experiences due to heavy bleeding. I had to stay in the hospital a lot. Each time the doctor would say that the baby might die due to the heavy bleeding. They also warned that I might die as well. Every time when the bleeding happened, unexplainable things would happen.

One time, I was lying on a bed, waiting for one of the doctors when I saw a pair of big golden hands on my stomach. I had no idea what was happening. The golden hands came with a voice and said, 'No, you have to survive for now. We need this baby. He is very important.' And then the bleeding stopped. Then doctors said, "Guess what? The baby is still there. There is a very strong heartbeat. You may go home. Everything is fine." These hands saved my baby and my life many times. I also received many visits from extraterrestrials during this pregnancy. I have no doubt they helped also.

The birth of my son was quite traumatic and I had lost a lot of blood. Afterwards, I had eight hours of surgery and ended up in a coma. When I woke up, only 40 hours later and to the astonishment of the hospital staff, I found myself in completely unfamiliar surroundings. I woke up knowing that I was me, Kaza, and that I am a walk-in from the 13th dimension. I began to lose my identity as Katze. My family, especially my husband, noticed something different about me almost immediately, as I began eating foods that I never eaten before and began drinking coffee for the first time.

When Katze was giving birth, she was dying, and we made an

agreement again. In our first agreement she agreed for me to come in during the so-called dream. She was happy to leave. This time, I came in with 80% of my energy and as she slowly passed away, I came in fully.

After three days, I returned home and my energy began to return. As soon as it did, I researched the term 'walk-in'. It surprised me because it was about spiritual stuff. I'm from Hong Kong and I wanted someone that speaks my language to talk more about this with. So I looked up on the internet and I found a radio host to speak with. He recommended that I contact Mary Rodwell.

In the beginning, I wondered why I needed to talk to her but I felt like it was the right thing to do, so I reached out. We set up a Skype meeting and during the meeting I was totally me, Kaza. I told her, "I'm a walk-in, from the 13th dimension. I came here because I have a mission to accomplish. I need your help to spread the message. I still feel confused, but I'm okay." I don't know why I said those words, but luckily Mary trusted and believed me.

After that I started to know more about myself and I feel more comfortable to be myself. It took me about one year to totally integrate. I was so excited about being on Earth and having a human body. I was like a crazy person telling every single person I knew and that would listen that I was a walk- in. I would say, "I'm so happy to meet you. Do you have something you want to share with me? I'm from the 13th dimension, do you want to hear more?" I thought it was a good thing and that it was safe to tell others. I thought people would be happy. But it was very different than I expected.

I had to tell people about ETs, and that they come in many forms. That's part of my mission. It's not just what you see on the TV, it also can be a walk-in. We can live together. We are here. We are here to learn, not to destroy things or cause trouble. Sometimes we just want to enjoy life like a human being here on this Earth.

I went to Hong Kong and was interviewed by a radio host several times. All I wanted to do was to tell people who I am, why I'm here and to tell people to start opening their minds. I wanted to tell them to take more care of themselves; to know more about the right way to live.

About six months after the interviews, the radio host started to tell people, during his show, that I was a liar and that all I want to do is ask for money because I offered healing. He said that even though I was a walk-in from the 13th dimension, I was evil. He told everyone I was a spiritual cult. But no one ever came forward to say that I overcharged them, or that they didn't receive help. But because he was a radio host, people started listening to him.

But many of my followers in Hong Kong, who still believe in me, wrote letters asking me not to stop, to keep helping them. Because of the persecution, I stopped charging any money for my healing services. I didn't feel it was worth it.

People began thinking that I was crazy, that I had lost my mind. My friends don't believe in me. My relatives don't believe in me. I was lucky that my children and husband thought that I was totally normal.

I made a second trip with Mary to Hong Kong to share the next part of my mission and to let people know about the star children and star people. They are just like us only in different forms. Many of them are on Earth today as walk-ins or they came in at birth. They just want to experience Earth or to help. It was quite successful and people were happy to see their research.

After that trip, I decided that I have finished spreading my message. I have a happy life in Australia. I live with my husband and with my family. I am safe there. I felt like I was betrayed and didn't want to experience that anymore. I started to doubt myself.

I keep a low profile now. I don't tell people anything about myself unless I know them very well. I don't feel ashamed; I am still very proud of who I am but I have lost the excitement when I first came in, full of passion and telling everyone about my journey. I am still open to helping and sharing my story with people like Sheila.

It sounded like human beings didn't want to hear the truth. I started reading a lot of books about how humans choose their belief systems. It is important to know because humans should have the free will to choose what they want to believe. I found that the belief system around this world is totally wrong. People have been brainwashed into thinking who they are, who they should listen to, what they should think. They do not know the truth of who they are or their true history.

I want to share that I come from the 13th dimension of another galaxy that I can't explain in language. There are no solid beings there. We are just pure light form. From where I came, I am a blue silverlight. We are very bright, luminous. I am split from there now, a smaller light, and in this body. When I leave my body and astral travel back home, I can download energy from my collective and can search the past or future. My language is like a frequency that can settle energy in a physical body. This is one way I can conduct healing on others.

Some people say, "Oh wow. You're like a goddess. You are pure light. You're really up there. The 13th dimension is the place of god." I tell them there is no up there or down there. We are all the same. Thirteenth dimension is no better than the third dimension. It is not bigger than or better than. We are all linked together. Without a level one, there cannot be a level two. I am not saying that we are more powerful than you. That's just where we came from. The 13th dimension. It's just a name. Everyone can connect with us and everyone will go there between lives to recharge before they recycle again.

My message, in part, is to tell people that we are real. One of the reasons that I came here is because I wanted to understand why we created human beings. Why do people have certain kinds of thoughts or certain kinds of feelings? Why do they act the way they do? So I became one. Now, I understand more and I can do my job better.

Every single being on this planet has a will, a desire, their love. Those things all create energy. Those energies all go into the 13th dimension. When all that energy comes together, it creates.

When someone cries out, "Oh God, please help me," the energy of that message is sent there and we receive it and give you the response. When you say that the 13th dimension is God's creation, you have to see that you helped create it. In the 13th dimension all communication is telepathic. There is total transparency.

Everyone has their own, different vibration. If we are not all linked together, we don't exist. Some people say that we are one. I can answer that statement and say 'Yes, we are one but we are all different.' We are all part of the whole. For example, take the human body. The body cannot exist without the lung. The lung is not the body but the body cannot survive without it. On Earth, we all have to work together because if not, we just fail.

That is why we have come to you. We feel and notice that a lot of you get lost in your relationships, health, your destiny. We are all linked together. It is time for us to all understand each other.

Our soul is made by a Creator. First, you have to understand that this Creator is not a statue or has many faces or even a name. As I was in the 13th dimension, I can tell you that this Creator had to create the first energy to prove that he was there because without that, he/she can't prove who he/she is. And then this energy started to split and became bigger and bigger but it left smaller packs of energy. These energy packs were left to start creating lives and different universes and different planets.

The 13th dimension is like a large cloud of energy, a mist. It is created by the first pack of energy or the first soul. That is how all the other souls are created. Souls go to different planets or universes to experience different lives. When it ends, they go back to the 13th dimension to get recharged and they keep recycling and come back together based on their karma.

I am unable to fit into human society. At the beginning, I tried very hard to fit in, so that I can do what I can. It turned out that humans are just unable to accept me. Luckily, my family fully accepts me and we have a better relationship than before. At work, I became more independent.

In the past, I was very aware of my emotions. The hardest thing about being a walk-in was learning to deal with human emotions. Now, I understand what emotions are all about. I am treating them like a movie – experience the feelings and let go. Before the walk-in, I would be very persistent on many things; now I am consciously experiencing life and I understand that everything is just an illusion.

The last part of my mission is to assist in human awakenings and the Ascension of Earth.

Maya Christobel

Maya did her masters and doctoral work and Harvard Graduate School of Education in developmental psychology and has been in private practice for more than thirty-five years. She is a pioneer in the field of biotechnology for healing trauma and is an award-winning writer and filmmaker. Maya is also an author who has been writing screenplays, ghostwriting novels, and coaching writers for the past 20 years.

As an independent transformational film producer, she just completed research and consulting on a film about teen depression and suicide and is working with young people around the world on a docuseries. Maya's entire professional career has revolved around helping people tell their stories and heal them.

Maya works with exoconscious experiencers through personal readings, offering direct transmissions from the 'Observers' who speak through her. Maya is available for speaking engagements and workshops on the topics of Living the Multidimensional life, Integrating your Life Experiences, and Parenting our New Children, as well as Writing your Story. She considers herself a global citizen and lives nomadically, currently residing in Santa Fe, New Mexico. Maya is a hybrid with a soul infusion walk-in and comes from outside the constellation Vega.

Maya's story

I still find it odd to say that I am a hybrid and a soul infusion walk-in. So, to assist the reader with these two very different, yet complimentary, components, I will first discuss hybrids, then my walk-in experience.

I was born a hybrid with the gift of knowing why I was here on planet Earth. From the age of two, I began to vividly remember things about an off-planet life. I possessed the gift of seeing energy, igniting people's hearts, and living empathically. By five years old, I began receiving continual visitations from my multidimensional guides and non-human spiritual family members who did not occupy 3D reality. These diverse unseen presences accompanied me until I was at a new stage of development where new beings would step in and remain with me until my next developmental shift and upgrade. I refer to this changing ensemble of non-human teachers and guides as the 'Observers' but when I was five, everything was entirely magical and mysterious. My life was filled with orbs, fairies, intelligent energies, and a telepathic link with animals. From an early age, my family described me as strange, overly emotional, and painfully sensitive. I was of grave concern to them.

Every decade or so, I had a turnover in my guardians and teachers. New guides and teachers would bring with them a new set of 'lesson plans' to speed my growth in consciousness, fine-tune my gifts and, little by little, reveal my history to me and my purpose for incarnating. But it was not just me learning from them.

What became clear was that I was a research balloon, a 'transmitter' of information for complex research into the human experience - especially the weather patterns of human emotions. Very clearly, I was on this planet for two reasons: To be a participant in a study of the heart-driven human experience, and to have a life filled with experiences for off-planet researchers to study. From passion and love to terror and death and everything in between, the full sweep of human experience was of interest to the Observers. I agreed to be this transmitter long before I was born. Yet, later in life, my presence here began to include becoming an energetic activator and stimulator of consciousness.

I possess the capacity to entangle or entrain my heart energy with another person's heart energy and create a kind of bio-resonance and ignition of a higher vibrational frequency. That being said, it is not always a pleasant experience for the person with an energetic imbalance or old patterning that needs to be neutralized. Old patterns must be deleted in order for the vibrational integrity of heart energy to become dominant. Like shedding old skin.

It is no small commitment to engage the full range of human experience. I faced certain death more than once. I had lots of money, then no money, experienced marriage, divorce, kidnapping, sexual abuse, abandonment, and a loss of everything I owned and every cent in the bank. I lived through betrayals by friends and lovers, despicable lies, being stalked, near-death surgeries, car accidents, and annihilating domination by powerful men. I have spent much time in the darkness of the human psyche, dealt with sociopaths, psychopaths and murderous people. I have seen into the darkest abyss and been in the light while there, only to find that both places are sacred.

I have also experienced the remarkable nature of motherhood, an advantageous Harvard education, exotic world travel, communication with animals, boundless love and compassion, miracles and serendipity, and loads and loads of love. I have lived in penthouses and I have lived in my car. Not one experience, no matter how wonderful, hard, or tragic, made me regret this incarnation. I learned spiritual resilience, courage and gratitude even for the most horrific experiences and count my life here as the supreme adventure.

My life growing up was in a conservative middle class military family. My youth was a constant experience of not fitting in and not belonging. I wanted to look beyond the obvious veil of illusion to the bigger picture and into the cosmos as it exists in every moment of being human. I never fit in at school and kept to myself. Yet, in the inevitable isolation that being a hybrid requires, my psychic life and my inner dialogues were always extremely dramatic, and surprising. I grew to prefer the unseen multidimensional world and the depth of my empathic and telepathic nature, over whatever was happening within my peer group or family or culture.

Yet, my greatest isolation was never being able to speak to anyone about my experiences. By my twenties I was told that I was to keep my non-ordinary nature and my experiences with extraterrestrial and multidimensional beings a secret. This felt like a prison sentence. Like running the gauntlet. A tall order for sure. I was then told that 'they' would let me know when it was okay to begin to reveal who I was and what I knew. I could never have guessed that they meant fifty years of waiting, recording my experiences, and scribing my learning.

What was the reason for all the silence and my living inside a proverbial incubator? It was simply not to contaminate the research project that I was, with other people's experiences, ideas, judgments, or drama. And there is a lot of drama in being a hybrid. The 'Observers' did not want me reading or, once the computer was available, searching for what was happening in the exoconscious world. I was mandated to remain un-swayed by other people's experiences, opinions or energy, or by the profound amount of fear that circulates on this planet regarding the unseen. I was to develop my human life 'organically' without any interference or influence.

I have often been asked why I have referred to my guides and teachers as observers. Countless entities have been part of my life that I learned to call whomever was in my life at the time, the 'Observers' or, my 'Dream Team'. I do not remember my life without them. I leaned in time that I am not an Earth-based human looking out into the stars to find my purpose or to develop a cosmology, but just the reverse. I am a cosmic being looking in on the human plane and I am often bewildered, dismayed, astonished, and disturbed by human existence, human beings, and how tragic most of civilization is due to a history of violence. The only things that feel familiar on this planet are nature herself and those I believe are the higher and more evolved beings - animals.

I came from an order of beings from an angelic/priesthood realm outside of the constellation Vega. I agreed to incarnate into the human experience for a very specific purpose. And at this very specific time in human history as we are poised on the brink of waking up as conscious humans. I possess human and non-human DNA, and my DNA configuration itself is a receptor or I like to see my DNA as a satellite dish that combs the universe for discrete messages and energy. I live a human life that is seamlessly interfaced with my soul from the angelic realm. This composite of energies is what makes a hybrid. Some people believe that all angels are hybrids.

Being a hybrid is being an ultimate outlier in a world where conformity and approval are impossible. I did not come to an understanding of being a hybrid but knew that this was my truth from a very early age. I realized that I was looking at a planet of people who called themselves Homo Sapiens, and that almost none of them were purely human, but genetically-altered humans that had been cross-pollinated by many off-world species. I found that walking in this world are beings from countless places, countless times, and with complex genetic imprints just like mine. Earth has been a giant laboratory and school since the beginning of time. And we are a petri dish for every kind of interstellar, interspecies, and intergalactic presences in one form or another. Humans are just a drop in the cosmic bucket.

I have a unique memory of my non-human self. I would not term the awareness I have as 'memory', but as simultaneous channels of information that run all the time. This 'simulcast' ability affords me other abilities. Clairaudience is a primary gift for me. Sight of the unseen, as well as being a radio transmitter that sends information to a team and receives constant information and energy, are all natural gifts that I have had to learn to incorporate into my daily life living under the radar. Being a cosmic scribe is a skill. Being an activator of the heart with a simple smile or gentle touch is my greatest gift. Any knowledge I brought in and continue to bring is beyond the scope of this interview. The cosmic knowledge that unfolds daily is my everyday reality. All this knowledge serves my real reason for being here: To love.

As I have shared, I am a hybrid. Yet, through a complex set of circumstances I am also a recent walk-in: a consciousness that was infused or implanted. I have angelic ancestry, angelic soul energy, a human mother, a human personality and combined DNA which contribute to being a hybrid. However, last year I experienced a walk-out of a karmically-patterned old self and then a walk-in of my future self, took over that space.

It happened during a harsh Maine winter when I had a physical accident and within hours, while at the hospital, I felt more than just different. I felt that I was enhanced in some way. Suddenly, I had a new kind of fearlessness and bravado and more traditionally masculine characteristics with a wicked sense of humor. Instantly I didn't care about what people thought of me, was bold in my opinions, highly analytical and bluntly assertive. I was totally incapable of enduring injustice of any kind and what had been a lifetime of responding to injustice with empathy and soft heartedness, I was suddenly fearless in my anger.

Once I was home, on crutches, and off my feet for nearly eight weeks, it was then made clear to me that I had merged with my 'future self'. This was no non-ordinary moment since while I was in the shower a voice so large rose up in me and began barraging me with detailed scientific information and requests. This voice was a far more integrated and slightly masculine self who had evolved new and more integrated capacities during my future timeline. My future self has a very distinct brash and take no prisoner voice, separate energy than the rest of me, and is very archetypally male. I can feel the subtle and not so subtle distinctions and my inner conversations are very different and quite brusque. I consider this synching with my future self, and the timeline brought with it, to be like an interface on your computer. Borrowing tech language, it is as if I have a dual processor navigating everything. I move back and forth seamlessly between these distinct processors, each serving distinct roles but moving in the same direction. There is a total recognition that we are not separate processors, but one magnificent computer of consciousness.

My future self, or walk-in, is called Uban. Uban is excited about being in a human body. I now see the world around me, which I have studied for decades, through his astonished eyes. He notices details in life that I have never seen, and he feels things about what I take for granted, which gives me a fresh perspective on the world around me. When Uban is excited I barely get through anything planned in a day. There is an innocence in him that, coupled with the child-like spirit in me, can get derailed, and runs headlong into experiences that are exhilarating and educational, all the while abandoning previous responsibilities.

Everything takes twice as long when I hear him say, "Oh, let's smell the flower." Or, "Oh my God, look how toes work." And if I need to grocery shop, he wants to linger and look at all the glass bottles and fondle the fresh fish at the open market. 'He is going to get me into trouble!' I think to myself. Because of his presence, I often forget that incarnation, is extraordinary. Uban is not a child, but it's like having those first eyes of a child who wants to play just a little longer, stay up a little later and is awestruck at how the sun is going down with all its subtle colors. I forget to simply stand still and remember that every one of those sunrises is a miracle. And for me, Uban is my miracle self.

Having made abnormal psychology part of my life and private practice for three decades I felt at home working with one of the most difficult 'diagnoses' in psychology: The multiple personality disorder (MPD). Sybil broke ground on how much psychology and neuroscience does not know about this phenomenon but I spent a great deal of my professional life working with people who had separate personalities, separate stories and were clinically deemed delusional. My 'at-homeness' with this difficult population of people was akin to Dr. John Mack's acceptance of the abduction experience being real and not pathological. For many MPD people I recognized past pathology and past the religious explanation of being possessed and saw people…much like me. For many of my patients the only crazy making part of their issues was not having any validation for their experience and once anyone was able to listen, believe and validate them, the anxiety and isolation of the patient changed in an instant.

When I asked Uban why he came into my life now. His answer was, "We don't have to deal with bodies like this in the future and I'm excited to be in a place that I am not from. I'm your more integrated self since in the future there is no distinction between mind, body, spirit, emotions, male, or female. I'm you're 'more' self." And oddly enough Uban is not that interested in emotions. He sees a moment when I might cry, or someone gets angry and then sad or hurt or confused, as neutral. He is not moved. He has equilibrium, balance and detachment. His experience is that there are no distinctions between the emotional body and the physical body, there is just presence.

I find this distinction in Uban fascinating because my emotional body has been the primary research satellite as I broadcast data about how humans are emotionally wired on planet Earth. The question for those off-planet researchers is to understand the biochemistry of emotion, how the brain works in states of emotion, and how the heart works. Uban says he does not have to worry about any of that.

I discovered early on that I am an activator. I can be with a person for a brief time and wherever the person is unconscious, they will have a wake-up call. It is not always easy or pleasant when a person comes out of unconsciousness. It is a lot like a person waking up after being in an extended coma. They are activated to move more deeply into love and compassion if that is their makeup. But if a person I am with is consumed by fear and anger and resentment, which creates a state of contraction and reactivity to life, they will move further into that state of imbalance so that transformation or transmutation can occur.

The people I have a heart-opening experience with usually remain in my life in some way. The people who, when their hearts are activated, come face-to-face with fear, memories, or unfinished karma, tend to distance from me and have a healing crisis. I used to feel responsible for helping those people get through a dark night of the soul or being stuck, but now I understand that is not my role

We are living at a time when the idea of 'the other' needs to be dissolved. These labels we try to use to describe anomalous experiences and identities will become archaic. Dis-evolved is an applicable word. The very nature of believing that there is 'the other' separates, polarizes and does not allow for the 'Ascension' trying to happen: Namely, unity and oneness. Fear is born out of the belief in separateness and look where our planet is right now.

Every single person with conscious awareness has within them, all the knowledge and experience that any one of these subjects suggests. Everyone can 'channel', can see, can hear, if they learn to practice the skills inside of non-ordinary reality and if the line between the seen and the unseen blurs until there is no demarcation. But, being human is a big variable that demands attention as well. Bodies are high maintenance and more disease than ever is cropping up when there is a lack of vibrational alignment between a person's essence and their human body. I call this lack of alignment, 'slippage'. The real disease is fear which keeps us out of that necessary alignment and living a low-vibrational life that attracts disease.

Living in the service of finding our true and authentic humanity is just as important as reaching beyond the stars. Imbuing the unseen with more power and wisdom than ourselves or listening to what Bashar has to share and making it more powerful and important a message than the message coming from each and every heart on this planet is missing a powerful point. This is faulty thinking and will simply get us more of the same mess we see happening right now.

How can we achieve this interface, this blurring of the lines of distinction? Let the labels go and allow for all things to be possible, allow for the mind and heart to expand and explode with the limitless possibilities all around, all the time. Don't just open the door to the unseen. Eliminate the doors altogether.

Daniel Teague

Daniel Teague is a distance healer at Vega Star Healing where he offers Seven Chakra Balancing, Chakra Hook Cutting, Emotional and Mental Block releases, Parasite Cord Cutting, and Energy Field Negative Energy Clearing. He scans the energy field of his client and adjusts their frequencies. He also offers paranormal services and pet healing services.

Through meditation he has discovered that he comes from the Lyra. He has the sense that he might have been involved with some type of military there as he has always presented a military presence.

Daniel has been interviewed by numerous radio programs where he shares his walk-in and paranormal experiences. His website is vegastarhealings.com.

Daniel's Story

I grew up on Long Island in New York and went to school in the 1980s and 90s. I was scheduled to graduate High School in 1992 at the age of 18, but that didn't happen as expected.

On the night of May 8, 1992, a group of friends and I went to the movies. Afterwards, I was driving everyone home. I had dropped everyone off and had only one friend remaining with me. He and I were in a car accident and basically, I was killed. I have no memory of the accident at all. The next thing I remember is waking up in a hospital a week later. I had been in a coma.

Over the next several months, I began to change. First, my personality changed from a shy personality into an outgoing one. Next, my memories changed. I still had all of my memories but over time, they began to feel as if they belonged to someone else. Something was not quite right. I became disassociated with my friends and family. New memories began to creep in, almost as if they were artificial or implanted.

One memory I experienced showed up months after the accident. Psychics have told me this is my walk-in experience. I remembered lying flat on my back. I couldn't see much of anything. Then I felt like I was in a dimly-lit room. I remember this unbelievably loud noise. It was a humming or buzzing sound that went straight through me.

The hum was so loud that if any other sounds were happening, the hum drowned it out. At the time, I couldn't even tell if I was breathing. I couldn't see anything clearly. I had no frontal vision, only peripheral vision. All I could make out were shadows and shapes moving about. I could see commotion near the lower half of my extremities. As I focused on that area, I couldn't find my legs! I had no memory. I couldn't move my head because honestly, my body seemed like it was gone and all I had was consciousness. I asked myself if I was dead. I didn't like the way things were going. This memory was very strange yet very vivid and very real. I remember it like it was yesterday although it has been over 20 years.

Regarding the personality change through the walk-in, I have a way that I like to explain what happened using the analogy of a computer. My background is with computers. That's what I did for many years. On a Windows operating system you have something called a profile. That profile has shell folders, like your desktop folder, your document folder, and various folders that represent different things. What if your soul is like the profile that houses different folders that make up the personality of someone? So, what if you took the personality profile out and stuck another personality profile in the same person? The personality would change and be completely different. I actually got a new personality.

The worst part of the personality change was that I lost all the good friends I made and the family connections that I had growing up. Those relationships slowly dissolved and I feel very disconnected to them now. They will never be the same. There will always be something missing. Especially with my family. I feel like I was forced into a family where I didn't belong.

People often ask me if the walk-in occurred while I was in the coma, and I tell them I don't think so. I think it happened during the car accident, in a split second. My consciousness removed me out of the whole deal. It was a bad wreck. I tell people: look, my physical body didn't die, or I wouldn't be here. Right? But the soul split and the new one came in.

For the next ten years everything in my life was pretty mellow. I knew nothing about psychic abilities or the paranormal. I didn't even know I was a walk-in, I just knew I was different.

I didn't know I was a walk-in until 16 years after the fact. I had no idea what was going on with me, I just knew that I was different. I went through a metamorphosis process that was absolutely surreal. This process didn't feel like a possession where something negative was taking me over. It just felt weird. I felt as if I was looking at myself through someone else's eyes. I'll give you an example. I was leaving a movie theater at night and as I was going through the exit doors to the parking lot, I didn't feel locked in my body. It was almost like a mentally drunken or fluid sensation, like I was floating within myself. I was looking at my hand, waving it in front of my face. It felt so disconnected from my body that I even asked myself if it really was my hand.

I had many surreal experiences in these early years. Growing up, I felt I was supposed to be in the military. I almost joined before high school ended, but I backed out. I've always felt like I have been a part of a militarized operation. Even today, I still feel like I am literally in a military attachment, even though I've never joined.

I tried to join the police department but couldn't because of the injuries my physical body sustained during the accident when I broke my femur and shattered my patella on my right side. I did become a volunteer firefighter in New York and was pretty active until I relocated outside the state.

It's strange, but I have been approached by people with some type of military background that have asked me if I am current or ex-military. It's the weirdest thing. When I tell them I'm not, they say to me that it's not a haircut thing, it's not my look, it's the way I present myself that caused them to ask. Maybe I was in the Lyran military.

Over the years, I have had many strange experiences. I have also had various gifts and talents emerge, and I have a few stories that I would like to share about them.

Several abilities started to surface. One of the first abilities that began to show up was a voice phenomenon. Within about a year of recovery, a voice, out of nowhere started talking to me and it scared the crap out of me. I didn't know if it was a spirit or ghost or what it was. It was with me for several months, but I was so freaked out that finally, I told it that it had to go. I ended up blocking the voice and it went away. But before I blocked it, I would be told things that ended up happening such as predicted negative events to people I knew.

Another time I was in Saint Augustine, Florida to participate in a midnight ghost tour at an old Fort along the beach. I was walking around the fort when I heard what I thought was rocks being thrown. I heard them whistling past as they hit the wall behind me. Then I heard popping noises against the wall. The next thing I knew, the tour guide was approaching me. I told him what had just happened and his mouth fell open. He explained that I was standing next to the execution wall.

My psychic awakening occurred while walking in a mall. I saw a small virtual window open in front of me. It depicted a man standing against a wall with crossed arms wearing an army jacket. This man then walked briskly toward this window which showed a mugging. The window vanished and in real time, I saw the same man from the vision and was able to avoid being mugged by slowing my walk.

Eventually, I moved to Arizona and joined a volunteer paranormal investigation company and began attending different psychic meetings and workshops. It was these groups that opened doors for me to be able to experience my gifts. Several things began to happen for me.

During one of the first group meetings, we practiced psychometry. This practice involves holding an object and receiving information about it. I discovered that I was a natural. The person with whom I was paired was amazed with my ability to know that the spoon I was holding was a military spoon from World War I. I was able to describe the person who was the initial owner.

The next thing that happened was that my dream life became very active. In one dream, I found myself in some type of posture, standing over a person laying on a massage table performing some type of gestures over the person's body. I called my friend the next morning to share the dream and she invited me to attend the next

Reiki share. This is a meeting where people practice energy healing on each other. She asked me to go into the same position as in the dream and show me what I had been doing.

I had a volunteer lay on the table. I stood in the stance and placed my hands about 2.5 feet away from him. All of a sudden, he freaks out on the table and asks what I was doing. Honestly, I had no idea what I was doing. He said he'd never felt energy like that before. My friend said that I had a gift and ought to develop it. That is when the healing ability began to manifest.

My first healing experience was working on my girlfriend's (now wife) headache. She was extremely prone to migraines. I began by formulating an intention for her that the migraine would turn it into a low-grade headache and that the body would just take care of it. Which it did. Since then, I have created an empire of energy work from just this one idea, formulating an intention in my mind and then allowing it to manifest.

Now, healing is now my life. I live, breathe, eat and sleep all the new ideas and concepts that I have adopted. It took a long time for me to accept who I am, but once I did, things really started to click.

I also started working with interdimensional beings. I'm channeling them and/or they're channeling to me. We open a channel and communicate in both directions. These interdimensional beings who I was talking to turned out to be my guides. I now call them my Counsel or my Collective. They do not speak all at once. They come through as individual voices and provide their name, constellation or star system initially. I also communicate with more spirit-based beings that were originally humans.

I communicate with them telepathically. I'll just formulate the thought or question in my mind and typically they are already answering it before I have completed the thought. They give me ideas for services. I feel like they sometimes implant thoughts or give me downloads. When this happens, I hear audible tones that go off in my ears, and then in about a week or so the new idea formulates. That's how the development of new ideas comes to me. I also have gone from being a non-empathic person to an extremely sensitive empath. I can literally sense and sometimes adopt people's negative emotions.

In 2014 I opened my business. Prior to that I worked in regular jobs. I never spoke of what was going on with me. I only opened up about who I was when I joined the psychic meetup groups. This is where I found a refuge in which to share my experiences.

Once I started working with the psychics, more and more psychic information came in. Basically the group I was in was not teaching me how to be more psychic, but helped to identify skills I already had developed on my own without giving it a label. I would look at a person and get a download of information about that person. The download was like a list of attributes about the person, their emotional mood, the negatives about them, addictions, if they were outgoing or shy. I didn't even have to know their name.

I thought I was profiling the person. It wasn't until I met another psychic lady who explained that I was not profiling the person but that I was reading their energy. What I was getting was called a psychic download.

I never really resonated with the whole psychic reading thing. I guess I did it for training purposes to prove I could do it.

Now I scan the energy of the aura and energy fields instead of read it. With a person, it's layers of dimensions, the skin and bones and all that. The blood, the brain, technically it's all frequency. It's just an extremely low frequency. That's why you can see it and touch it. As frequency rises, at a certain point it disappears. It's not that it's not there, it's just it's not visible to the naked eye. So with extraterrestrials or interdimensional beings, why can't people always see them? You only see them when there is synchronicity between your subconsciousness, your consciousness and the dimensions.

Being a walk-in is a unique experience for each person. For me, it set me on a course of healing. The worst part is that chances are, you are going to lose all the good friends you had when you were growing up. Those friendships slowly dissolve. You may still know them, but it won't ever be the same. There will always be something missing. Being a walk-in is almost like those *Matrix* movies. Once you're out and you know everything, when your soul is released it can't go back. Ignorance is bliss. That is 100% true.

To do this sort of work, you have to step out of fear, especially if you're prone to being skeptical or jumpy. If certain individuals cause you fear, don't do this type of work. It's not for you. If you can't work by yourself, if you can't take yourself out of a group setting, if you can't walk on a mountain trail on a hiking trail by yourself, it's not for you. You have to be able to have enough moxie in your system to say, I'm ready for the unknown. In order to do the specialized type of work that I do, you have to have an open mind, and be able to set up rules with limits and boundaries.

Be kind to strangers and kind to animals. Someday they may be in a position to help you. You never know when you might need their help.

Yvonne Perry

Yvonne Perry is a Nashville, Tennessee, based minister, author, healing sound therapist, light language workshop facilitator, and galactic practitioner of light codes. Her shamanic methods help people retrieve and reintegrate multidimensional soul aspects. She does this through her books, light language sessions, seminars, coaching, and other spiritual services.

A graduate of American Institute of Holistic Theology, Yvonne holds a Bachelor of Science in Metaphysics. During her five-year involvement with Toastmasters International, Yvonne earned the recognition of Distinguished Toastmaster Award for her exemplary speaking skills. She attained every level of accomplishment the organization offered as well as many awards in speaking competitions.

She is a licensed minister through Universal Life Church. As a light language activator and galactic shaman, she offers coaching to empaths (highly sensitive people), walk-ins, star seeds, and those who are dealing with Ascension symptoms.

Yvonne's books include *Light Language Emerging, Walk-ins Among Us, Whose Stuff is This?, Shifting into Purer Consciousness, More Than Meets the Eye,* and The Sid Series, which is a collection of holistic stories for children. You can purchase these books from her website, weare1inspirit.com.

Yvonne became a walk-in on December 3, 1999. She has had multiple soul experiences including a soul exchange and a soul infusion with her higher self. She brought in the gift of light language in 1994.

She believes that our souls are an accumulation of each and every one of our life experiences. We originate with Source Energy but have many, many lifetimes on this and other planets. Yvonne believes that since she holds a piece of each place that she has visited or lived, that she is an accumulation of them all. But she does resonate with the Pleiades and Arcturian origins.

Her mission is to be a light bringer and way shower. She says that we are here to help each other to wake up to the truth of who we are, to heal ourselves and the planet. You may reach her via her website at weare1inspirit.com.

Yvonne's Story

I will never forget that night. It was December 3, 1999. I had gone to a movie with a friend. This activity was something new because I had been so busy trying to be a supermom, raising a family and being the perfect wife, that I had not spent much time with people outside of the spiritual community. So, going to the movie with a new friend was a big deal for me. When I returned home, and before I could even get in the door of the house, I was met by my husband who immediately began questioning me about where I had been. He knew where I was, and it was only 10:00 pm. We got into a heated discussion, all the way into the house and into our bedroom. I couldn't understand why he was yelling at me. The argument was so horrific, and I became so emotionally distraught that I literally passed out and dropped to the floor. I don't know exactly how long I was out. I could hear my husband and daughter talking to me and to each other, but their voices seemed so far away. That is when the walk-in happened.

I was on the floor, paralyzed and afraid. Then I heard a voice say, "Things will be alright. This is for your own good. You will understand later." I didn't know if I was hearing God, an angel, or who was speaking to me, but the voice immediately sent calming waves of unconditional love and peace throughout my entire body. I lay there just bathing in this sweet sensation.

When I was able to move, I stood up feeling totally different. I felt stronger, rested and empowered. I also felt oddly detached from the situation, from my husband and daughter. As if nothing had happened, I got ready for bed. I decided to sleep in my son's old room as I could not stand the idea of going to bed with 'that man'.

I don't think I slept at all that night, but I was comforted by a very strong presence which brought in love and sweet peace. It felt amazing. The next morning, I knew what I had to do. I packed a bag and left in such a hurry that I forgot to say goodbye to my daughter. Looking back, I know that I was so detached that I wasn't thinking as a mother or wife. I just knew I had to go. I went to another friend's house that I had only known for a few weeks. After that, my new short-term home was an Economy Inn. Staying there was good for me to rest and recuperate. My dream life supported me with comfort.

Over the next few months, I hardly recognized myself. Everyone noticed the changes. My daughter told me that she did not have to mind me because I was not her mother! My mom did not understand me or anything I was doing. People at church judged me so harshly that I stopped going to church or small group meetings. They couldn't believe that I was divorced. I was living in the Bible Belt of Tennessee and no one, not even me, understood what was happening.

I felt disassociated, and in a zombie-like state. I had been very sick earlier in my life and had experienced a near-death experience. Because of that, I thought that I had died and come back in the same body. I did not believe in reincarnation at the time, so coming back from the dead as a different person was the only acceptable explanation I had for the change in my belief system, habits, and behaviors. I even stopped playing the keyboard which I had enjoyed for most of my life. I felt like I was looking at myself through someone else's eyes. Everything in my life was different. My childhood memories were gone; I only remembered a few snippets. My mom helped to remember bits and pieces of growing up by sharing old photo albums. When I saw the photos, it was as if I was looking at something from a long, long time ago. Slowly some memories returned.

For the first 40 years of my deep southern life, I was enmeshed with the fundamental dogma of religion and lived according to the interpretation of the Bible, my family, society, and church leaders that taught me. Before I had the label to put on me due to my empathic abilities, I was what you call an intercessor in the church, meaning that I carried the burdens of others to the throne of grace (in church terms). It was not uncommon for me to be locked away in my prayer room for half the day, singing, playing keyboards, writing worship songs, interceding, and laying in trance. While praying for others, I empathically took on their suffering until it severely challenged my emotional and physical health.

Once the walk-in has arrived, it begins to clear the old imprinting and the cellular memories that no longer serve the new higher vibrating soul. I believe this clearing attributed the new health issues that I began experiencing. I began having horrible pain throughout my neck, shoulders and back, and I was diagnosed with fibromyalgia. Sometimes it hurt so bad that I felt like I was being ripped apart. My nerves were fried as I watched myself make changes that I would have never done before. People thought I was having a nervous breakdown. I might have agreed if it were not for the inner knowing that God was guiding me through this.

It wasn't until Roni Angel shared her walk-in experience with me that I began to understand that maybe I, too, was a walk-in. I read Ruth Montgomery's book, *Strangers Among Us*, and for the first time since this all began, I began to feel like I understood what was happening to me. As this new realization became my reality, my nervousness and fibromyalgia went away.

During this same time, I was driving by a building that was holding church services. I had had such a bad experience with the last church I attended that I really did not want to go to another one. But every time I drove by, the urge to go grew stronger and my intuition was telling me that it was important for me to at least visit this church. Finally, I decided to go. There, I met a man that ten weeks later I married. The old me would never have married so quickly.

The traditional church beliefs that I firmly held, slowly began to melt away and I was filled with a new expansiveness. I began to understand God in a much bigger way and as the source of all things. We are, each one of us, individual expressions of Source Energy having our own experiences to benefit all. I think that the walk-in process is part of the overall Ascension process. By that, I mean we ascend or progress on an individual basis as we are recollecting fragmented parts of ourselves, and then coming into wholeness. The

Ascension process is about moving upward through less dense timelines and bandwidths. 3D is a denser, egoic, patriarchal, male dominant frequency. As we move into Ascension, we move into a more divine feminine unity where we are helping one another, having less conflict, and moving into a place of acceptance and unconditional love. So, what that looks like for me may be different for someone else, but I think we are headed to that place of unconditional love for ourselves and for others and being able to flow without the racism, bigotry, and judgement that is not part of the Christ Consciousness. The condemnation that we have lived with is what we are ascending out of, and we are coming into more acceptance, a more loving and nurturing expression of our divinity. All of it is multifaceted, so whether we are experiencing walk-ins or soul exchanges or rotations or shifts in consciousness, it is bringing us back to a place of remembering ourselves as one.

Then in 2005, I was diagnosed with a potentially malignant tumor in my colon and would have to have surgery. I had no fear and even my guides reassured me that everything would be okay. In fact, they were going to use this as an opportunity to upgrade my existing walk-in while I was under. This time, more of my higher self entered and no doubt assisted in my healing process. And my soul was better prepared to handle the massive energy changes that would continue to come. Despite these wonderful changes I was grieving and felt as if I would be going away. What I have discovered years later is that it was the former soul aspect that had left. For all these years, it had been hanging out, recharging, and observing until the appropriate time to go.

The embodiment or joining of soul aspects is a natural part of the Ascension process. Therefore, anyone who is becoming more sentient and spiritually aware may naturally have shifts or walk-ins. As we vibrate in alignment with the frequencies of higher bandwidths, we take on the identity of ourselves in those realms. We may still have memories of our former soul aspects, but the trauma associated with that lifetime is neutralized.

In 2013, I embodied another soul aspect and began using light language in my client coaching sessions with walk-ins. Big shifts started happening for me and my clients afterward. The codes and the vector movement of light language supports the physical body, the personality, and soul aspects in the quest for unity or homecoming to Source.

Jeremie Leckron

Jeremie was born in Glendale, California in 1943. She spent her childhood years in Salt Lake City, Utah and on Hopi Third Mesa in Arizona. Her undergraduate education was at the University of Utah where she received a master's degree in anthropology. Later, she attended the University of California, Berkeley where she received her doctorate in psychology and postdoctoral work in religion from the California Institute for Integral Studies. She considers herself a lifetime student of the work of Carl Jung and Rudolf Steiner.

Growing up, she spent her summers with her grandmother on Third Masa, learning the old ways of the people until her grandmother's passing. She then resumed her training with her uncle and great aunt. Jeremie is the seventh daughter of the seventh daughter of the seventh daughter and to the Hopi people, that is highly significant.

Some of the teachers Jeremie apprenticed with include: Chief Dan Evehema (Hopi); Sun Bear (Chippewa); Fire Dog (Navajo); Grandfather Rolling Thunder (Shoshone/Cherokee); Grandmother Snowdeer (Olgala Sioux); Grandmother Moon Shadow (Zuni); Her Grandmother, Violet (Komokpu kroanix) (Hopi, Third Masa); Her Great Aunt, Tish (1/2 Hopi 1/2 Anglo); and Her Uncle Tom Banyanca (Hopi, Second Mesa).

She was given the name Grandmother Medicine Song (So'o

Ngahu Taawi) at a council held in Zuni, Pueblo in the summer of 2017. She was also given permission to share her knowledge of the medicine teachings she holds in the oral tradition to a global community online. She takes the title of 'grandmother' very seriously. Grandmother (So'o) is both a term of endearment as well as a sign of respect bestowed upon a woman.

Jeremie is a spiritual teacher (and is mine), a storyteller and a ceremonial leader. Her heritage is both Anglo Saxon and Hopi American Indian. She says she was blessed to grow up in two worlds: the world of her white Mormon ancestry and that of her maternal Hopi Indian ancestry. Beginning in 2019, at the age of 75, she decided that now is the time to make the necessary bridge to a larger global community by co-creating a website with the help of a few students. The website hopiwisdomteachings.com provides Hopi Wisdom Teachings. Jeremie is a soul exchange walk-in.

Jeremie's Story

I was five or six years old, and highly precocious. That year I was convinced that my parents had hidden the Christmas presents in our barn loft, so I went in search of them. We had horses so there were stalls inside the barn. It had a hard-packed dirt floor, scattered with hay from feeding the horses. I took a ladder and began to climb up to the loft, which was around two storeys high. As I reached the top the ladder began to swing backwards and we both hit the floor. The back of my skull was crushed. I don't remember who found me, but I was told that my mother became hysterical and neighbors were called to help. My father was at work. Somehow, I was taken to the Latter-Day Saints Hospital in Salt Lake City, Utah. Shortly after my arrival, the hospital called my father to inform him that I had been pronounced dead. It was approximately 45 minutes before my father could get there. When he arrived, I was on a gurney in the morgue. I am told he dropped his head down and began to cry. Apparently, I opened my eyes and said to him, "Sir, why are you crying?" I had no awareness of who he was or where I was. Also, by the time my father arrived, my skull was completely healed. I have no memories of the event or prior to this time, but I was young so if I forgot things. It was okay because I was still building my memory.

During this same time, I was just beginning my journeys to go to Third Masa to study with my grandmother. As soon as everyone felt I was well enough my visits resumed. I didn't know what had happened, but my grandmother did. She understood that I was a walk-in because this is part of her Hopi beliefs and part of their tradition. They didn't call them walk-ins. The translation means 'soul exchange', or 'huuya'. When she introduced the concept to me, she held up two fingers, the index and middle finger, and this is where my life memory really starts. I can't really remember the incident myself so this is all family hearsay. That happened over 70 years ago.

I only came to really understand the gravity of it all I was after reading Ruth Montgomery's book, *Strangers Among Us*. That is when I really began to put the pieces together with my Grandmother's teachings, and things became clear to me.

The Hopi people generally believe that their galactic origins are the Pleiades. So I consider myself a Pleiades star seed being. Many of the teachings that I give talk about them. The Kachinas are star beings. The teachings I give about the Vibratory Centers that the Hopis practice is Pleiadian in its origins. It's completely vibratory. It has to do with sound and color and guardians. The whole notion of the ancient 20 count teachings is directly out of the Pleiades. Their energy is very feminine. It's very artistic. Typically, it's very intuitive and very telepathic.

The Pleiades would be considered my star origin and that goes directly back to the ties with the Sun Clan of the Hopi. My grandmother passed this information down to me from her mother. And she received the information from her mother and so on down through the lineage.

The story of my Earth lineage has also been passed down from generation to generation and I will share with you an abbreviated version of my most recent lineage. When the Mormon missionaries first arrived at the Mesas, they were trying to convert the people to Mormonism. It is the brief of some Mormon forefathers that the Hopi people (as well as some other American Indians) are the lost 12th tribe of Israel. Because of this belief, it has always been very important to the Mormons to send Missionaries to the American Indian Reservations. My great grandmother, who was of the Bear Clan, wanted nothing to do with them. The only course of action to take was to leave the Mesas. She gathered a small group together, including my grandmother and mother, and left. They ended up somewhere in the Grand Canyon. There is a story that tells of the Hopi emerging from a hole or a sipapu (sipapus are found at the bottom center of the kivas for people to climb in and out of) in the bottom of the Grand Canyon. This was at the beginning of the Third World after having lived underground with the Ant people. But that's another story.

This group lived in the Grand Canyon for five to six years. Some died. The rest were tired and hungry. That is when the missionaries found them. This was in the early 1900s. My great grandmother was converted to Mormonism, and married the man who converted her. That man became my great grandfather. The family adopted my grandmother.

After the walk-in, things started to happen to me that were really profound. There was one incident that occurred at the Mormon church that I was attending with my parents. I had a terrifying, pre-cognitive awareness (vision) of one of the leaders committing horrific acts and I screamed. My father took me out of the sanctuary and I explained what I had just witnessed.

My father was my Mormon mentor and he very much wanted to know what was going on with his daughter. This happened in the late 1940s and there was little information known about this type of event/behavior. My father searched for answers and ended up contacting the Edgar Cayce Institute. He found that there was a research facility in Colorado.

I remember my father putting me in the car and driving me to the facility. It was just a home, not a big facility, but I remember them testing me. They conducted a lot of cognitive and pre-cognitive awareness tests. This was a lot for a young child but I continued going there from the time I was around five or six until I was almost 14 years old. That's when my grandmother died and my great aunt began taking me to the reservation.

Because of the intensity of the work, I still have a strong memory of the kind of testing that they did. They used cards. At that time, we didn't have the technology that we do today, so we did a lot of testing with me sitting in one room and the tester in another. Sometimes they would hold up a card and in the other room and I would identify it. They ran a battery of tests day-in and day-out, as well as meditations. Finally my father took me back home and said, "No more tests." He wanted me to live as normal a life as possible.

All the while, I continued to do my spiritual work with my grandmother at Hopi land, until my great aunt took over.

I believe that walk-ins arrive at a predetermined time. In my case, my body had to be a little older so that it could contain the new, high-vibrational energy that was coming. This energy could not unfold or begin to release its true potential until I was older, more mature. I believe walk-ins have a higher vibration than the original soul, so the body has to be at a certain vibration just to be able to hold that energy. Walk-ins arrive to people at different ages so their physical body can hold the higher vibration. In certain cases, the walk-in soul has to wait until the time is right, or a certain level of maturity has been achieved, before it can begin to reveal itself. In my case, I think I arrived at a young age because of the genetic connection with the Hopi tribe and my Hopi people. I believe that every walk-in has a purpose. I've always felt that my purpose was to be a bridge between these two very different worlds. You could even think of me as a bridge between the world of spirit and the world of humanity. Maybe that is part of the reason that I am a walk-in and why I came in so young - to integrate at a young age so I could help others with their process.

From my perspective, when someone experiences a true walk-in, it is a soul exchange, it's permanent. There is no going back, ever. No reversal. It is an amazing process. I am unfamiliar with any other type of walk-in as my teachings say a walk-in is a soul exchange. I do know there are other types of soul experiences that people have but from my perspective they are not walk-ins. That doesn't mean their experience is more or less impactful. Just different.

I believe that we come here with a purpose. I don't believe in accidents. I think there's a plan and if we make the right choices, then the plan unfolds.

I had a vision or a dream when I was in Asheville, North Carolina, of a piece of property. I didn't know where it was, but chief Dan had always wanted me to go to Kentucky. So in January 1999 I did a road trip with Davis, my husband until he passed in 2009. We found the property that I have dreamed of, in a little town in Kentucky. We purchased the property and moved there, though I didn't know anybody and there was no obvious reason to be there. But I knew that this move was important.

In the spring of 2000, I needed to get the word out about the work I was doing, but I didn't have a way of advertising myself. There was no one there doing anything similar, nor with the background that I had. I took out an ad in the Yellow Pages and pretty soon I received a phone call from a young woman, you, who was living in southwestern Virginia. I returned your call, introduced myself and asked how I could help. The very first words out of your mouth were, "I think I'm going crazy." Then we talked and I said, "You know, I don't think you're going crazy. I think you've got some questions." And we made an appointment. You were in the process of moving to the town I was in to take a job.

When the day of your appointment arrived, here you came, up the step to my door. You were this teeny tiny person. You had your back to the door and the whole door just filled up with light. I remember this so well. The light was almost blinding. You came in and sat, and we started talking. As we did, the light got really big as you started talking. Then, it just kind of came down and settled in.

You began to explain what was going on in your life and I said that I thought you were a walk-in. You should have seen your face. You had no idea what I was talking about.

Because of my grandmother's teachings and the fact that I had lived in California and had been a part of many spiritual organizations, I knew a lot more about this. I had been working in the evolution of the spiritual new age movement since the 1960s and you, like a lot of people, had never heard of a walk-in.

Like I say, I do not believe in accidents. You were the only person that responded to that ad. It was strange because I knew I had to place it. But not surprising, as we are all connected.

I believe that we are all part of the Creator and that our souls are an expression of the Creator. This expression is our divine spark. Our spirit self is what I would call our essence of the Creator. Our souls are the masks that we wear, our personality for this lifetime. And are so very connected to Earth, to our Earth walk.

When we come here, I think our spirit and maybe our spirit family, grandmother, grandfather our family origin helps to make the decision to incarnate. Maybe we need to have a full life experience or there needs to be a life experience in order for us to progress or there needs to be a life experience because we have a particular wisdom that is necessary on Earth at this time. So this spirit group helps to choose an earthly father and a mother. They help choose the right physical body. Then we will help the soul aspect go into that body for that particular lifetime or for as long as the message that we are given or the learning that we need to receive or the experiences we need to grow and have taken place. At the end of our life, when we drop the robe, my belief is that my soul essence, my soul self is going to go back and join with spirit and go back to essence. And I may or may not decide in that essence form that there needs to be another incarnation.

In the Hopi tradition, when we come into human form, the soul does not enter the body until the moment of birth. It enters the body through the fontanelle, the soft spot in the top of the head. There is a belief that while the baby is in the womb, the possibility for life and the essence of life is made possible through the connection within the mother. It's purely physical at that point; the soul does not enter until the moment of birth and exits at the moment of death unless there is a walk-in experience.

One of the teachings of soul spirit essence (higher self as most call it) is that everything drops down into soul, and soul drops down into human life. At the end of life, the soul goes back up into spirit essence and shares all of its information with all of the overlay of the spiritual essence. Therefore everything goes up.

In the prayers that I say and in the prayers that the Hopi say, we don't necessarily pray to God. We say grandmothers and grandfathers because we are talking to our spirit essence family. And so it's, "Grandmothers and Grandfathers, can you hear me? Here I am. Remember me. I am a part of you." So the individual part of us never dies but it is a piece of the greater collective that gathers information and has experiences and has its own particular talents. And that's really what the Hopi belief is too.

I think that we are all on what I call the Ascension path or the path to higher change. Every billionth of a second, everything changes. Everything. You and I are different people every second of every day. Earth is a new Earth every billionth of a second. Right now, as you read this, we are evolving into new human beings that are evolving into new Earth. And we are helping people to get there.

The new human being is going to be much higher vibrationally, much more evolved. It will almost come to a point that we're not going to need a body. When people talk about the light body and this energetic body, that's our etheric body. But, it's been with us all the time. It is my belief that what we are really going to do is drop our physical body by vibrating ever higher and move into our authentic body. We won't have that lower fourth aspect. We'll only need our etheric body. As we evolve every second, I think that we're going to draw up, move through this lower, denser physical vibration, because it is that vibration that is using up all the resources of the Earth.

We cannot continue to do the same things in the same way, because if we do we're going to eat up the Earth. She will not be able to survive. She is struggling right now. We are drawing energy from her etheric body, living off her life force. So we are becoming more highly evolved so that we don't have to do that. That's when we're going to see this new human and this new Earth because we're going to be existing more in balance. We will then be using more in our etheric body than we are in our physical. When we talk about the new Earth and the new humans, and all the other 'newness' things, the newness time is now. The change needs to be now. We need to be way more aware that one, we are totally insignificant, and two, we are simply a part of everything that is. everything changes every billionth of a second based upon all of the information that is coming forward. No one is going to do this for us. We have to be the change. Remember, we are the ones we have been waiting for. We have to walk the beauty way.

Miguel Mendonça

Following his work as a researcher, author and campaigner on sustainability, Miguel wrote a series of books on the field of consciousness and contact. He has written seven books to date: *Meet the Hybrids* (with Barbara Lamb); *We Are the Disclosure*; *Being with the Beings*; *Quick! Act Normal* (as Michael Ford); *Feed-in Tariffs*; *A Renewable World* (with Prof. Herbert Girardet), and *Powering the Green Economy* (with Dr. David Jacobs and Dr. Benjamin Sovacool).

In 2019 he experienced a jumper walk-in for three weeks. He is the only person that I interviewed that kept real-time notes during this period on what he was experiencing emotionally, mentally and physically.

His website is wearethedisclosure.com.

Miguel's Story

On January 7th 2019, I woke up different. The first thing I noticed is that I couldn't curse. I realized that I couldn't even think of words. I was baffled because anyone that knows me knows that cursing is a lively component of my vocabulary. That day I was talking with my closest friends, Matt (Thomas, from *Meet the Hybrids*) and Dave, who also swear like sailors. Every time they said variations of the 'F' word, it physically hurt to hear it. It was bizarre. I knew something was up.

I just didn't know what.

In the next few days I realized that I was seeing the world very differently. I'm not sure how long it took before the possibility of a walk-in experience occurred to me, but I know I was never in fear about that possibility. My altered consciousness was in fact uncharacteristically serene.

I felt the desire to attempt to work out what was happening, and to whom. Was Miguel still in there, or had he been somehow overlaid with a new consciousness? I began to journal, which then developed into a major research effort. As part of this I put together a complete narrative account of all my metaphysical experiences, writing over 40,000 words in under three weeks. I wanted to see if I could understand how I got there.

But who was the 'I' in that sentence? The more I contemplated the question, the more I felt a familiarity around the consciousness. It took me back to an event which occurred when I was three years old. It was the summer of 1976 and I had just moved to England from Rhodesia, with my parents and sister. We were staying with my Auntie Joan in Eastbourne, and I was alone in her living room. Suddenly I was aware of a presence, all around me. I could see nothing, but I knew something was there. And I was aware that it knew that I was aware of its presence.

And then I became aware that our physical senses only perceive certain layers of reality, but beyond those senses exist many other layers that are available to each other at all times, if one is able to connect by other means. I now understand that moment as a crash course in multidimensional awareness, despite lacking the language to express it at the time. That is the last thing I remember about that event, but it was so profound that it has shaped my entire life. I mention it because the energy of what occupied me had a familiarity, and I have wondered if the two events are closely connected.

One crazy moment from the walk-in experience took place in the center of Bristol one dark, cold and rainy evening. I was with a close friend in the city when something drew my attention to a little sign inside a pizzeria. It read 'Gluten free pizza bases available'. Due to dietary restrictions I hadn't eaten pizza in nearly ten years, so I had to enquire. They had vegan cheese too so I ordered one and waited for it to cook. We were sitting facing Park Street, a busy shopping street in central Bristol. You see across the street to the Council House and College Green, and over to Bristol Cathedral and the Central Library on the far side. The architecture of the latter is beautiful. I remember staring at them thinking, 'This is so crazy. I'm on another planet in the skin of a local. I'm watching regular humans living their lives. I'm seeing these buildings and these neon lights and I'm looking at all the different types of architecture and the different people drifting up and down the street. I'm sitting inside a pizzeria having this experience and these people have no idea of what is happening inside me!' It was like being a spy. I could experience it as the planetary tourist, but also as Miguel, seeing it as absolutely mad, but in the fun sense.

Obviously situations like this were tripping me out, so I decided to start talking to some well-versed people in the field, as well as sharing it with friends and family to get their perspective on what might be happening with me. I remember talking to Matt, Dave and Lou, and my mother, who was incredibly sweet about it, though she knows very little about this realm. Her love was enough to bridge any gap in understanding, and that was a beautiful experience. I then talked with Robert Fullington, Jacquelin Smith, Barbara Lamb, Mary Rodwell, Leo Sprinkle and CristiAnne Quiros, among others. Then I started researching to see if there might be walk-in groups and I found one on Facebook. In the journal below I describe what happened with that.

I also reference a dream in the journal, which I'll share here, for context. It came some weeks or months before the experience. I was at Hadlow College in Kent, where I had studied Landscape Management in the mid-90s. It was the last day of term and I was leaving for the summer. Then a moment later I was going into the canteen and some classmates were asking, "Hey, how was your summer?" I said, "What are you talking about? Summer's just starting." In the canteen everything was different to how it had been a moment ago. I tried to leave but the former exit had now become an entrance only. I was spinning out. Where had the time gone? Then, a young woman who worked there saw me, and understood what was happening. I got a coffee and she took me outside. She led me down a yellow brick pathway that spiralled down to the base of a Norman castle. I was freaking out by this point, because I knew I was a walk-in and felt totally lost. I said, "I can't do this."

So I squatted down and whipped my index finger in a circle, creating a little dust devil that rapidly grew into a towering tornado. It began lifting us up through the branches of an enormous tree and the woman and I were reaching out to each other, trying to hold hands, while guiding ourselves up through the branches. The crown grew denser at the top and we pushed through to find ourselves by railroad tracks. A beautiful, ornate yellow and orange train came by so we floated up the side and onto the roof and rode it went to the end of the track, where it reached a turntable. We floated off onto a circular brick wall around the turntable area and found ourselves looking out over the incredible city below us, which I think is based on Ljubljana in Slovenia. I recognize it from a work trip a decade earlier. In both realities the city was surrounded by spectacular mountains.

I took the woman's hand and we flew over the city, down into the streets, then into the shops. For some reason I wanted to buy a battery and it only cost me five pence, which I thought was really cheap. We then flew out and up and past a gigantic waterfall plunging from mountains of unreal scale. As we continued our flight, it started getting colder and began snowing. I said something to her like, "Oh, cool. Just up ahead there's the …" and then I woke up. We were going from level to level in the dream, from a world I did not understand to one that I did. It was some months before the jumper experience, and perhaps it was preparing me for what was to come. But honestly, I don't imagine you can be prepared for something like that. I know that some time after the dream I had said out loud that I welcomed a walk-in, that I was happy to leave this body. I do in some ways wish it had been a permanent arrangement, though I can see I still have things to contribute here.

I will now share some of the most pertinent parts of the journal, before adding some concluding comments.

Today is Thursday the 24th of January 2019, day 17. I spent the last couple of days reading through the first nine chapters of this exploration. It's been a lot of fun, actually, to see how the experience has developed since beginning the writing on the 8th of January. It is hard to tell at this point how much contradiction there may be, as my perspective is shifting continually. The one constant is the feeling of difference. I simply do not feel like the Miguel prior to January 7th. The review has also been useful in finding the views of others that have most resonated.

Jacquelin Smith:

"A higher-level, larger, more evolved aspect of your soul has come in - the higher portion of energy. And this is clearing out the older aspects of the personality of Miguel; the old construct is dissolving. It is not negative, but it could feel scary; it could feel like you are being taken over. But it is a purifying, a releasing of the personality in some sense. But you're here on Earth, you're in a body, so there has to be some kind of construct for the personality. This is part of your own evolutionary process as a soul, an opportunity to experience this kind of evolution in a more involved way, now. This aspect also came in to help give you a way to stay here for now, to remain here on Earth so that your soul can continue to do work, to express, to be creative, to love. It's like your soul is bringing you in a level of energy physically, as well as expanding you creatively and in other ways to continue here - which is awesome. This is what happens to a number of people. It is creating a balance. Miguel is not gone, but is more in the background, as the other aspect is making over and integrating. It is a co-consciousness - creating balance and integration. I feel really excited for you. Miguel is not going to totally disappear - people will adjust to who you are. And I want to welcome you as a new consciousness on this planet. I love and embrace all of you."

Barbara Lamb:

"It sounds like you're really having an experience of enlightenment. Over the centuries people have talked and written about enlightenment, and it really sounds like this is a wonderful enlightenment experience. I'm fascinated by your thinking back about Miguel's personality and reactions to things and relationships as if you're a whole different being. There's a separation in a sense from you and Miguel. And yet here you are living in Miguel. That must be really fascinating."

Dr. CristiAnne Quiros:

"I think people used to call this 'possession', like it was something bad, rather than someone coming into your house and working with you. They're a companion, or they're learning about life on this planet, what it's like to be a human being. So they're looking around and trying to get you to show them how things are. At the same time they're downloading stuff that they know to you too. So it's like a back-and-forth conversation of higher planes. It's like if we are trying to understand dolphins, and we can go into their body and live their experience for a time, we would see things totally differently to what we would see from the outside. To be a dolphin and have that dolphin experience for five days, you would have a totally different consciousness about dolphins, and other fish, and the ocean environment. It would change so much. So it's not necessary to join for a lifetime. Sometimes they just come and hang out for a while to learn. And then they move on and take that knowledge someplace else."

"If it's feeling good for you, and working for you, then enjoy it while it's there. Like anything else in life. You never know how long it's going to be there, like your house, or your car or your job. If you live each day as if you might lose it, then it makes you appreciate it, and really connect with it. Love it, and when it needs to go, gracefully let it go. And that's really hard to do, with anything we've learned from, or are enjoying. It's like the empty bowl gets filled. Be willing to empty out and let go, trusting that the bowl will be refilled, and maybe with totally different content. Just enjoy it. Write about it. It seems like that's the way it's supposed to be."

"There are a lot of stories that sound way out there, and unless you've had experiences you might think, 'This person's nuts.' But if you have had experiences, oh my God, there are layers and subtleties, all those things you were talking about. And yes, it's all of that. But it's like being able to perceive different wavelengths. Not all TV sets can get the same channels, not all radios can get the same stations.

[...] So this integration of another being, it's like a wavelength, like being able to pick up a signal that not everybody else can. It comes directly to you. It sits in there and feeds off information. And sometimes people can't handle this shift.

"What a gift. It may not be anything you did, but it may have been the right time, to see if you can handle it. Who knows? It may be higher self, it may be a portion of who you are, it may be another energy coming into you, amping up everything. Just enjoy it."

There are several observations here which resonate. Jacquelin's sense that this is an aspect of myself. Barbara seeing this is a form of enlightenment. CristiAnne discusses ideas around visitors sharing consciousness, experience and information, and the idea of being able to tune into two wavelengths at once.

Some of these are personal - aspects of my soul, and some are external - other 'beings' popping in briefly to learn, teach and share. But the real question I am left with, at this point, is that of agency. To what extent is this my doing? Is it just a gift bestowed by a separate agency, for reasons as yet unclear to me? Or is this part of me, which I had on some level agreed to join with? Is it just a brief teach-in, a living workshop for consciousness sharing? And how could I tell the difference?

Right now it feels less like Miguel has entirely gone. But I do not know whether or not that is due to experiencing so many of his regular patterns and processes. If this is an upgrade, then it is not a total replacement, and clearly I am able to experience the full sweep of Miguel's emotions, if in a somewhat muted, detached fashion. Here is an example. I spoke recently with someone who claimed to be researching walk-ins. When I explained the experience thus far, she immediately belittled it, laughing in a derisory manner, and telling me that it had only been a couple of weeks, and she had been working with this for almost a decade. Over the next half hour she went into anger repeatedly, scolding me for my attitudes, reactions to my situation, word choice, responses to her and so on. She seemed keen to make everything an argument if I did not agree immediately and entirely with her 'advice'. It was tortuous. And shocking, as she has set herself up ostensibly to 'help' people going through these huge shifts.

This has of course given me something to work with - my first negative response. At the time I had to remind myself not to fall into Miguel's habits of mind, and submit to the rushes of adrenaline caused by feeling attacked and bullied. Discussing this event with other people, one view was that maybe it was an agreement between us, to give us something we both needed. Another was that it could be that she must be left free to give other people the same negative experience so that they might gain something from it. Right now, Friday the 25th of January, I am still undecided on whether or not to message the person concerned and share my observations on the experience, if not for her then for others who might be damaged by her behavior. But, the likely outcome is a smearing on social media, a rant on Facebook. And it always seems rather crude and lacking in self-respect when people engage in trading insults in such settings. So there is a moral dilemma there. Do I willingly attract more of her negativity, on the slight chance that she may be willing to look at herself and do the work necessary to improve her manner when dealing with vulnerable people?

In the 'cosmic' field, this lady is one of five people I have met who have that angry, bullying, controlling personality. None of these people are happy. The redirection of our unhappiness toward others is, as a human, apparently all but unavoidable. This is in part due to living in cultures that avoid self-examination. We are not commonly taught in school to do meditation, to learn mindfulness, to develop honesty with ourselves and others. This is apparently not valued by those that make policy. There is in general an issue with truth on this planet. I researched and wrote a novel about truth, and while I never felt it publishable as a story, the process itself was very illuminating and affecting. I shared the manuscript with two other people and both of them quote it to me occasionally. It was called Truth Time, and now seems somewhat prescient, thinking about the #metoo movement. Suddenly there is a pouring out of truths that had been kept hidden for reasons of shame and fear. It is exciting to think where this may lead us, though the main takeaway from my research is that humans have a major problem with truth. And it is killing us. Political systems are filled with so many lies it is breathtaking. Given that political processes everywhere are captured by existing wealth and power, this should be no surprise. 'The people' are not the real constituency of the politicians, certainly beyond a certain threshold of power. There may be exceptions, but this is, I believe it is fair to say, the rule.

By contrast to the above experience, yesterday I had two wonderful exchanges. The first was with Dr R. Leo Sprinkle, a pioneer in working with experiencers, during his time as a professor of psychology at the University of Wyoming. In 1980 he founded the Rocky Mountain UFO Conference, an annual meeting for experiencers to tell their stories. When I told him my story so far, he asked a few questions on how it started, if anything happened the night before, and then he said that he asked his guides if there is any information that might be of use. And the message he got was, 'He is waiting for a female.' He asked if it had any meaning and I said, "Well, it's kind of the story of my life." He cracked up laughing. I then explained that in the walk-in dream I had, there was a young woman who acted as guide to me, before I took her into my world. He then asked how I live through each day with this new experience. Do I focus on it, or try to apply it to what goes on around me? I explained that it is allowing me to see Miguel's mechanisms, habits, processes and history, with a clarity that Miguel never had. And that I've been recording, discussing and studying the process. I told him that I have received several theories from others on what may be occurring, including interaction with the higher self, or a walk-in. He asked if I'm any closer to complete understanding, or whether it is something I have to accept as I go along. I said that I am simply documenting and analyzing in order to make this useful to myself and others, but in some ways this feels like a continuation of Miguel's sense of social mission. That was kind of his thing, but at this stage I'm not sure what my thing is. At present it's just to make the adjustment, but after this I don't know what happens. I said that in terms of relationships I feel the same. Certainly the people I love and care about. There is an unfiltered, uncomplicated love for these people.

Leo said it's almost as if I'm being taken on a journey, as a participant, but am becoming somewhat enlightened, evolving and transcending as I go.

I said that it's hard to tell because I have a theory that in a sense it is not the original person that get enlightened. The new state is so different that the old version does not get to experience or enjoy it. The person is so changed that the way they experience and enjoy will be different in fundamental ways. So with my situation, it is just how it is. It is difficult to celebrate it. I can recognize that it is a good thing, and it feels good, but it doesn't feel so incredible that I want to shout it from the rooftops. It's a much more subtle appreciation, rather than a firework display of joy.

He asked if it feels as if I'm becoming something beyond human, or does it feel like it's expanding or developing my human potential. I said that's interesting because I know Miguel never really felt human. So it's almost like I don't know enough about humans to know if this is a thing that humans experience. I don't have memory of being for example a Pleiadian, and being here to do something specific. Perhaps I scrubbed my memory so that I could. Unknown. This made Leo wonder if this is part of a process of moving all people in this world forward. He asked if others feel they are going through something similar. I told him that numerous people have told me that they have indeed gone through significant shifts in the last month or two, leading to several hypotheses relating to a preparation of sorts. This could be towards dealing with catastrophic or otherwise consciousness-shifting large-scale events. This could involve Earth changes, mass ET contact or other such events. In Strangers Among Us, Ruth Montgomery's guides told her that a nuclear war and a pole shift were both coming by the end of the 20th century. Neither came to pass, certainly in this timeline. But who knows what may be coming our way. It feels to me that there is much left to run in the human story, though what nightmares may manifest within it, we do not know.

A friend of Leo's was saying to him that Trump is precipitating a transformative process, through the pressure that he is causing to build up in the American people. He said that not only do I seem to be going through a transformation myself, but that I am helping others through their process. I said that I hope so, that it has to mean something. That it is not without purpose. And if there is purpose to it, then it doesn't take much to step back and consider to whom this is happening. A construct that is a writer, researcher, analyst, someone who talks to people experiencing all kinds of different states of being, encountering all sorts of metaphysical and spiritual phenomena. So it feels like this is happening to the right person in terms of being able to document, analyze and report.

I then voiced interest in the idea that I am 'waiting for a female.' He said that I may be waiting for a female process, as it seems I am incorporating the attributes of the goddess. The typical description of a god is strong, firm, whereas the goddess is often described as more open, fluid, so that the process is always changing, but the product - our human awareness - continues to expand.

I said to my girlfriend that I feel this is a feminine energy that has come in. The awareness of that had settled into place the previous weekend. And this is constantly in process, so it takes moments of quiet reflection for certain things to become clear. So I'm thinking I should be getting back into meditation to see what comes in. Leo observed that it is as if I am the voice that I am hearing. Like both processes are being experienced at the same time.

I described it as a two-track consciousness, like I can be in one or the other, but not quite both simultaneously. And it's like I don't know how much of Miguel to keep alive. Do I need to finish up things that are recognizably Miguel, and then step into this other aspect entirely? Leo said that he feels he has to accept my situation, because he can't seem to analyze it, it is beyond his intellectual awareness. I said that I sympathize - I feel the same. The only thing I can do is to just be, and as illumination arrives, document it. And there is value in that. More so than in simply publishing a one page document at the end that says 'here's the final answer'. If I was looking for answers I would be more interested in looking at other people's processes.

Leo then painted the picture he was seeing in his mind's eye, that of a little kid and an old man. The old man can incorporate the kid, but the kid cannot incorporate the old man. He had the sense that I am the same but very different.

I said that feels true to an extent, though there are limitations in what I can access from Miguel. Because I just am different. I can see Miguel's mechanisms, but I can't experience them. I can try, but it would just be an act. In a sense I feel like I'm walking around in a Miguel costume.

Leo said it's strange and beautiful at the same time. My view is that it's been an oddly neutral experience, as if I am embodying that neutral observer being that I first experienced at age three. Like it moved into Miguel's body, having patiently waited since 1976 until 2019 when he finally said okay. So I wonder if that same kind of consciousness that I feel around me now - has it swapped over? Did it take up residence in the body, while Miguel gets to be the neutral observer? It's hard to know, but Miguel's consciousness certainly needed a rest.

We then talked about age. Leo said that his body is 88 years old, but some say his mind is adolescent, and others say it's childish. But his spirit feels ageless. When he talks with others of like mind, he hears the view that the shift of consciousness that is underway will transform everyone. But right now he feels anxious, yet accepting at the same time. Afraid, yet courageous. As in my situation, getting rid of the old and welcoming the new. He is told by his guides that the entire Earth and everything on it is changing, moving from one level of awareness to the next, and he hopes it happens soon, ending with his customary, "Yeehaw!"

Afterwards I spoke with Wendy Wolfe, a light language singer with whom I made a music track last year, and she had an interesting take. She said she has experienced what I'm going through on a fairly regular basis.

"The way I understand it, from my guides and listening to Bashar, it's as if we finally understand that our mind is not our consciousness, that it exists within our consciousness and we have multiple minds within that consciousness."

She said that one day she woke up and it was as if she was being herself from a different perspective. It now happens on a pretty regular basis, but it's more intentional. It's a function of her consciousness. She paraphrased Bashar, saying, "It's not really someone new walking in, it's just your consciousness is looking at this from a different perspective, and you as a consciousness are becoming aware that this is what is going to happen to you. You will be able to see how you create time. How time is flexible and malleable and you're going to be able to see yourself from different perspectives.

"And for all of us who are connecting to other multidimensional aspects of ourselves, it's not that we're seeing ourselves through their eyes, it's that we're matching the frequency and being able to see ourselves from a different direction. Because everything is frequency, vibration. So once you start to pick apart the physics of reality, the things we are trying to apply this logic to become illogical. And this is why they can't be with us yet, because it starts to fall apart and we begin to see the 'blueprint' reality of how you're creating it, and you're able to see it from different points of view. We're trying to come close to it without freaking ourselves out. Some of us can handle it, but most cannot."

So there it is. A great deal of information from some very experienced individuals. Reading it back, it is interesting how 'I' was able to frame things either from the strong Miguel perspective - as in the discussion about the novel Truth Time, or the soft Miguel perspective, as in the majority of the piece. I mean that I could get closer to Miguel's core perspective when I discussed things from his past, things that defined him.

CristiAnne's comment about gracefully letting it go also struck me. The desire to slip back into that experience is powerful. It was so peaceful compared to my usual life, which has most emotions cranked way up. It brings to mind the post-meditation clarity and calm. It's like the difference between the raw and the refined versions of myself. It seems clear that a blend of the two would serve me well. Can I stir that other aspect, and bring it into alignment with the rest of Miguel? There are pros and cons, undoubtedly. In a sense I would have to be willing to let go of Miguel, as I knew him. The ego immediately freaks out at the idea. So I feel pulled in two different directions. Perhaps it will simply pop back in at some point, and circumvent the ego.

The most potent desire is to gain full understanding of the experience. Who was involved, and why? What triggered it? What was Miguel's role, and that of the 'other'? Was it connected to the spirit of '76? Perhaps there is a good reason I do not know, but as a researcher, a questioner, it's particularly frustrating. It's about self-knowledge, after all. Most people reading this book wish to know themselves better. It's a natural impulse for many of us. We know there is so much more to us, but virtually all of it is beyond the veil. We glimpse some of it, by various means, and for many, it seems it is about that feeling of being homesick, of being cut off from our people. I never felt that I was a regular human, though I have no sense of a single home, just a sense of coming from a place defined by love and wisdom. Hence, humans have always been strange and frightening to me, despite our capacity for such powerful love and compassion. We are in the midst of a pandemic that is bringing human nature into sharp focus. Fear, paranoia, anger and selfishness, but also love, connection, generosity and selflessness. We can only try to be better versions of ourselves throughout and beyond, and perhaps that was ultimately what my experience offered me.

The Cosmology of the Soul

One of the blessings I have received from this book is the opportunity to meet amazing people. People whom I have connected with and am honored to call friends. I have learned so much from them.

Being a walk-in was a hard concept to wrap my head around. It went against everything that I previously thought was true. My mind was expanded in such a way that at times, I found that I had to just stop thinking and drop into 3D as deep as I could just to feel comfortable and to ground myself. I have expanded over the past 20 years more than I could ever have thought possible. I have expanded even further again, thanks to my new friends.

During the writing of this book, I had the privilege of having sessions with Barbara Lamb, Darlene Van de Grift, Jacquelin Smith, Maia Christine Nartoomid and Rob Gauthier. You will be introduced to Rob, Maya and Darlene in the following section. You heard Jacquelin's story in the previous section and in the foreword you were introduced to Barbara. I was enlightened by these sessions and want to share with you the profound effect they had on my life. The truth is, that these sessions helped set me free in my search for my multidimensional family and home. They also helped broaden my understanding of the origins and nature of my soul. At times, I have felt so lonely over the past 20 years that all I wanted to do was to go home, wherever that was. Don't get me wrong, I love this planet and its people. I have a wonderful family and I am so blessed to have their love and support in my life but at times, my heart longed to know where my other family was. I had so many questions like, where am I from? Do I have other family members here? Am I the only one? Am I alone? I was looking for a connection of a different kind. I believe that many of you reading this book may be looking for the same type of connection and answers. If so, I hope this book helps but please, reach out to people who can support you on your journey. Find a teacher, have a session, meditate, pray, connect with your guides.

For me, the truth that I heard from the lips of others during my sessions helped me validate my origins and brought me peace. I discovered that I have lived for a long, long time. I began my journey in the angelic realm and have lived numerous lives as a Pleiadian, Sirian, Arcturian, Mantis and in the Andromedan system, and possibly more. I learned that I am in the soul lineage of Thoth and I discovered that between lifetimes, I integrate back into the Christic energy (Christ Consciousness path of self-awareness and love) and work with Earth's grid system. When I leave this planet I will return to the collective once more.

Prior to embodiment, I lived in a collective composed of all of the star cultures I mentioned above plus a few more. I was in essence operating as my true multidimensional self. My job, if you will, was to assist with the grid system of Earth's collective consciousness by sending unconditional love and spiritual awakening energy to it in order to consciously and energetically prepare the planet and humanity for spiritual Ascension. This was all profound news to me and resonated at the deepest level of my being. It also helped to explain my drives and motivations.

When I incarnated from my spiritual collective, I brought with me the blending of all these cultures but most strongly the traits of the Arcturians. I was told in a meditation in 2012 that I was Arcturian but to hear it from others that had no knowledge of what I had been told was affirming. Not just by one person but many.

It is a very Arcturian attribute that I have chosen to bring forward in this lifetime for it is a path full of urgency and desire to achieve the 'mission'. To 'just do it' and 'get it done'. My life's mission, my passion, my desire to be of service to others, all makes sense to me now.

It is the collective's traits that fuel my desire to be a way shower and to help others on their spiritual evolutionary paths. To be the teacher and adviser. All these energies combined drive me to hold space for the healing of humanity, the Earth and the Ascension, where we will move into higher states of consciousness.

I do not feel nor believe that this information makes me special or unique. It actually humbles me. It is just information. However, knowing the cosmology of my soul, who I am, where I am from and that I am on mission, brings great peace to me.

I do believe, however, that we have all lived, many, many lives. We are all multidimensional beings. I also believe that we are all here on planet Earth at this time to experience the mass spiritual awakening of humanity. We are each special and unique with the gifts and talents we share. Sometimes, it only takes a smile to change someone's day. We never know the ripple effect a simple act of kindness can make. It can be something as simple as music, poetry, art, a healing session, authorship or anything that warms the heart. We all have contributions to make.

Whether you are a CEO or a laborer, we are all the same. We are all one. Some of us just don't remember who we are, yet. But our souls remember. Our souls are pure consciousness having temporary experiences of inhabiting a series of human, extraterrestrial, angelic, light being forms. I believe that we all have or will have experienced every life form available to us before reuniting with Source.

Some of us traveled through the cosmos to incarnate on Earth, while others incarnate on different planets, star systems and dimensions. Regardless of where the soul travels, it gathers knowledge. It gathers information. It evolves.

One of the reasons I feel so strongly about including this section in the book is because one of my goals is to help open people's minds to understand that it really doesn't matter if you are a walk-in, a multidimensional being, a hybrid or an extraterrestrial being. We are all here to work together, for the betterment of humanity and planet Earth. We are here to grow and experience together. If we can accept this fact and really take it to heart, then we can begin to understand that the ethnicity, the color of people's skin, our gender, our political or religious beliefs, where we come from, really doesn't matter. Prejudices fall by the wayside.

Additional Perspectives

In preparing this book, I wished to seek other perspectives on the walk-in phenomenon. I reached out to a number of experienced, respected figures in this field, and asked them about their views on walk-ins and the cosmology of the soul. I have summarized their perspectives.

Mary Rodwell

Mary is recognized as one of the leading researchers and writers in the field of consciousness and contact phenomena. She is the Founder and Principal of the Australian Close Encounter Resource Network (ACERN), counselor, hypnotherapist and author. In 2002, Mary wrote her first book *Awakening, How Extraterrestrial Contact Can Transform Your Life* and *The New Human, Awakening to Our Cosmic Heritage* in 2016. She is currently working on her third book, due to be released in 2020. Her website is alienlady.com.

Walk-ins: The concept of walk-ins is another step in one's conscious evolution. My research tells me that a walk-in is when one soul enters into the biological container (my term for the body) and the other soul exits. For a lot of people, it's one thing saying you've seen spaceships or met non-human intelligence, but it's another to accept a soul swap because you are moving into the intangible realm of belief. Some people might say to prove it or validate it to them. My research shows that it's all about the experience. I'm not proving anything to anyone. People have to decide what they believe based on their experience. They are the ones proving it to themselves. At the end of the day, the only tangibility is our experience. Everything comes back to experience and soul. When you say to me, what's the evidence that somebody's having an experience? The evidence is the shift in awareness. And you don't do that from a fantasy, from imagination. You only have a shift when it's real.

Cosmology of the Soul: My research indicates that we operate and interact in multidimensional realities, a multiverse, quantum hologram of consciousness. It suggests we are energy consciousness/soul/spirit that, when incarnated, inhabit a physical biological form to experience a material density for our learning and growth as a soul. We incarnate with a physical, energetic, spiritual frequency that embodies a multidimensional DNA to create a template for our physical incarnation. We may resonate with a label such as star seed, hybrid, walk-in, or wanderer.

I believe we are all aspects of Source, a collective universal consciousness, that some call God. It is this consciousness that seeks experience and sends aspects of itself (souls) to all levels of realities to experience and grow. We are multidimensional beings. As a soul consciousness, the soul itself resides within the matrix of the collective universal consciousness. The soul chooses to inhabit a particular body or container for experience. Research has suggested the soul does not inhabit the fetus all the time but will move between the body and the non-physical realm and does not become fully embodied until after birth.

Everything goes back to the soul. It is all very fascinating. The reason that I check on people's multidimensional self during a session is simply because we come from an inaccurate understanding of psychology that doesn't allow for multidimensional awareness. We are all multidimensional beings so let's start looking at every experience from a multidimensional perspective. Rather than going around thinking we can work out why somebody has an issue because of X, Y, and Z, when in fact, it may be something completely different in terms of our multidimensional world. Some of the things through my life have given me pause for thought but I'm a bit of a rebel, you know.

Darlene Van de Grift

Darlene is the Executive Director at the Institute for Exoconsciousness. She is a respected medical intuitive and multidimensional mediator with nearly 40 years of experience. Darlene assists her clients with discovering what they truly need by helping them unravel the stories surrounding their physical, emotional and spiritual pain. She is the founder of A Way to Better Health Massage School where she taught anatomy, physiology and massage. She is also the founder of Soul Union, where she assists people to discover their blockages, gain clarity and define steps toward wellbeing. Darlene is certified in teaching of kinesiology, massage, anatomy and physiology, nutritional counseling, plant medicine, Matrix Energetics, Touch for Health, Intention Muscle Balancing, Reconnection Therapy, and Vibrational Arts. She is in the process of writing her own book and is featured in the book *Being with the Beings - The How and the Why of ET Contact* by Miguel Mendonça.

Darlene offers private sessions from her home. Her website is soulunion.com.

Walk-ins: I believe that we are multidimensional beings, with different aspects of ourselves simultaneously having an experience in multiple dimensions and on multiple planets, in the past, present and future. Some of us are assimilating one or more of these aspects into our current self.

When a walk-in happens, I believe it occurs during a time when the physical body is at a disadvantage. The body is compromised somehow, whether it is in a possible death situation, trauma, grief, an accident or whatever. I also believe that walk-ins have to be in resonance with the physical body and the person's soul. There has to be an alignment or sorts. Walk-ins are not random happenings. There has to be some kind of structure in relation to who gets invited in and on what level. There is an unconscious process on a spiritual plane of invitation and agreement by both souls. The soul can choose to leave with the walk-in coming in, owning the full essence of the person and all the physical aspects of assuming the person's life. Or there can be a merging with a different part of the soul or a multidimensional part of the soul as part of the whole. Either way the soul is not going to have a new, freshly vacated body, because the body carries the cellular memories and soul imprinting of the original soul.

There's an understanding or an agreement that has to take place when the new soul or soul aspect(s) come(s) in. If there is still a part of the original soul's energy left, the two souls have to agree to share the space and cohabit. I have had a client who, during a session, identified as being both the person that walked in through the door and the walk-in. They see themselves as two different entities.

It is important for walk-ins to know they are walk-ins so that integration can occur. The new being has to be able to acquaint itself with the nuances of the new living quarters, so to speak. Not everyone is conscious that they are a walk-in. They think the changes are a result of the situation that caused this action to begin with. Sometimes our psyche denies the new existence and sometimes it embraces it. It all depends on the individual.

Within our auric energy field there can exist additional parts of our soul that chose not to incarnate. Not that they are walk-ins, although they certainly could be, but actual soul parts of the greater soul of the person. Some may call this a guidance system or your higher self. Whatever you choose to call it, it is a containment field of the soul. There exists the possibility that soul aspects that do not incarnate choose to become part of the matrix of this field. They become an observer and may cycle in and out of the body if we open up to the availability of connecting with them.

These aspects are just a different part of us that exist on their own timeline or within their own dimension but because we are connected as one on a multidimensional level they also exist with our own energy field. They are soul parts of us, fragments, frequency matched threads that can communicate with us, if we are open to hearing.

Cosmology of the Soul: I believe that we are multidimensional beings, with different aspects of ourselves simultaneously having an experience in multiple dimensions and on multiple planets, in the past, present and future. Some of us are assimilating one or more of these aspects into our current self.

There is a direct connection with each soul and the body, as if there was a cord holding them together. When the time is chosen to enter, the soul comes in. Whether the entering is during conception, in utero or just as a baby takes its first breath, life can enter. One of the things that I learned from the Council of 28 multidimensional beings that I work with, is that we all have a soul or the life force that governs us, whether we are humans or not. Each soul contains all the information about who we have been in past lives, the lessons we have learned, our past missions, and so on. Based on the desired outcome for the next lifetime, bits and pieces of the soul or the soul's DNA begins to be put together. This DNA will help the soul unfold in such a way that it assists to achieve its goal. I am told that the soul anchors into the body when it takes its first breath. But being anchored does not mean that the soul decides to stay. It travels in and out of the body and if it decides to leave, the baby dies. But if a soul decides to stay, if its frequency is a match with the physical body, it anchors and begins to unfold. It begins to become aware, and out of that awareness, vapors arise and become the consciousness. Consciousness, in my opinion, is the awareness from our soul. It is our guiding force.

Rebecca Hardcastle-Wright

Rebecca is a leading expert in cosmic consciousness and extraterrestrial contact. She is committed to building an Exoconscious Civilization co-created by humans, ETs, and multidimensional beings. She is the Founder and Director of the international non-profit Institute for Exoconsciousness (I-EXO) whose mission is to advance entrepreneurial experiencers who are inventing next-era, co-created technology/science, communication, education, art and healing.

Her graduate degrees include an MDiv in Philosophical Theology from Boston University School of Theology and a PhD in Parapsychic Science from the American Institute of Holistic Theology. Her undergraduate degree is from Otterbein University. She studied Continental Philosophy in Basel, Switzerland. Rebecca was ordained in the United Methodist Church and served as an interfaith chaplain at Wright State University, Dayton, Ohio. She is certified as a hypnotherapist and coach from Southwest Institute for Healing Arts. While working in Washington, DC, Rebecca was a member of Dr. Edgar Mitchell's Quantrek organization's international science team. Rebecca taught one of the first ufology courses in the nation at Scottsdale Community College.

Rebecca has written several books including: *How Exoconscious Humans Guide our Space-Faring Future*; *Exoconsciousness: Your 21st Century Mind*, and *The Exoconscious Human: Claiming Psychic Intelligence in a Transhuman World*, to be published in 2020.

She practices as a therapist at the MindBody Medicine Center in Scottsdale, Arizona where she specializes in healing trauma. Her website is exoconsciousness.com.

Walk-ins: In the context of exoconsciousness, walk-ins represent the material and physical manifestation of an ET or multidimensional being into a person, thereby shifting their human identity and being. In spiritual language, walk-ins are an incarnation, where the essence of the ET or multidimensional integrates, or dwells, in the flesh of an individual, such that the person is fully human and fully ET, multidimensional. They are not watered down, homogenized or blended, but are a fully embraced new being.

The walk-in experience may result from 1) a co-creative process where the individual intentionally commences a transformative process of reordering their beliefs and matrices of their perception, for example through desired spiritual or consciousness work. In this case, the intent of the individual invites the ET, multidimensional being, who enters via a collaborative process. 2) The individual may come to Earth life with an explicit contract to engage at some point in their development to be a walk-in. This contract may be unconscious, but grows to be conscious, especially as the walk-in opens their understanding and expression of their new identity.

When what happened can no longer be ignored, the contract becomes visible and real. 3) The individual may experience a 'soul emergency' or undergo challenges such that a walk-in appears as the most healthy solution. For example, this may be an illness challenge that is resolved through becoming a walk-in. The individual may be intensely aware of the challenge and either consciously or unconsciously open themselves to the walk-in experience. Walk-ins form a community, supported by I-EXO. It is essential that walk-ins nurture and guide one another through their common experience of the loss of former emotional, spiritual, physical beliefs and abilities. A common feeling of loss, and need to reorient, leads to new grounding, balance and physical reconfiguration. The energy and possibilities generated by the walk-in community accelerate the development of exoconsciousness across humans.

In the exoconscious community, walk-ins provide essential experience and wisdom. They stretch the boundaries of our understanding of consciousness, as walk-ins represent an expansion of the field of consciousness and human abilities. They stretch the boundaries of our understanding of the soul, as walk-ins represent a 'soul plasticity' —the transference of one soul into another—not recognized in either spiritual or religious doctrine. Finally, they stretch the boundaries of our understanding of the physical body as a vessel, which through the walk-in experience accommodates new energies, information and spirit.

Cosmology of the Soul: For me, spirit and soul are different. I view spirit as the part of me that is connected to a field of consciousness or the field of All That Is, the field of Source. It is the part of me that is connected to the bigger part of everything. Soul on the other hand is something that is personal. It is individual. It is the accumulation from every lifetime, every thought, every action. This accumulation of knowledge is different for everyone, and everyone evolves a distinct soul. Some souls are brand new while others are older, some even ancient.

The soul is a person's individual Akashic record that holds their biological, emotional, physical, kinesthetic, relational, consciousness and spiritual experiences. The same holds true for beings everywhere, not just on Earth. We may have lifetimes on other planets and in other dimensions and that knowledge is held in the Akashic record of our soul.

Everything you experience in life has a profound effect. The experiences that you're accumulating on Earth or multidimensionally influence you and your soul. These experiences may be on Earth, dimensionally, under the ground and off planet—all are about who you are, and contribute to who you will become.

Soul life has a circular path that spirals forward. Your soul's journey is on a quest to sort out and discover what you know and what you don't know. Hitting that significant awareness of what you don't know brings you a wonderful gift of humility and respect for others. Cherish your humility and be grateful that an exoconscious community travels with you. Remember, we are all one in this soul journey, whether we recognize one another as humans, extraterrestrials or multidimensionales.

Maia Chrystine Nartoomid

Maia is a Mysterium Teacher under the etheric Temple of Thoth, a spiritual consultant, akashic translator (reader) and digital artist. She has been translating from the Akasha consciously as a profession of Spirit since 1967. Maia received a diploma from the Sophia Divinity School for the Independent Catholic Apostolic Church of Antioch-

Malabar Rite in 2000, and was ordained as a priest in that church. She currently serves as a priest in the Ascension Alliance (an independent Catholic movement) and is Dame of the Johannine Templar Priory of the White Stone. Maia is the co-founder and sole operator of the Spirit Heart Sanctuary, a non-profit ministry. Within the New Earth Star Inner Academy, she provides translations from the Akashic Records on planetary transformation and self-awareness, employing heart Ascension principles. Her internet services extend to members and participants globally. The intersection of quantum physics and conscious evolution of her writings was validated in meetings with Dr. Edgar Mitchell, Apollo 14 astronaut and founder of The Institute of Noetic Sciences, and through close correspondence with L. George Lawrence, the inventor of the first laser engine. She has published two books. *Red Tree* is an Akashic setting for high spiritual science, and *Blue Star Love* is a spiritual biography of Elvis Presley.

Currently she is the Spiritual Director for the Academy of Geo-Energetics (SAGE) as well as counselor to the SAGE community in Crestone, Colorado. Maia offers private past-life readings via Thoth. All information that she shares is received through her transmissions with Thoth. Her website is newearthstar.org.

Walk-ins: Walk-ins are identified as souls which have traded places upon agreement with a soul currently inhabiting a body. Thus, as the current body soul leaves, the new 'tenant' enters. The switch is made, and the individual feels suddenly different and not at all who they were before, although they will retain most memory in the cellular consciousness of that physical life prior to their entry into it. According to Thoth, such walk-in experiences do occur, however they happen with far less frequency than presently believed. Some people think souls trade places when the current body's soul is not able to fully do its work in that lifetime, and wishes to move on, and the disincarnate soul is in a hurry to become physical for its own purposes, not wishing to go through the tedious stages of birth and maturing. Thoth tells us that this is not exactly so. If such an exchange of realms were allowed to take place exclusively for these reasons, souls would be in constant exchange, playing musical chairs to the extent that no karmic resolution would be possible. Walk-in, or what Thoth prefers to call 'absalom', meaning to pass through, is dictated through the command center or iid, as a means for balancing an entire grid of soul placement. When these grids become imbalanced due to karmic saturation, certain tensions must be released through a re-ordering process.

Often this requires rapid transitional methods. In the light of this purpose, there are points upon the grids which become energetically de-centralized. This allows a more highly evolved soul to assume the embodiment of one which is in a lesser evolved state, so that the grid-point that embodiment is holding may become more rapidly activated. A walk-in then takes place when a soul, not previously in the current incarnation, comes into the body as the former soul moves out.

Cosmology of the Soul: The Creation Universe is the matrix in which all other universes, including our own, are given the Light mathematical codes for existence. As all souls stem from the One, in order to move forward in cohesion with such a process as incarnation, light code bondings bring souls together into units that are able to 'fit' with other units, similar to a child's building blocks, until all souls are ultimately linked through families. Through this giant family tree all is still one within the greater template. The iid (oversoul) is continually cognizant of the light codes in all stages of the soul's evolution, or what we would define as past, present and future, and it then links that soul to it.

The iid then, is an energy-pyramid containment field for the highly evolved intelligence and consciousness of the universal builders, or Elohim, of the Creation Universe. The iid intelligence is in constant symbiotic contact with all souls in all universes. It is therefore what you might call the command center for the evolutionary experiential flow of all souls. This concept may be staggering to our linear way of thinking, but we must understand that the incredible number of souls involved means nothing to the greater realities which move within the One Consciousness. As Thoth has told me, "Only the matter-bound must count the sheep to know how many there are or where they pasture." The iid is at one with every single 'sheep'. Yet each soul is very individualistic in its incarnational passage as it moves into realms that separate, distinguish, select and individuate all experience. The soul must become one among many in order to find its way back to the eternality of the One.

Gayle Mack

Born into a Hungarian Gypsy lineage, Gayle Mack has been delivering profound messages, channeling and offering hands on healing since the age of three. She channels the Divine Mother and her many aspects, as well as, angelic, Christic and multidimensional light beings. She is trained as a 'Mary' and works with the etheric Templar Knights. She is an ordained minister of the Sisterhood of the Emerald Fire. Gayle believes her divine purpose is to assist the Planet and humanity on the journey to achieve enlightenment and Ascension.

Gayle received her Doctorate in Natural Medicine from the Southern College of Naturopathic Medicine and a Doctorate in BioEnergetics from the Academy of BioEnergetics.

She is the founder of Body & Nature (an alternative wellness center), which incorporates Young Living Essential Oils, the BEMER (microcirculation technology) and electrodermal screening. She has been in the bio-energetic field as a practitioner and educator for twenty years.

Gayle has had phenomenal spiritual experiences throughout her entire life. She is a healer, international speaker, workshop facilitator and author of *Spiral Breath: Activating Higher Consciousness, Healing and the Glia Brain*. Her website is keystoAscension.com.

Walk-ins: I have worked with many walk-ins and believe that there are different types of entry. As I understand it, most walk-ins come into a physical body only after the original natal soul of said body has given their permission and made an agreement to do so.

On occasion, a lingering soul will slip into a body during the last breath and soul transition of the natal soul. I was taught by my grandparents to create sacred space and hold the person who is leaving this physical realm in prayer and light until they have made their transition.

I have worked with people in the hospital who had died and been resuscitated, and have said that they 'picked up' a soul on their way back into their body. With one person, we were able to trace the energy back and received the name of a person who died just a couple of days before.

I believe that the chemical memory from the original soul is still present in the tissue and cells. The chemical memory is being accessed and shared with the new walk-in.

Cosmology of the Soul: Consciousness, in my opinion, is multi-layered. There is the waking consciousness, the subconsciousness, the higher consciousness and the divine consciousness. Our waking consciousness is utilized in this physical realm while the subconscious is accessed without our conscious even knowing. The higher consciousness allows us to tap into our extrasensory gifts, which allows us to rise above the physical striving and achieve balance and peace. The divine consciousness connects us to the oneness and part of the Realm of Imperishable Stars. This Realm is pure consciousness without matter. The energy is kinetic and extremely high in frequency. It is equally as light as it is dark and the souls have individuality, though no form.

I believe there are higher realms above this realm and that they all have a connection to this physical realm. When we are consciously going through this life, our consciousness drives us and our spirituality is the unconscious piece that is working and co-creating experiences that trigger our memory that there is something better. There is something grander than just existing in this three-dimensional realm.

The remembrance of, and the return to our divine higher selves, is encoded within the essence of our being. Within our cells we hold our original soul signature frequency and the knowing of all that is. Before we form a cell, the 'essence' is present and holds all the information of the Divine. A thought sparks the 'essence', which begins a shift from energy into living matter. The spark of life continues to condense the living matter into cells, which eventually forms our physical being. We are fractals, like a microcosm of a macrocosm. Our creation goes back to the spark and tachyon, the subtle organizing energy fields. We have all of creation, everything that exists, exists in our cells and in ourselves.

Everything that Divine God, (All That Is; however you call 'it', he, she, it being androgynous) has created, we have within ourselves. Within our essence' we hold the knowledge of the universe, the knowing, and the ability to remember who we are so that we can become, and return to, our divine light bodies and be the greatest that we can be.

In a 2018 DNA study, a researcher was studying a DNA strand on a microscope slide. He observed that when he removed the DNA, the energy and holographic imprint remained on the slide. Citation: Gadbois, L. 'DNA-the phantom effect, quantum hologram and the etheric body.' MedCrave Online Journal of Proteomics & Bioinformatics (MOJPB). 2018;7(1):9-10. DOI: 10.15406/mojpb.2018.07.00206. This holographic imprint replicated a new physical DNA strand from the hologram. To me, this demonstrates that the information, the divine consciousness found within the DNA of our cells, and the remembrance of our light bodies, does not necessarily have to be physical to be in our cells. The Divine knowledge is energetically imprinted within our essence.

During an intense meditation, while lying in an Egyptian sarcophagus, I visited a location called the Realm of Imperishable Stars. I actually stopped breathing for 21 minutes, and became only essence. This proved to me that the essence of our soul is everlasting. The Bible says this also. Our physicality is really just a cloak that we wear while traveling through this earthly journey.

Rob Gauthier

Rob Gauthier, known as the ET Whisperer, has channeled more than 250 different extraterrestrial beings, but mainly two: TReb Bor yit-NE, a fifth-density being, and Aridif, a sixth-density being.

He has been interviewed on a variety of radio shows and YouTube channels, and has been featured in multiple shows on Gaia TV. Rob has his own YouTube channel called the E.T. Whisperer where he shares hundreds of hours of channeling videos, classes and workshops.

He co-authored three books with Jefferson Viscardi entitled *Plee-Na-Ki and The Plenatalaka - Pleiadian Soul Reflection*; *Benevolent Hybrid Reptilian Humans*; and *Extraterrestrial Life - Galactic Humans*. Rob also has a chapter in the book *Being with the Beings - The How and the Why of ET Contact*, by Miguel Mendonça. He is currently authoring his own book in partnership with Aridif.

Rob lives in Michigan with his son Jeremie, his beloved Kalina Angell and their daughter, Lilith. His website is etwhisperer.com.

Walk-ins: According to Aridif, walk-outs are souls that are able to leave the physical body and have a new soul walk in. Hence the name walk-ins. The walk-in is able to take the place of the first soul of the physical body and the walk-in can pick up directly where the other left off.

Walk-ins are either in the same oversoul or a different one, but most come from the same oversoul. They can also be high dimensional beings, star seeds (extraterrestrial beings) or members of a collective that sent fractals of themselves into the walk-in soul.

Cosmology of the Soul: Through my own understanding, and by working with TReb and Aridif over the years, I have come to understand some significant universal knowledge about densities and the incarnation cycles of the soul. I have learned so much and continue to learn. You have to remember that what I see and know, and what TReb and Aridif experience and know, are shared from our personal perspective. If you spoke with a being from a different planet or different star system, their knowledge about the same subject might vary as does any knowledge, especially about incarnation cycles and densities. We all have our own way of seeing things. But as for densities, there are thirteen in total. Our cosmology is found in our incarnation cycles on our way back to Source.

The first entities upon this planet were fire, rock, water, air, electricity, minerals and of course molecules which everything is made from. These are the foundational building blocks of all of life, where consciousness begins. This is the density where consciousness moves from a state of beingness to becoming aware of itself. It is a very exciting stage. It can take billions of years and 100,000,000 incarnations to move through this cycle.

Second density is home to single-cell organisms: all biological life, plants and eventually animals. This is where life operates instinctually and lives in the moment. Life evolves quickly in the second density. To reach this stage of evolution on the Earth, it takes approximately 4.6 billion years. To experience it from beginning to end takes approximately 100,000 incarnations.

Third density is currently where humanity is. This is one of the most difficult and intense of all the density cycles because we struggle to become self-aware. We explore ourselves, time, community and all things. That's what we're here to do in the third density. We actually began moving out of this density in 2012 and are third-density beings operating in the fourth dimension. I know this is a tough concept to grasp, but things are really shifting. The entire incarnation cycle can take anywhere from 75,000 to 100,000 years or approximately 500 incarnation cycles.

Fourth density is where we begin the journey to explore love. It's the place to explore intimacy, not just with other people but with yourself. Typically, we think of the fourth density as being height, width, depth and time. It vibrates at a higher frequency than the third density, so even if a fourth density being was standing right in front of you, you would not be able to see it. Actually, you can only see the things that are in the same density or in the densities below you. It takes about 100 incarnations before we move from the fourth to fifth density.

Beings of the fifth density are still operating in bodies but they are of a much higher vibration, so they are semi-physical. In this density, they are learning about the deepest love and wisdom. At this level, they focus on wisdom and learning to experience and extend unconditional love. They are all about finding full connection to themselves and to everything around them. Fifth density beings are not bound by the laws of time and space. It takes 20 incarnation cycles to move through the various fifth-density phases. Sixth density operates outside of time and space and the beings that live there can actually bend space and time to travel. The focus here is on the mastery of love and wisdom. Not just knowledge but the wisdom of all things. It's where you learn the wisdom of anything that you could ever love. You will want to know everything about it, and anything you want to know about, you'll instantly be intimate with that. That's the mastery of physical reality.

The beings within the seventh through the thirteenth densities are purely non-physical and only concerned with experience. They're neither good nor bad. They are 100% neutral and indifferent. If they create a planet and its people, it doesn't matter if that planet ends up going into really bad experiences and its people kill themselves off very quickly or if they survive and thrive and make it all the way through their evolution, through sixth density to rejoin nonphysical consciousness. It doesn't matter because to them, all experiences are valid and important.

The seventh through the thirteenth density is where we operate as pure consciousness and where souls and soul groups reside. If an entity desires to experience and express itself further, it can manifest as planets and moons towards the end of its incarnation in the seventh density. The eight density is the density where consciousness expresses itself as stars. This is the last true point of individualism as a singularity. The ninth density is known as the Galactic Consciousness. The tenth density is the consciousness where entities of densities seven through nine come together to form a higher co-consciousness level. The eleventh density is the culmination of a complete cycle and it encompasses densities seven, eight, nine and ten to create the universal consciousness. Known as the Creator Brain, the twelfth density is all forms of matter that are conceived. The thirteenth density is the return to Source.

Robert Schwartz

Rob is a spiritual facilitator, hypnotherapist and author. He offers Between Lives Soul Regressions in which people can find out what they planned before they were born, why they made those plans, how they're doing in terms of fulfilling their plan, and how they can better fulfil their plan. His website is yoursoulsplan.com.

He is the author of *Your Soul's Plan* and *Your Soul's Gift*. Rob works to assist people in their healing process, resolve life issues, and helps people understand their life plan.

Walk-ins: My understanding is that the walk-in souls are a very high-vibrational soul with a tremendous amount of support on the other side for what the soul is undertaking. I should explain first that I researched people's pre-birth plans for the two books, by working just with mediums and channels. And in these channeling sessions we would ask spirit if this person planned their challenges before he or she was born. And if so, why? And then in the books I present all the information that came through from spirit. Sometimes in the channeling sessions, the subject of walk-ins has come up for one reason or another. I remember clearly it came up in one of these sessions we did for the death of a loved one. What they were told by spirit in that session was that a walk-in often comes in during a severe illness or a severe accident. And so that will be used as an opportunity for the soul.

Cosmology of the Soul: We all have multiple aspects of ourselves and so a single soul can incarnate many times on the same dimensional plane on the same planet.

I interviewed a woman in the Netherlands who channels Jesus. When he speaks through her and uses his given Hebrew name, which is Yeshua. Through regressions, I've spoken with him extensively on the subject of pre-birth planning. He explained that there are basically three levels to the soul. The highest vibrational level is the level at which all souls are one, and then they take a notch down in vibration. You have the individuated souls and then another big notch down. And individually, in vibration, you have the personality, which is a portion of the soul's energy placed in a physical body. And what he's explained to me regarding the incarnation process is that the life plan is created by the person's soul.

The person's higher self, in consultation with God, spirit guides, angels, masters and so forth develop the plan. Once the plan has been created, the personality that's going to be in the body is created by the soul. And then the soul informs the personality of what the life plan will be.

According to Jesus, the vast majority of personalities will agree to the life plan largely because they can sense from their higher self and from their guides, tremendous wisdom and great unconditional love. And so this reassures them that even if it's a challenging life plan, it is for the highest good of all beings.

Again, according to Jesus, there's a small percentage of people who start to experience human emotions of fear, anxiety, doubt, and they express concerns that the life plan may be a bit too much. If that happens, the life plan is revised to make it more acceptable to the personality. And then at that point, the vast majority of personalities who express concern now agree to the revised life plan. There's still a small percentage, those who express concern, that remain concerned that the life plan may still be too much. And if that happens, it's either scrapped or substantially revised. The bottom line here is that nobody is forced to do anything and the personality always has to agree.

Julia Cannon

Julia began her service to humanity as a registered nurse, for over 20 years. At the same time her mother, Dolores Cannon, was developing her hypnotism techniques.

Julie opened her own healing center but was being urged to do something else. That something else was to work with her mother and help her grow her business.

She is an author of the book, *Soul Speak*, and has taken over the world-renowned Quantum Healing Hypnosis Technique (QHHT). Julia is an international speaker and offers hypnosis training sessions. Her website is qhhtofficial.com

Walk-ins: My understanding of walk-ins and the soul exchange come from my mother, Dolores Cannon, and her work. According to the research she gathered there is an agreement between two souls: the one that is currently in the body and the soul that will swap places. The current soul for whatever reason, just can't take it anymore. Life is too much. It is more than they can handle and they need a break. So there is an arrangement made with another soul. The other soul agrees to come in and take on everything that the previous soul had, all the spiritual growth projects they are working on, agreements, whatever they are learning and whatever they are doing. If they weren't finished then those projects have to be finished first. Once they have completed them, they can move on with whatever else they have as their own personal mission.

My understanding is that walk-ins could be part of the three waves of volunteers that Dolores spoke of in her books. "The first wave of these souls is the Baby Boomer generation. They have had the hardest time adjusting to life on Earth. They are horrified by the rampant violence of our world and want to return "home" – even though they consciously have no idea where it is. Strong emotions like anger and hate deeply disturb them. Some rebelled against the status quo and even committed suicide to escape the chaos of Earth. They are the pioneers who paved the way for the second and third waves of volunteers.

The second wave found their transition to life on Earth much more easily than the first wave. The second wave souls tend to work behind the scenes, often on their own, creating little or no Karma. In the sessions I conduct as a hypnotist, they have been described as antennas that unconsciously channel energy onto the Earth. They do not have to do anything; they just have to be. Their energy affects everyone they come into contact with. Their paradox is they are supposed to be sharing their energy, but they do not like being around people.

Many first and second wave souls unconsciously realize that having children creates Karma. Many do not marry in the first place, unless they are fortunate enough to meet another soul to whom they can relate. They just want to do their job and go home. The third wave is a group of exceptional new children. This advanced group arrived already equipped with enhanced DNA compatible with the frequency of the New Earth. They need challenges to keep them interested, not drugs to treat their misdiagnosed illnesses such as ADHD. They are the new "hope of the world."

There are walk-in volunteers from all kinds of different groups that have been coming here. According to regression sessions, so many of them know they are not from here.

Cosmology of the Soul: I think a soul is a small part of a much bigger part of ourselves. This much bigger part of ourselves takes a piece of itself and puts it into this body. That much bigger part can be having many experiences and expressions at the same time multidimensionally. All those expressions and experiences and everything that is going on feeds back into the larger part. The smaller piece could be called a soul. The thing my guides show to me is the smaller pieces keep coming in and going out of the bigger piece so there is a constant flow of learning, in and out.

Consciousness is like different states of awareness or different states of being awake. Spiritual consciousness is how aware you are and how awake you are. We all wake up more and more to who we are so we have varying states of that consciousness. I believe consciousness originated from the Source, the great computer in the sky.

My feeling or my experience about Source or Creator or whatever you want to call it, is this hugeness, this great all-encompassing being. It is the complete being that we are all part of, that we have all come from. It is our home and it's where we return. They're saying life source.

I really want people to know who they really are and really want them to understand how great they are. You know you couldn't get on this planet without a golden ticket. You had to be a master manifester to get here. That's why there are lines waiting to get here.

Some people feel like, "Oh, who am I? What am I? I've got all these things happening to me and oh gosh, you know, I'm the dredge of society" kind of thing and I just really want people to know you are much greater than you can ever believe and ever imagine. Claim and embrace your greatness. Don't let these other things get in your way and stop you. You are magnificent and you are here for a reason.

Conclusions

The journey from September 1999 to now, 21 years later, has been extraordinary. In this book I have written about my process, and how it has brought me to the desire to study the walk-in phenomenon in detail. The only effective way to do this was to simply listen to the way others have experienced their walk-in event, learned to integrate their new life, and identified and pursued their mission. This conclusion is my attempt to analyze their stories and find the commonalities and differences, and discover their sources of strength and direction. My greatest hope is that what we have shared will be of benefit to others, especially those who are going through their own walk-in experience.

The conclusion reflects the structure of the book. I begin with a brief discussion about what I have learned through writing about my own journey and what came up for me. I will discuss this more at the end of this section. I then move into a discussion about the key organizing themes of the book: consciousness, form and purpose, and discuss the typical elements surrounding the walk-in phenomenon. Next, I examine the experiences of the 15 walk-ins I interviewed. Then, I analyze the perspectives on walk-ins held by a group of eight people who have been involved in this field for some time. They derive their information from a variety of sources. These include: channeling, receiving downloads and information from guides, information from clients' counseling and regression sessions, and information from experiencers in informal settings. The conclusion ends with some final thoughts, and then a prayer and a poem which for me capture the spirit of this book.

What I Discovered

My Journey - When this process began, I thought I had lost my mind. Knowing about past lives, healing, ceremonies, the soul leaving the body and so on, completely freaked me out, because the old me did not believe in any of those things. I was raised to believe in the standard Christian model of existence; birth, life, death then heaven or hell. But the new me knew that was not true because I remembered being in an afterlife state. My psychic abilities, including clairvoyance, clairsentience and clairaudience were also challenging to integrate at first. I fought against it, but in the end, accepting this new reality saved my sanity. I decided to take only the good things in my life, my children, and built a new life for us based on love.

Over time I came to terms with being a walk-in, yet the full integration process, including clearing out the cellular memories, dysfunctional behavior patterns and thought process, took over ten years. But knowing who I was, within months of arriving, made all the difference. In that state of openness I discovered my mission and actively integrated it. Life has since unfolded in ways I could not have imagined all those years ago. I now accept that part of my mission is being a wayshower, including sharing my story and the stories of others with similar experiences.

In writing about my own journey, I felt honored to have experienced all that I did. I felt grateful to the universe for granting me the experience to be human, to be a mother, a wife, a teacher, a healer, and now an author. I have come away with a deep sense of appreciation for my first spiritual teacher, Jeremie, and know beyond a shadow of a doubt that I am a walk-in.

I came to the understanding that we are eternal souls having a temporary human experience. We are all an aspect of Source. This universal truth allows me to live on a solid foundation of forgiveness and non judgement. Does that mean that I have always walked my path with grace and ease? I wish I could say yes. But I am just as human as the next person. Emotions rule this planet. Frustration, anger, fear of the unknown, feeling like I didn't belong, all these things plagued me for the first few years. I did not understand then or now, how humans can be so hurtful and murderous toward one another; why there are wars, poverty, and inequality. But I made a conscious choice with each and every experience to try to operate from my true essence. If I can do it, so can you.

When I look back at those first few years, the 'crazy days', I am so grateful for them. My main takeaway is that yes, the experiences are important teachers, but most important is the way we handle the experiences, how we move through them. We can allow them to shape us into a better version of ourselves.

Consciousness, Form and Purpose - This is the conceptual foundation of this book. In essence it is the theoretical side of the subject. In this section we talked about the anatomy of the soul, and the way that we are structured as beings. I discuss the sheantiaskaan (oversoul), the container of all our experiences from all our incarnations; the higher self which is our guidance system, and the soul which is the personality of this lifetime. All of existence can be defined in these terms. From Source to the sheantiaskaan to the higher self to the soul, we are part of Source, and Source is part of us. Everyone is a divine reflection of Source, so when you get angry or upset, ask yourself: what in that person is me?

Going Home - Sharing about the death process and about how it is just a transitional phase with nothing to fear, filled me with the sweetness and remembrance of being released from the body. This sensation sometimes lingered with me for days. It was an excellent reminder that no matter how tough things might get, there is no right or wrong way to experience. Experience 'just is.' So, what does this mean? It means there is a spiritual reality beyond the body. It says that we are not identified solely with the body, but are one part of the vastness of creation, part of Source. It means that we are eternal beings having a human experience, not a human with a soul.

I was also reminded that this life is a holographic projection of a reality that we all agreed to experience together. It is not real. It looks and feels real but it is not real. You bleed when cut but it's all part of the game of life. Yes, we cry, laugh, feel pain and joy. But we chose all these experiences. Shakespeare said it best, when he said, "All the world's a stage. And all the men and women merely players."

What is a Walk-in - The other educational piece in this book is about the different types of walk-ins, types of experiences and their origins. In this section we looked at the loosening of the energetic bodies so the walk-in can enter into the body. I was excited with how this section turned out. It discusses the various types of walk-ins: soul exchanges, soul infusion, soul overlay, soul braids, jumpers and soul layering. This information flowed freely so I knew it was inspired by spirit. I was thrilled when Robert McWilliam shared his memories about the exchange of the energetic body of the walk-in host as it was being prepared for his soul's entrance because his memories echo my own. Writing about Earth seeds, Source seeds, dimensional seeds and star seeds, and the multidimensionality and galactic origins of souls, stirred a deep remembrance in me. I seemed to experience my galactic guides near and believe they helped guide my thoughts and hand as I typed. Waves of feeling connected to and with them would periodically wash over me as I contemplated each line.

Walk-in Interviews

This book is broken down into two interview sections: firstly my story and those of other walk-ins, and secondly the perspectives about walk-ins by other people. Below are brief highlights from each of the walk-ins, which look at the event, integration and mission.

Marilyn Harper went from being a radio advertising salesperson, playwright and party girl to understanding over time that she is a 17th dimensional channel. The shift was precipitated by a medical emergency. During a hospital stay the walk-in entered her body. Only later did she begin to notice changes in her personality, behaviors and tastes. It took her several years to understand who she was. Marilyn became a channel for a 17th dimensional collective called Adironnda. She now travels all over the world, changing the lives of people with the message from the beings. Her mission is to serve as a channel for unconditional love from the other side. Marilyn retained most of her memories and believes that her walk-in chose it that way. She believes that walk-ins are here for a higher purpose.

Hildegard Gmeiner's life changed dramatically when the walk-in event occurred. She experienced a NDE when she collapsed and witnessed her body being raised into the back of the ambulance. She remembers the transference of her new soul and the conservations around her. When she awoke in the hospital and the doctors questioned her about what had happened, she said matter of factly, "I am a 7th dimensional consciousness scientist from Andromeda, here to anchor higher vibration on this planet." Although she retained most of her life memories, she had to learn everything about being human, with the help of her Andromedan guides Ashtar-Athena and her lifelong companion and guide, LuiMar. She discovered that she was a volunteer for the walk-in program. Hildegard came in with a firm mission that was twofold: To raise her children to the light; To tell her life story and in so doing help others who had similar experiences. Her mission of raising her children is complete and now she is telling her story and assisting others.

LivingSoul's memories began when she was back on her home planet as a little girl who ran away from home only to find herself in the body of a seven-year-old human child. As a child, she was very protected and since she was so young, integration was seamless. Throughout her childhood, she practiced meditation, sometimes for hours at a time. LivingSoul believes her mission is to experience the fullness this human life has to offer and to bring light and positivity to this world. She feels the concept of a mission is a typical human way of looking at it and believes that she will return to her home planet when she is complete with her life. She believes that walk-ins are here to experience.

Jacquelin Smith experienced a series of walk-ins. She was told they removed 85% of who she originally was, left 15% of the natal soul and then replaced the 85% with multidimensional aspects of her star being soul. It was a very difficult integration process for her. She has a mission to help the animal and human kingdoms on the planet. In addition to being a walk-in, Jacquelin is an ET-human hybrid. Jacquelin feels that we are all different aspects of the creator and the creator is learning and expressing itself through every form of consciousness.

Dylan Kuczko became a soul-infused walk-in with aspects of himself from the angelic realm at age seven. Around age nine or ten he began seeing into other dimensions and learned that he was a walk-in. He knew he was different and tried to hide his abilities from the other kids and his teachers. As a young adult, he has fully stepped into being his authentic self in service to humanity through the healing work he offers. Dylan believes he is here to experience being human and as such lives life to the fullest and feels that each walk-in arrives with their own purpose.

Robert McWilliam is a walk-in from the Pleiadian star system and arrived when his host was 18 years old. It was not until he was an adult that he discovered that he was a walk-in. He remembers volunteering to swap places with Robert and to complete his contract for this life.

Robert has not revealed who he is to anyone other than a few select spiritually-minded friends. His family did not know he was a walk-in, only that he was different from the rest of the family. Robert believes that walk-in missions vary from soul to soul, depending on what they need to grow and evolve.

Nicole Richmond walked into the body of an Ojibway, First Nations attorney. She entered during a car accident and took several years to integrate. Now knowing who she is, she is determined to stand in her personal truth and to be of service to humanity. Nicole has dedicated her life to assisting her indigenous community and humanity as a whole. She affiliates as an Arcturian. Nichole also feels that each walk-in arrives with their own mission.

YnDon Clark received a soul infusion with a future aspect of himself. His integration process took about two years before he began sharing who he was. Since then, he has opened himself up to being in service to the universe and follows the callings, wherever they may lead. YnDon believes that experience and integration of the multidimensional aspects of ourselves are what the walk-in experience is all about.

Scott Mathias is a soul exchange walk-in from the star Antares. He exchanged places with Scott due to extreme trauma brought on by the death of his child. He became so overwhelmed with grief, that he gave up the will to live. The Walk-in is an EL'an known as ANKHA'ra with memories of his non-Earth lifetimes. He is here to help humanity raise its consciousness to prepare for the upcoming shift in human consciousness. Scott views walk-ins as beings which are here to assist humanity.

Kaza Blizz is a walk-in from the 13th dimension. She entered the body of a comatose woman with four children and integrated very quickly, knowing exactly who she is. Kaza enthusiastically shares the information she brought from the other side with anyone who is interested in hearing her story. She speaks at workshops, online events and conferences. She spreads her message of hope, love and the fact that walk-ins are here to help raise awareness and consciousness. Kaza's mission continues to unfold for her.

Maya Christobel was born a hybrid who encountered a walk-in soul layering. She speaks about living a multidimensional life. Maya believes that walk-ins have their own experiences to live out and that in doing so they are helping to raise the consciousness of the planet. Recently, she began sharing her story with her family and now the world.

Daniel Teague is a walk-in from Lyra. He entered his host's body following a car accident when he was 18 years old. Since then, he has had many metaphysical and paranormal experiences. Stepping into his gifts, he is now a healer and offers a variety of services. Daniel feels that the experience and mission of each walk-in is unique.

Yvonne Perry's life was turned upside down when she became a walk-in with a totally different personality. She has experienced a soul exchange and a soul infusion with her higher self. When she became a walk-in she lost a great deal of her memory but has regained most of it. Now, she is a minister, author, healing sound therapist, light language workshop facilitator and galactic practitioner of light codes. One of Yvonne's greatest joys is being of service to humanity. She feels that everyone's core mission is the same: to be unconditional love in motion. She believes that we are all here to remember our oneness.

Jeremie Leckron is of Hopi lineage. She walked into the body of a deceased five-year-old child due to an horrific accident. When her father arrived at the hospital, over 45 minutes after she had been pronounced dead, she opened her eyes. As a child, she didn't know that she was a walk-in and her life was filled with a multitude of psychic events and spiritual training. Jeremie stepped into her mission of being in service to humanity by becoming a spiritual teacher. She is from the Pleiadian star system. Jeremie feels that each walk-in experience is unique to the experiencer.

Miguel Mendonça experienced a soul jumper that entered his body for a period of three weeks. Part of his natal soul remained the observer while the other consciousness took over his body and had a variety of experiences during that period. He does not know where the jumper was from or its true purpose. He believes it is possible that the jumper wanted to experience being human and states that he may never know for sure. He believes it is possible that it was a formless consciousness he first encountered at age three.

None of the walk-in experiences are the same, yet several had similar settings. Marilyn, Dylan, Kaza and Jeremie all experienced their walk-in's arrival while in a hospital. Hildegard's walk-in event took place en route to a hospital. Emma, Jacquelin, Miguel, Robert, Scott, Yvonne, and myself all experienced our walk-in events at home. Daniel, Maya and Nicole became walk-ins as a result of a car accident. YnDon's event occurred while he was awake and connected with a spacecraft. He witnessed a future aspect of himself being lowered into his body. Each situation was somewhat different. Based on the sharings of each of these people, I believe the walk-in scenarios happen when the body is ready to expire, in a deep sleep, through trauma, during death or near death. I also believe that there is typically an agreement for the walk-in to occur.

When looking deeper into the integration process, each person experienced something different as well. Dylan, Emma, and Jeremie were so young that they did not notice a major difference. Robert and Daniel were in their late teens and attributed their integration to a normal adolescence. YnDon was a young man in his twenties who was going along with the flow. Hildegard, Kaza, Miguel, Jacquelin, Marilyn, Maya, Nicole, Scott, Yvonne and myself were all adults when the walk-in happened and all noticed immediate differences, as did our family and friends. It seems that the older you are, the more dramatic the personality and lifestyle changes are.

Maya, Jacquelin and YnDon report their walk-ins being future aspects of themselves while Jacquelin and Yvonne merged with multiple aspects. Marilyn, Dylan and Kaza came from a different dimension. Hildegard, Emma, Robert, Nicole, Scott, Daniel, Jeremie and myself come from different planets. Miguel is unsure where his walk-in originated from.

Allowing the mission to unfold was another common theme. Everyone came in with a mission to either be of service to humanity, Gaia or to animals. This verifies that walk-ins are here to be of service.

Most discussions added information on the idea that reality is multidimensional in nature, and so are we. And most underlined the fact that all things are Source, and arise from and return to Source.

Other points that they share included:

- There are soul exchanges, soul infusions, overlays, braids, jumpers and soul layering
- If the walk-in occurred during adulthood, their life changed more dramatically
- If the walk-in happened during childhood, the person may not have known they were a walk-in but they knew they were different
- Prior to incarnating a contract is made with the walk-out soul for the walk-in to arrive at a specific time. There are, however, instances where the walk-in event occurs instantaneously without an agreement
- Most experience some type of memory issues
- Our souls are eternal and incarnate many times on this and different planets
- Extraterrestrials are us and we are them
- All of the walk-ins, except for Miguel, recalls being from other planets and other dimensions. However, Miguel is the only one to be able to provide a day to day accounting of his walk-in experience
- None of the walk-ins are from planet Earth
- Two of the walk-ins are human/hybrids.

I cannot begin to explain the kinship I felt with the people that I interviewed. I connected with each one, at some level, and recognized elements of their stories in me. It was most gratifying to connect with my own people.

Other Interviews

I also interviewed eight other people who have been involved in the metaphysical field for a long time. They are Mary Rodwell, Darlene Van de Grift, Rebecca Hardcastle-Wright, Maia Chrystine Nartoomid, Gayle Mack, Rob Gauthier, Robert Schwartz and Julia Cannon. I have included a brief synopsis of their interviews.

They derive their information from a variety of sources including: channeling, receiving downloads, information from their guides, information from clients', counseling and regression sessions, and information from experiencers in informal settings.

Mary Rodwell said that her research shows that walk-ins are here for the experience. "It's all about the experience. Multidimensional experience. Everything comes back to soul."

She believes that the soul attaches when the first breath of a newborn baby is taken.

Darlene Van de Grift believes that the walk-in souls could be multidimensional aspects of one's self. She feels walk-ins occur when the body is compromised and an alignment of energy occurs.

She believes that walk-ins are not random occurrences and that a structure of some type must be in place and the event cannot occur until the walk-in soul is invited.

Rebecca Hardcastle-Wright is of the opinion that walk-ins can represent the material and physical manifestation of an ET or multidimensional being. Walk-ins occur through a co-creative process between the natal soul and walk-in soul. It is important for walk-ins to know they are walk-ins for the sake of integration.

She believes that the spirit is connected to the universal consciousness whereas the soul attaches to the body. Rebecca states that the soul is a person's individual Akashic record.

Maia Chrystine Nartoomid feels that walk-ins occur when one soul leaves and another soul enters. She said Thoth said that everything that is labeled a walk-in but not a soul exchange is something else. Thoth suggests that most often souls are infused with future or multidimensional aspects of their higher soul. Our souls all stem from the larger soul. She states, "Each soul is individualistic in its incarnational travels."

Gayle Mack believes that walk-ins swap souls with a soul that is ready to leave and that there are many different scenarios in which this can occur. Walk-ins typically carry a much higher vibration than the soul that is leaving and is here to help with the spiritual evolution of its own soul as well as with the souls of others. She also believes that all of creation originates with God or Source, and states that we are souls or fractals originating from God. Our souls are everlasting.

Rob Gauthier states that walk-in souls most likely come from the same oversoul but not always. They can be high dimensional beings, star seeds or members of a collective that sends fractals of themselves into the walk-in soul. He discusses densities rather than dimensions and believes that there are thirteen levels or densities of an incarnation process whereby an entity experiences all levels until it reunites with Source.

Robert Schwartz's understanding of walk-in souls is that they are very high-vibrational souls that incarnate for a variety of reasons. Each soul has its own pre-birth plan before incarnating. He feels that we all have multiple aspects of ourselves and that a single soul can incarnate many times.

Julia Cannon understands that walk-ins are part of three waves of volunteers that have come to the planet to assist humanity in raising their spiritual consciousness. According to hypnosis sessions, walk-ins come from all over the universe and from different dimensions. She believes that the soul is a small part of a much larger soul. The information the small soul receives is fed back to the larger soul for its overall growth and evolution.

Other common understandings about walk-ins include:

- Walk-in events occur when one soul leaves the body and another one walks in
- Walk-ins either swap souls or they bring in higher aspects of themselves
- In order for a walk-in to occur, some type of trauma to the physical body takes place
- Walk-ins then to carry a higher vibration than the soul that left
- Walk-ins come in with a mission
- Walk-ins can come from different dimensions, different times, be a multidimensional aspect of the natal soul or be an extraterrestrial

Cosmology of the soul common thoughts are:

- We are all aspects of Source. We are all one
- We are multidimensional and extraterrestrial beings
- Everything begins and ends with Source
- Souls attach when the first breath of a newborn is taken
- We incarnate to learn, grow and experience
- Each soul is different and unique

It is fascinating that the walk-ins and non-walk-ins interviewed hold similar beliefs in all areas. To my mind, this serves as confirmation that, as I already understood, we are all connected.

Final Thoughts

The two years leading up to the writing of this book were filled with longing to connect with my own kind. Having now met other people who have had a variety of walk-in experiences, I wanted to know what they remembered and how they had integrated into this dimension. Hearing their stories served as confirmation and validation for me.

One of the confirmations and validations that I received is that yes, walk-ins are from off-planet. When this truth first began to make itself known to me I had difficulty accepting it, because that meant that I, too, came from off-planet, a thought that should have resonated easily but didn't.

I had dreams, visions and meditations where I was aboard spacecraft, speaking with other beings. In one meditation I was told that I was Arcturian, a word I had never heard of, and had to research its meaning. In another meditation, I received spiritual gifts from a Mantis beings. I felt only love in its presence. I didn't know why initially this was such a struggle for me to accept. After all, my parents have always believed in and talked about UFOs and the off-planet beings that piloted them, but there was no evidence or proof. In fact, several members of my family have seen spacecraft.

My dad reported seeing several unexplainable sights in the sky that he thought were spacecraft. The most memorable was when he and his partner at the US Forest Service, Cliff, saw a long, slender craft with windows all around, hovering over a mountain top near Sugar Grove, Virginia. My dad said, "It was moving erratically, then in a flash it was gone." My dad also said that his mom talked about seeing spacecraft her entire life. On one occasion she witnessed a craft landing in a field behind a hill near her house. She did not go out to investigate but watched the location for half an hour before it slowly rose up and in a flash it was gone. After that, she would go outside at night and stare in the sky. My grandmother is said to have talked about the ships over LA in the 1950s. She had family and friends there that saw them, but I don't know if she saw them personally.

My cousin Ken Langston and his friend Eddie Hodges saw a glow in the sky that followed them and slowed, stopped and sped up just as their car did. Another cousin crested a hill while hunting and in a flat spot ahead, he described seeing a 'saucer' about the size of a house with flashing lights all around. It was glowing and spinning slowly as it hovered above the ground. He was so afraid that his knees buckled and he fell to the ground. Very slowly the craft moved over his head and he feared for his life. When he looked up, he described the undercarriage as being a honeycomb-like structure with lights around the periphery, and he said there was a humming. The craft began to slowly rise higher into the sky and in a flash, disappeared. He was so shaken that he barely made it to his car. He told this story for the rest of his life. I share this because these UFO-related stories were told around the dinner table. One would think that it should have been easy to accept myself as Arcturian, having grown up with these stories throughout my family.

Now that I have integrated, I am happy to share about my off-planet ancestry. I relish the family stories and they have spurred a new excitement to begin to speak with the rest of the family to see if they have any stories that they would like to share.

Another confirmation/validation that I received from writing this book is that nothing happens by accident. The universe has put amazing people in front of me. People who needed to be a part of this book. People who needed to tell their stories and to share with the world that we are not alone. We are all connected. We are all one.

My sessions with Barbara, Darlene, Jacquelin, Maia and Rob, mentioned in the Cosmology of the Soul section, is where I discovered my collective consisted of Pleiadian, Sirian, Arcturian, Mantis, Angelic, Andromedan and Christic energy. This solidified some things within me and I began to understand that all the beings that had reached out to me in dreams and meditations were trying to let me know that they were here for me. I was never alone. They are part of my galactic family and I am part of theirs. Sometimes it is hard to see what is right in front of you.

I am now inspired, more than ever, to tell my story. To share the truth of who I am and that we are part of each other. I am encouraged to learn everything I can about the collective consciousness. I want to study more about ley lines, vortices and gridding. I want to visit power places around the world and breathe in their energy.

I am also inspired to share more about learning to live from a place of heart, not head. When we overthink our minds seem to create drama that doesn't exist. We become anxious, we worry and can't sleep. Our endocrine systems begin to respond by adding pounds to our frames and overall we feel yucky. But when we drop into our heart space, we operate with a clear mind and a balanced persona. When we are able to step into our true natures, we begin to extend love to all those around. Most importantly, we remember that we are souls having a human experience, not a human with a soul. There is a big difference.

We are souls that are here to experience, to operate from a place of heart. To laugh, dance and act silly. To drink a little wine, feel the sun on our face and gaze up in the night sky in wonderment. To remember who we are and live from our heart space is a sacred gift.

If we can learn to operate from this place of heart, then the world will change because we will become love. We will not worry about who said what about whom. We will not care what others think of us because we know this is all temporary. We will know that we are souls and live from that place.

The sad truth is that people still believe they are only humans. They get caught up in the 'must have, must do, must achieve' mentality. Possessions mean nothing, really. We also are not our jobs, our titles, our homes, our relationships, our cars, our money, or the lack thereof. These things will pass. If we can remember that we are divine sparks of Source and our only purpose is to remember who we are and experience for Source's evolution, then that is when we will find true happiness. We are just along for the ride. So why worry? What does it really matter?

I look at the times we are in now and I see a direct correlation to the phases of the transformation I went through. Just as I was sick, our world is sick. Just as I felt like I was going crazy, the world, for most, feels like it is going crazy - economically, politically, socially, ecologically and spiritually. Just as I dropped into acknowledgement of my situation, accepting and then created a new, healthier reality for myself, the world is going to have to do the same.

We are living in times when our world is experiencing turmoil. And it is this turmoil that gives me hope. Hope that we, humanity, are on the cusp of shifting our consciousness to a higher level and are beginning to create a new Earth. An Earth where prejudice does not exist, where sickness is met with love and compassion, without forcing people to become sheep and just do what we are told, such as take medicines that are not good for our bodies. An Earth that operates from a place of soul and heart, not from the me-me-me, more-more-more mentality. If I can shift my entire paradigm, you can too. If enough of us shift, then the world changes. May this planet experience the shift that I did.

Now it is time for you, the reader, to draw your own conclusions based on the information and experiences that I have shared with you. Begin to ask questions for yourself. Perhaps the questionnaire in the appendix will be useful.

It has been my honor to share the words in this book with you. I hope they serve to expand your mind and bring peace to your heart. I am in gratitude to all those that have shared their stories. It has been my privilege to work with them.

I leave you with a Navajo traditional prayer and the words of Chief Seattle, who said:

"This we know: the earth does not belong to man,
man belongs to the earth.
All things are connected like the blood that unites us all.
Man did not weave the web of life, he is merely a strand in it.
Whatever he does to the web, he does to himself."

On the final page I added the poem *Walking In Beauty* to leave each of you with a prayer and blessing to send you off on your own journey. It is a Navajo/Dine traditional closing prayer and blessing.

Walking in Beauty

Today I will walk out, today everything unnecessary will leave me,
I will be as I was before, I will have a cool breeze over my body.
I will have a light body, I will be happy forever, nothing will hinder
me.
I walk with beauty before me.
I walk with beauty behind me.
I walk with beauty below me.
I walk with beauty above me.
I walk with beauty around me.
My words will be beautiful.

In beauty all day long may I walk.
Through the returning seasons, may I walk.
On the trail marked with pollen may I walk.
With dew about my feet, may I walk.
With beauty before me may I walk.
With beauty behind me may I walk.
With beauty below me may I walk.
With beauty above me may I walk.
With beauty all around me may I walk.

In old age wandering on a trail of beauty, lively, may I walk.
In old age wandering on a trail of beauty, living again, may I walk.
My words will be beautiful.

Appendix

Walk-in Questionnaire

Once a walk-in event has occurred many people are left bewildered for day, months and even years. Some people may not even be aware that such an event has occurred as they retain the memories of the previous soul; however, they know that something has changed. They feel different; they know things without knowing how or why; they have new tastes in food; their limits and boundaries have changed; their behavioral patterns change; their spiritual beliefs dramatically change; or their belief systems change. Some people suddenly disconnect from family and friends and change jobs, get divorced or move to a new town or city.

There are many common traits among walk-in souls. Are you one of them? The following is a series of questions designed to help determine if you may be a Walk-in. Please circle the number to all the statements or questions that you identify with.

Have you or are you experiencing any of the below:

1. Have you experienced a near-death experience, major emotional trauma, illness, undergone surgery and felt totally different after the experience?
2. Do you or have your friends/family noticed changes in your personality?

3. Do you suddenly feel differently about family and friends?
4. Have you made sudden lifestyle changes for no reason?
5. Have you changed jobs, career, relationship(s) without a reason, other than they no longer feed your soul?
6. Are you disinterested in previous hobbies?
7. Have you developed new interests in spirituality, astrology, tarot, extraterrestrials or other esoteric topics?
8. Are you experiencing almost euphoric feelings of expansion, a connection to all things, a feeling of oneness?
9. Have you had an instantaneous awakening of spiritual gifts?
10. Have you ever looked into the mirror and not recognized the person staring back at you?
11. Do you remember things you didn't know before without studying them?
12. Have you experienced missing time?
13. Do you feel that you don't belong anymore?
14. Do you intuitively know things that you didn't before?
15. Are you hypersensitive to others' thoughts and feelings?
16. Do you know when people are not being honest with you?
17. Do you feel like something is different or has happened but you don't know what?
18. Do you have mental confusion?
19. Are you experiencing partial or full memory loss?
20. Are you feeling like you know something that other people don't, but you can't remember what it is?
21. Do you have a new sense of mission?
22. Do you have a feeling of being more balanced?
23. Are you experiencing unexplained bouts of sadness or depression?
24. Do you experience feelings of being disconnected to those

around you?

25. Have you experienced changes in your health, either of symptoms going away or a host of new symptoms arriving?

26. Are you hypersensitive to other people's feelings and emotions?

27. Do you have new talents and skills?

28. Are you having out-of-body experiences (OBE), astral travel or astral projection?

If you answered yes to a majority of these questions, it is possible that are a walk-in. But there is only one way to know for sure. Ask yourself. Trust your inner knowing. Develop a relationship or stronger relationship with your guides and ask them for verification. And it may help to seek out someone who might be a walk-in themselves.

Recommended Reading

Andrea Perron
House of Darkness House of Light Trilogy
In a Flicker (co-authored with George R. Lopez)
A Wonder to Behold

Alma Daniel, Timothy Wyllie, and Andrew Ramer
Ask Your Angels

Barbara Lamb
Crop Circles Revealed (co-authored with Judith Moore)
Alien Experiences (co-authored with Nadine Lalich)
Meet the Hybrids (co-authored with Miguel Mendonça)

Brian L. Weiss, MD
Many Lives, Many Masters

Dolores Cannon
The Convoluted Universe Book One, Two, Three, Four, and Five
The Three Waves of Volunteers and the New Earth
Keepers of the Garden
The Custodians: Beyond Abduction

J.J. Hurtak
The Book of Knowledge: The Keys of Enoch

Jacquelin Smith
Animal Communication - Our Sacred Connection
Star Origins and Wisdom of Animals: Talks With Animal Souls

Julie Cannon
Soul Speak - The Language of Your Body

Lee Carroll
Kryon Series

Maia Chrystine Nartoomid
Red Tree
Blue Star Love

Mary Hardy
The Alchemist's Handbook to Homeopathy
Pyramid Energy: The Philosophy of God, The Science of Man

Mary Rodwell
Awakening: How Extraterrestrial Contact Can Transform your Life
The New Human, Awakening to Our Cosmic Heritage

Maia Chrystine Nartoomid
Blue Star Love

Miguel Mendonça
Meet the Hybrids: The Lives and Missions of ET Ambassadors on

Earth (co-authored with Barbara Lamb)

We are the Disclosure: A People's History of the Extraterrestrial Field

Being with the Beings: The How and the Why of ET Contact

Rebecca Hardcastle-Wright

How Exoconscious Humans Guide our Space-Faring Future

Exoconsciousness: Your 21st Century Mind

The Exoconscious Human: Claiming Psychic Intelligence in a Transhuman World

Rob Gauthier

Co-authored three books with Jefferson Viscardi

Plee-Na-Ki and The Plenatalaka - Pleiadian Soul Reflection

Benevolent Hybrid Reptilian Humans

Extraterrestrial Life - Galactic Humans.

Robert Schwartz

Your Soul's Plan

Your Soul's Gift

Ruth Montgomery

Strangers Among Us

Aliens Among Us

Scott Mathias

The Antares Seals: Return of the Holy Grail

Scott Werner

The Next Step in Human Evolution

Take Back Your Health
Vicki Werner
The Secret to Healing and Recovery

Yvonne Perry
Light Language Emerging: Activating Ascension Codes and Integrating Body, Soul and Spirit
Walk-ins Among Us
Shifting into Purer Consciousness
Whose Stuff is This?
More Than Meets the Eye
The Sid Series
Celestial Shaman Book

Printed in Great Britain
by Amazon

12992662R00178